IN HIS OWN WORDS

Messianic Insights into the Hebrew Alphabet

———————— Revised & Expanded ————————

L. Grant Luton

BETH TIKKUN PUBLISHING

Copyright © 2018
Beth Tikkun Publishing

Scripture quotations are loosely based upon the NEW AMERICAN STANDARD BIBLE, © 1960, 1962, 1963, 1968, 1971, 1972, 1973, 1975, 1977, by the Lockman Foundation. Used by Permission. Throughout this publication the name *Jesus* is rendered 'Yeshua', *Christ* is rendered 'Messiah', *the LORD* is rendered 'Adonai', *Law* is rendered 'Torah', and *church* is rendered 'kahal'.

All rights reserved. No part of this book may be reproduced in any form, except for the inclusion of brief quotations in a review or article, without written permission from the author or publisher.

First edition, August 2018

ISBN-13: 978-1724916457
ISBN-10: 1724916459

Beth Tikkun Publishing
1501 Lomalinda Cir. NW
Uniontown, OH 44685-8209
mail@bethtikkunpublishing.com

Teachings by the author are available at
www.bethtikkun.com

Cover: Tim Pell
Illustrations: Phil Rose

To **ROBIN**
my woman of valor

To **JOSHUA**, **CALEB** & **LINDSAY**
for teaching me the most

In memory of
MOM and **DAD**
for starting me on the journey

And to
BETH TIKKUN MESSIANIC FELLOWSHIP
for taking the journey with me

Contents

Preface vii
Preface to the 2018 Edition xi
Introduction xiii
Hebrew Alphabet Table xxi

Series One – The Gospel of God
1. א *Aleph*, In God's Image 3
2. ב *Beit*, God's Word, God's Dwelling 23
3. ג *Gimel*, A Voice in the Wilderness 45
4. ד *Dalet*, A Witness at the Door 57
5. ה *Hei*, The Breath of God 71
6. ו *Vav*, A Man of the Word 83
7. ז *Zayin*, The Sword and the Seed 91

Series Two – The Spiritual Walk
8. ח *Chet*, Life Abundant 105
9. ט *Tet*, A Matter of Life and Death 113
10. י *Yud*, The Hand of God 127
11. כ,ך *Kaf*, God's Work in Messiah Yeshua 137
12. ל *Lamed*, A Light to the World 143
13. מ,ם *Mem*, Living Waters 151
14. נ,ן *Nun*, Humility, Fish and the *Kahal* 163

Series Three – Promises and Warnings
15. ס *Samech*, Supporting the Fallen 177
16. ע *Ayin*, The Window of the Soul 183
17. פ,ף *Peh*, The Power of Speech 193
18. צ,ץ *Tzaddi*, The Righteousness of the Saints ... 199
19. ק *Kof*, Holy Unto the Lord 211
20. ר *Resh*, Human Reasoning vs. Obedience 221
21. ש *Shin*, Peace and Protection 229

The Cross of Yeshua & Return to *Aleph*
22. ת *Tuv*, The Power of the Cross 251
23. א Return to *Aleph* 267

Appendices
Appendix A: The number 26 283
Appendix B: Fire and Water 289
Bibliography 297

Preface

It has never been God's intention to hide Himself from us. On the contrary, we have been the ones to hide ourselves from Him – a habit we inherited from Adam and Eve. Our determination to hide, however, is no match for God's ability to seek and find us. When He does draw us from darkness into light and as we surrender ourselves to His love and grace the roles of hide and seek are gradually reversed. Instead of God having to seek us, we begin with our whole hearts to seek Him. We have an amazing Savior who makes the process of getting to know Him life's most rewarding adventure.

God assists our quest for Him by revealing Himself to us on many levels – the grand as well as the microscopic. The entire creation, from the expanse of space to the elegant mathematical balance of a molecule, proclaims the wisdom and love of our great Creator. Paul wrote: *"For since the creation of the world God's invisible qualities – His eternal power and divine nature – have been clearly seen, being understood from what has been made, so that men are without excuse."*[1] The evidence is apparent to any person with a seeking heart.

Because many remain stubbornly indifferent to nature's proclamation of a wise and loving Creator, God has provided a more articulate expression of Himself in the form of a witnessing people who demonstrate His presence in their lives. Messiah refers to these godly ones as lights of the world.[2] But even the most dedicated believers are fallible. As lights of the world, God's people sometimes produce precious little wattage. Therefore, God has provided the world with a timeless, supernatural, and

---

[1] Romans 1:20 .
[2] Matthew 5:14

infallible witness – His Word the Bible.

Many inspirational books have been written which help open our understanding to the wonders of God's Word. But I hope to take the reader a step closer to God's heart by examining some of the minute, untranslatable features of the Hebrew scriptures. As we take this journey of discovery, we will encounter letters in the *Tanach* that are printed oversize or undersize for no apparent reason. We will encounter letters that are printed upside down, broken in half, or suspended in mid-air. We will discover why nearly every column of a Torah scroll begins with a letter that symbolizes a hook, and why some passages of scripture are printed in such a manner so as to look like a brick wall. These peculiarities, and many more, are found only in the Hebrew scriptures and were validated by Yeshua when He said, *"...until heaven and earth pass, not the smallest letter or stroke shall pass away from the Torah until all is accomplished."*[3] In other words, Yeshua was saying that neither the smallest letter of the Hebrew alphabet (the *yud*), nor the seemingly insignificant decorations on the letters (the *tagin*) are accidental – even the smallest details contain a message. Thus, the purpose of this book is twofold: to examine some of the intimate details of the Hebrew scriptures, and to explore the spiritual principles which are reflected in these details.

This book is the result of an adventure that began in 1992 when I made my first visit to Israel. I had been a student of the Bible for nearly 25 years, but visiting Israel provided an entirely new perspective on the Scriptures. Having grown up in western society, I was prone to view God's Word through the lens of 20th century western civilization. But visiting Israel changed that forever. As a result of exploring the rugged beauty of the land God gave to His chosen people, my mind was opened to a dimension of His Word that had till then been entirely foreign. Visiting the birthplace of the Bible indelibly impressed upon me that the things of God are Hebraic in nature. I learned that if I wanted to embrace God's Word in its fullness, I must also embrace its Jewishness. I began to study the history of Judaism in order to gain a better understanding of the Jewish roots of my own faith. This study opened my eyes to the differences between the Judaism described in the Torah, and the Judaism practiced by the legalists of Yeshua's day. Moreover, I discovered how very similar biblical Christianity is to biblical Judaism. In fact, in their pure forms they are nearly indistinguishable.

In order to complete my studies, I began to learn Hebrew, which opened up a new world of insight into the Scriptures and the ways of God. Though I have much to

---

[3] Matthew 5:18

learn about this fascinating language, my efforts thus far have been richly rewarded. One rabbi has said that studying the Bible by means of a translation is like kissing a woman through a veil. Through the following pages I hope to lift the veil a little so that the hidden beauty of God's Word may to some degree be perceived by the reader, for the ruggedness and stark beauty of the land of Israel are reflected in the sounds, textures, and rhythms of the Hebrew language. But more importantly, many spiritual insights are contained in the shapes and arrangements of the Hebrew letters. Rabbi Abraham Joshua Heschel said it best when he wrote, "It is not enough to know how to translate Hebrew into English; it is not enough to have met a word in the dictionary and to have experienced unpleasant adventures with it in the study of grammar. A word has a soul, and we must learn how to attain insight into its life."[4]

I suggest that you read this book slowly and meditatively so that you may not only grasp the truths it set forth, but also that you may do so despite the deficiencies of the author. This book also requires you to think open-mindedly about concepts and insights which are "strong meat"[5] and need to be chewed carefully. One will certainly find things which raise a question or perhaps an objection. In such cases, just press on to pursue God through the revelation He has given us of Himself through His holy Word. My prayer is that of Paul, that *"…the God of our Lord Yeshua HaMashiach, the Father of glory, may give unto you the spirit of wisdom and revelation in the knowledge of Him."*[6] With God's help we will gain insight into the lessons contained in the Hebrew letters as we study God's eternal message to us … in His own words.

---

[4] Moral Grandeur and Spiritual Audacity, Farrar, Straus, Giroux, 1996, pg. 116.
[5] Hebrews 5:14
[6] Ephesians 1:17

Preface to the 2018 Edition

I can hardly believe that it has been nearly twenty years since I wrote the previous Preface. My children are grown, I am now a grandfather, I am preparing to return to Israel for the sixth time, and the small Bible study I was leading has now become a congregation of the most wonderful people it has ever been my privilege to know.

But, it is a strange experience to pick up a book I wrote nearly two decades ago and read it from the perspective of time. I confess that more than once I winced at what I had written (or at *how* I had written). I remember well the struggle I had trying to juggle my evangelicalism with my evolving Hebraic understanding of truth. Some of the theologies I held then have come into sharper focus, while others have been replaced with a more scriptural understanding. However, the fundamentals of God's love and grace, Messiah's power to save, and the Torah's timeless brilliance, wisdom, and reliability have become even more profound and beautiful to me.

Rabbinic literature describes study of the Hebrew scriptures as "swimming in the sea of Torah". Anyone who has jumped into the deep end of God's Word understands exactly what this means. As one of those swimmers, I realize that I will never see it all, know it all, or understand it all. God's Word is the revelation of God's mind. Who can truly know it? Though we are commanded to know God and to love Him, thankfully, we are not commanded to understand Him. That will take eternity. It will also take eternity to get to the bottom of God's Word, it is that infinite.

My own spiritual journey over the past twenty years has resulted in a deeper intimacy with God's Word and, hence, with God Himself. He has been utterly faithful to reveal Himself through His Word in the most beautiful and inspiring ways. This has been made possible by developing ever greater proficiency in biblical Hebrew. Hebrew, which the rabbis refer to as "the language of transcendence", has become the language through which I view everything I encounter in the Scriptures. It has made my reading of the Bible change from black and white to living color. Also, what was merely intellectual before, has become spiritually dynamic and alive. This has not been my experience only, but also that of my brothers and sisters at Beth Tikkun Messianic Fellowship. It has been the adventure of a lifetime.

When I first published my book, I had no idea how it would be received, but I never expected it to become something of value in so many lives. If nothing else, I figured it would prove a cure for insomnia. (And, in this, it has met with success.) But, I have also made many new friends through *In His Own Words*. It has been a great (though greatly undeserved) pleasure to receive so many kind and encouraging words from readers around the world.

Returning to my experience (i.e. wincing) while reading my book after all these years – my goal in editing my book and expanding greatly on its content is so that, should God grant me strength, rereading this book twenty years from now will be a less painful experience. Not that it was all painful, mind you. I must admit, it had its good parts, too. But, I hope that the reader will find this edition to be (a) more homogenous and coherent, and (b) more inspiring with its many new insights and discoveries.

Unlike the first edition of this book, this one has benefited from the input of several talented friends. I must thank Brett Tipton for bringing his editing skills to bear and for exorcising my many typos. Thanks also to two talented artistic friends – Tim Pell for the cover, and Phil Rose for the illustrations.

May God richly bless you in your study of His Word.
L. Grant Luton
July 2018

Introduction

Readers who are unfamiliar with the Hebrew language will find it beneficial to carefully read this introduction. Here, we will address issues which are essential to understanding what follows. You may wish to return here occasionally to review a topic referred to in the body of the text. However, those readers who are familiar with the Hebrew alphabet, Bible translation, and the basic tenets of Judaism may opt to skip the Introduction and proceed to Chapter One.

Hebrew Reads from Right to Left

The reader will often be instructed to examine a certain letter of a word or phrase. In order to identify the correct letter and avoid confusion, remember to follow the text from right to left.

Letters and Pictures

Each Hebrew letter is actually a picture, or symbol, of an object, animal, person, or body part. The interpretations of these symbols are based upon centuries of tradition. Some of these are easily recognized (such as *hei*, ה, which is a 'window', and *peh*, פ, which is a 'mouth'), but others are more obscure (such as *yud*, י, which is a 'hand').

xiv

There are seven basic "simple" letters that are used to construct the more complex letters. These seven simple letters are: ז,ו,י,ג,ד,כ,ז. The other fifteen letters (the "complex") are formed by combinations of these seven.[7]

Letter Names

Unlike the English alphabet, most Hebrew letters have a name which is itself a word. Hence, when a Hebrew word is spelled, a string of words must be used to give the spelling. For example, the word for 'father' is אב (pronounced *av*). If we spell this word aloud, the names of the two letters are *aleph* and *beit*. But, if we translate the words *aleph* and *beit* into English, they are 'master' and 'house'. Thus, together they render "master of the house". (And isn't a *father* intended to be the '*master* of the *house*'?)

The Scriptures

Terms that I frequently use to refer to the Bible, or segment of it, are as follows:

> **Torah** –The first five books of the Bible. These five books are sometimes called the *Pentateuch*, or *Books of Moses*. The word *Torah* is often mistranslated 'Law'. Though it does contain laws, the word *Torah* means 'instruction'.
>
> **Tanach** – This is the Hebrew name for the Hebrew Scriptures, usually referred to as The Old Testament.[8] Its name is derived from its three divisions: the <u>To</u>rah (the five books of Moses), the <u>Nevi'im</u> (the Prophets), and the <u>Chetuvim</u> (the Writings). These same three sections were recognized by Yeshua: *"Now He said to them, 'These are My words which I spoke to you while I was still with you, that all things which are written about Me in the Torah of Moses and the Prophets and the Psalms must be fulfilled.'"*[9]
>
> **Apostolic Writings** – These are usually referred to as The New Testament. This is a misnomer. The Apostolic Writings are *not* the New Covenant. They tell us about Yeshua and the new covenant He instituted. (See footnote 3.) At times, I

---

[7] Coincidentally, dividing the number of the complex letters by the number of simple letters (22 divided by 7) renders the number known as *pi* (π = 3.1415926....).

[8] I prefer not to use the terms *New Testament* and *Old Testament* when referring to the Scriptures. These terms refer to covenants contained within the Scriptures, but are not used of the Scriptures themselves. The "Old Testament" is actually the Bible that the "New Testament" writers instructed us to study and to follow. (James 1:22-25, for example.)

[9] Luke 24:44

may refer to the Apostolic Writings as the Messianic Writings, or the Greek Scriptures.

The Scriptures – I use this term to simply refer to the entire Bible.

Gematria

The ancient Hebrews lacked numerals, thus they incorporated the letters of the alphabet to serve in this capacity.[10] They devised a simple system wherein each letter represents a numeric value: א = 1, ב = 2, ג = 3 ... and so on. (The numeric values of the letters are given in the chart following the Introduction.) Since each letter has a numeric value, each word of the *Tanach* also has a corresponding numeric value. For instance, the word for 'father' (אב, *av*) has a numeric value of 3 because א = 1 and ב = 2. The Sages developed an entire field of study involving the mathematical patterns of scripture called *gematria*. Beyond the simple calculation of a word's numeric value, they developed additional methods of calculating numeric values of words in the Torah. The only form of *gematria* used in this book is the simple form set forth above called "primary" or "simple *gematria*".

Do not confuse *gematria* with numerology! These have nothing whatsoever to do with one another. Numerology is a branch of the occult used to, supposedly, tell the future and tell one's fortune. Gematria has nothing to do with this forbidden practice.

Talmud

Second only to the *Torah*, the most sacred writing in Judaism is the *Talmud* (literally 'Study'). It consists of more than 6,000 pages of lore, insights, anecdotes, stories, illustrations, Torah commentary, and conflicting rabbinic opinions on an array of subjects that rambles unpredictably from topic to topic. There are two versions of the *Talmud* - the *Babylonian Talmud* (*Bavli*) and the *Jerusalem Talmud* (*Yerushalami*), which are named after their place of origin. The *Talmud* is divided into 60 sections called *Tractates*.[11]

The *Talmud* is comprised of a central core called the *Mishnah* (which is commentary on the Torah) and *Gemara* (which is commentary on the *Mishnah*). The stories and

---

[10] This is also true of *koine* Greek, the language in which the Apostolic Scriptures were written.
[11] Some versions have 63 sections.

illustrations contained in the *Talmud* are rich in wisdom and historical anecdotes, making it a useful resource for better understanding Jewish thought. It also provides rich background for a better understanding of the culture in which the Apostolic Scriptures were written. In fact, the Gospels contain many occasions of Yeshua citing material in the *Talmud*.

Do not take these comments as a blanket endorsement of the *Talmud*! There are many things contained in it with which Yeshua disagreed. Although I have included several quotes from the *Talmud*, in no way do I endorse it as inspired.

Sages

The term 'Sages' refers collectively to the long line of Jewish theologians stretching back over the last 3,000 years. These men are responsible for a vast body of work, including the *Mishnah*, *Talmud*, *Midrash Rabbah*, and many other writings. So as not to tire the reader with a litany of names, I have followed the common practice among Jewish writers and commentators of simply referring to these men as "the Sages". The reader may consult any one of a number of works providing biographical data on the Sages.[12]

Torah Scrolls

The most sacred object in a synagogue is the Torah scroll (or *Sefer Torah*), which is comprised of the five books of Moses. Though older synagogues may own several Torah scrolls, every synagogue has at least one. A Torah scroll is prepared today exactly as it has been for thousands of years. The text is hand-printed on parchment (made from the skins of kosher animals) using a quill pen and special ink. The letters must be printed according to exacting specifications so that every Torah scroll is letter perfect. The letters used in a Torah scroll lack vowel signs (see below), and are more ornate than those found in printed Hebrew books. Even though Torah scrolls have no chapter and verse designations, they do contain many unusual markings, letter arrangements, and other features not normally found in printed Hebrew Bibles. These peculiarities have been faithfully copied by scribes for thousands of years and are the focus of many of the insights contained in this book.

---

[12] Interestingly, one of the Sages still studied today is Gamaliel, who was the Apostle Paul's mentor. (Acts 22:3.)

Vowel Signs

Printed Hebrew contains no vowels. The twenty-two letters of the Hebrew alphabet represent twenty consonants plus two silent letters. This makes pronunciation of a word difficult for a reader not familiar with spoken Hebrew. The development of vowel symbols (called *nikkud*) came about during the early Middle Ages due to concern that readers would forget the correct pronunciation of the words of the *Torah*. These vowel signs are now included in all printed Hebrew Bibles. Since they were not part of the original Hebrew and are not found in Torah scrolls, I have generally omitted them as well.

Final Forms

Five Hebrew letters assume a different form when they appear at the end a word. For example, *kaf* (which appears as "כ") changes to "ך" when it occurs at the end of a word. The five letters with final forms are:

		Final Form[13]
kaf	כ	ך
mem	מ	ם
nun	נ	ן
peh	פ	ף
tzaddi	צ	ץ

Hebrew Verb Roots

Every Hebrew verb is built on a three-letter root word (or *lemma*). Additional letters are added to the front, back, or middle of the root in order to change its tense, gender, or make it plural. In most cases, when discussing a verb, we will consider only the three-letter verb root.

God' Names

Several of God's names will be addressed within the pages of this book, but some explanation will be helpful before we begin our study. I use the word 'God' to refer only to the God of the Bible. However, if this word is in lowercase – 'god' – it refers to false

---

[13] Called *sofit* (סופית).

gods. In Hebrew, there are two names that are most commonly used in reference to God. The first, *Elohim* (אֱלֹהִים), is the most commonly used name of God in the *Tanach*. It is the name used exclusively in the story of creation in Genesis 1.

The proper name for God, however, is YHVH (יהוה) – a name that we do not know how to pronounce, and are warned not to. In scripture quotations using YHVH, I generally substitute the name *Adonai*, which means 'Lord'. This is common practice in Judaism so as to avoid mispronouncing God's name YHVH.[14] On some occasions, the *Tanach* uses the shortened form *Yah* (יה), which consists of the first two letters of YHVH (יהוה).

The Name *Yeshua*

The term 'Jesus Christ' is derived from Greek rather than from Hebrew. Hence, it seemed fitting that in a book dealing with the Hebrew alphabet, the Hebrew designations for the Messiah should be used. Therefore, throughout the text, the Hebrew name *Yeshua* is used for 'Jesus', and *Messiah* for 'Christ'.[15] These names (used by the early believers) are used in the Messianic community today.

A Word About Translations

I am constantly asked what translation I use when I teach. It may surprise you to learn that this is a non-issue in Jewish circles. Since most Jewish students can read Hebrew, an English translation is unnecessary. Subsequently, it is common for a Jewish commentator producing a work in English, to render the Hebrew passage into English himself, and not rely on someone else's translation.

Though not as proficient in Hebrew as an orthodox Jew, I nevertheless find myself adopting this practice more and more. Therefore, what I have done throughout this work is use the New American Standard Bible as a platform translation, and then made modifications as necessary. Some of the changes I have made consistently throughout this book are the following:

> Jesus = *Yeshua*
> Christ = *Messiah*
> The LORD = *Adonai* / YHVH

---

[14] Another common practice in Judaism is to use the term *Hashem*, which means 'the Name'.
[15] The Hebrew pronunciation for 'Messiah' is *Mashiach*.

Law = *Torah*
Old Testament = *Tanach*
New Testament = *Apostolic Scriptures / Greek Scriptures*
John the Baptist = *John the Immerser*

One of the things that has also guided my forays into translation is awareness that the writers of the Apostolic Scriptures were Hebrew thinkers. In other words, being Jewish men who were trained in synagogue and steeped in the Hebrew Scriptures, they thought in Hebrew terms while writing in Greek. The Complete Jewish Bible does an excellent job of restoring the Hebraic 'flavor' of the Greek Scriptures, and I occasionally quote it here.[16]

References to the Holy Spirit

Concerning the subject of the 'Holy Spirit', the traditional convention is to capitalize this term. Therefore, so as not to give offence, I have followed suit. However, when the words 'God's spirit' or 'spirit of God' or simply 'the spirit' occur, I have printed 'spirit' in lowercase.

Why, you may ask, is this even a concern? Though gender is not a major issue in English grammar, it is in Hebrew and Greek. Hebrew incorporates two genders: masculine and feminine. Greek, on the other hand, incorporates three genders: masculine, feminine and neuter. In Hebrew, the word for 'spirit' (רוח, *ruach*) is always feminine. In Greek, the word for 'spirit' (πνευμα, *pneuma*) is always neuter. But, never is it a 'he'.

Due to the suppression of these grammatical facts, translators have bowed to tradition and capitalized 'Holy Spirit' as if it were a proper name. So as not to offend the sensitivities of some readers, I have done the same.

Pre-Temple Script

A standing debate among historians and Hebraists concerns whether the present form of the Hebrew letters is the same as that originally used to write the Torah. One camp claims that the present script is of Babylonian origin and came into popular use among the Jewish people during the Babylonian exile. The opposing camp contends

---

[16] The author also highly recommends The Delitzsch Hebrew Gospels (Vine of David, 2011).

that the two scripts developed simultaneously – one for common use and one for sacred.

Regardless of which theory is correct, we may safely assume that God, in His sovereignty, orchestrated events so that the present script is used in all Torah scrolls. Even if the script presently used was borrowed from the Babylonians, this is by no means contrary to God's ways. After all, Abraham – the father of the Jewish people – was also called out of the area of Babylon. God has always been redeeming things from Gentile culture for sacred use. Greek itself was ordained as the language in which the Apostolic Scriptures were recorded.

These examples, and others that space limitations preclude, are consistent with the verse describing how God the great Redeemer *"...sent His own Son in the likeness of sinful flesh."*[17] It should not surprise us that God, who clothed the *incarnate* Word in the *"likeness of sinful flesh"*, would also clothe His *written* Word in letters taken from the secular world.[18]

Interrelationship of the Letters

Your first reading of this book will introduce you to the fundamental lessons contained in the letters, but a second reading will help to develop an appreciation of the connection each letter has to the others. Therefore, I recommend that your first reading be followed soon after by a second. This second reading will allow you to more fully appreciate the interrelationship of the letters and the logical progression of their lessons.

---

[17] Romans 8:3. See also Titus 2:14.
[18] Furthermore, the script used today is the same as that used in the days of Yeshua when He stated that each "jot or tittle" would be preserved. (Matthew 5:18)

Letter	Name	Numerical Value	Signification	Pronunciation
א	Aleph	1	Ox	(silent)
ב	Beit	2	House	v, b
ג	Gimel	3	Camel	g
ד	Dalet	4	Door	d
ה	Hei	5	Window	h
ו	Vav	6	Hook	v, u
ז	Zayin	7	Weapon	z
ח	Chet	8	Fence	ch (as in "Bach")
ט	Tet	9	Snake	t
י	Yud	10	Hand	y
כ,ך	Kaf	20	Palm of hand	k, ch (as in "Bach")
ל	Lamed	30	Ox-goad	l
מ,ם	Mem	40	Water	m
נ,ן	Nun	50	Fish	n
ס	Samech	60	Support	s
ע	Ayin	70	Eye	(silent)
פ,ף	Peh	80	Mouth	p, ph
צ,ץ	Tzaddi	90	Fish-hook	tz
ק	Kof	100	Back of head	k
ר	Resh	200	Head	r
ש	Shin	300	Tooth	sh, s
ת	Tuv	400	Cross	t

Series One

The Gospel of God

1

א | *Aleph*

In God's Image

"Hear, O Israel! Adonai is our God, Adonai is One."
DEUTERONOMY 6:4

For centuries, Jewish scholars have perceived the individual letters of the Hebrew alphabet as containing important spiritual lessons, and *aleph* (א), in its exalted position at the head of the alphabet, is considered to be the repository of all the alphabet's wisdom. *Aleph* (א) is much more than merely the Hebrew equivalent of the letter 'A' – the first in a series of letters. It is considered by Jewish theologians to actually be made in the image of God and is thus the holiest of all the letters. *Aleph's* name means 'lord' or 'master' thus making it the lord of all the letters – a father with twenty-one children.[1] In fact, the first two letters of the Hebrew alphabet – *aleph* and *beit* – together spell אב (*av*) 'father', thus teaching that all things begin with God, the *Father* of all.

The One-In-Three

The cornerstone of Jewish theology is *"Hear O Israel! Adonai is our God, Adonai is One!"* However, the writings of the Sages acknowledge that *aleph* (א, the letter which traditionally represents God) consists of three parts. In turn, these three parts are

---

[1] Rabbi Michael L. Munk, The Wisdom of the Hebrew Alphabet, pg. 43.

themselves individual letters of the alphabet.[2] The three letters that comprise the *aleph* (א) are two *yuds* (י) separated by a slanted *vav* (ו) as shown below.

Thus, it can be seen how *aleph* (א), which consists of three parts, nevertheless has a numeric value of one. Some will see this as support for the idea of a "Trinity", whereas others will see this as an illustration that God manifests Himself in both the physical and spiritual realms. Regardless of your particular point of view, the day is coming when such notions will become moot since we will all know God as He is, and not how we imagine Him to be. As John stated, "*Beloved, now we are children of God, and it has not appeared as yet what we will be. We know that when He appears, we will be like Him, because we will see Him just as He is.*"[3] In other words, there will be no need for further discussion as to God's "make up". We will know Him as He is.

John may have based his statement above on Zechariah prophecy: "*And Adonai will be king over all the earth; in that day Adonai will be one, and His name one.*"[4] In a similar vein, Paul prophesied: "*When all things are subjected to Him, then the Son Himself also will be subjected to the One who subjected all things to Him, so that God may be all in all.*"[5]

Unlike the English alphabet, each Hebrew letter has a numeric value: א = 1, ב = 2, ג = 3, etc. Therefore, if we calculate the numeric values of the letters comprising *aleph* (א), we find that they have a total value of twenty-six (י + ו + י = 10 + 6 + 10 = 26). But what is the significance of twenty-six? It is the numeric value of God's name – יהוה (י + ה + ו + ה = 10 + 5 + 6 + 5 = 26) – which we denote with the letters YHVH. This once again demonstrates how *aleph* (א), the first letter of the alphabet, represents God.

God's Name — YHVH

The name of God, יהוה (YHVH), is the Bible's grandest example of the principle: "*It is the glory of God to conceal a matter; to search out a matter is the glory of kings.*"[6] There is much

---

[2] Rabbi Yitzchak Ginsburgh, <u>The Alef-Beit</u>, pgs. 24, 378.
[3] 1 John 3:2
[4] Zechariah 14:9
[5] 1 Corinthians 15:28
[6] Proverbs 25:2

in God's great name for us to explore, and to do so is to walk on holy ground. Moreover, the name יהוה is regarded so holy that Jews dare not speak it. Whenever the Torah is read aloud and the name of יהוה is encountered, the word *Adonai* ('Lord') or *Hashem* (literally 'the Name') is substituted in order to avoid uttering this holy name – which is just as well since no one knows with certainty its correct pronunciation.[7] Also, a scribe exercises the utmost caution when printing God's name in a Torah scroll. Before printing the letters יהוה, he says aloud, "I am about to write the name of God in honor of His holy name." If a king should address him as he writes the name of God, he is not permitted to pause for a reply, but must first complete the printing of these four sacred letters. And, should a scribe make the slightest error in printing God's name, he is forbidden to correct his mistake. The sheet of parchment must be set aside, and the scribe must begin again with a new sheet.[8]

Bible translators have long struggled with how to translate יהוה (referred to as the *tetragrammaton* – a Greek word meaning "the sign of the four [letters]"). The King James Version of the Bible makes no attempt to translate the word יהוה, but simply substitutes the word LORD printed in capital letters.[9] Other translations use 'Jehovah' or 'Yahweh', but the accuracy of these translations is dubious at best. The difficulty arises from the fact that the consonants comprising יהוה (YHVH) may be pronounced in various ways and we do not know how God pronounced His name when He revealed it to Moses. For instance, depending upon the speaker's accent, the *yud* (י) may be pronounced as a 'y', or, some think, a 'j'. And *vav* (ו) may be pronounced, depending on the speaker's accent, either as 'v' or 'w', or as the vowel 'u' or 'o'. *Hei* (ה), on the other hand, is always pronounced with an 'h' sound. Thus, there are many possible pronunciations for יהוה, but no one knows which one is correct.

To further complicate the matter, we do not know what vowel sounds should be inserted between the consonants. Though vowel markings (in the form of dots and dashes placed above or below the letters) were later developed and added to all of the other words of the Torah, no vowel symbols were added to יהוה since no one knew how this word was originally pronounced. In recent times, however, some printed

---

[7] Even the word *Adonai* is not used conversationally among the orthodox because of the holiness it derives from being a substitute for YHVH.

[8] Each sheet of parchment in Torah scroll normally contains three to four columns of print.

[9] There are four exceptions to this rule in the KJV: Ex.6:3/Ps.83:18/Is.12:2/26:4.

editions of the *Tanach* will add the vowel markings from the word *Adonai* (אֲדֹנָי) and apply them to the word יהוה as in the illustration below.

> וַיֹּאמֶר עוֹד אֱלֹהִים אֶל־מֹשֶׁה כֹּה תֹאמַר אֶל־בְּנֵי יִשְׂרָאֵל יְהוָה אֱלֹהֵי אֲבֹתֵיכֶם אֱלֹהֵי אַבְרָהָם אֱלֹהֵי יִצְחָק וֵאלֹהֵי יַעֲקֹב שְׁלָחַנִי אֲלֵיכֶם זֶה־שְּׁמִי לְעֹלָם וְזֶה זִכְרִי לְדֹר דֹּר׃

Exodus 3:15

What's in a Name?

The name יהוה was first revealed to Moses when God commissioned him to deliver the children of Israel from Egyptian bondage. In the Biblical account, Moses argued with God that he was not the man for the job.[10] Among Moses' excuses for not wanting to return to Egypt is his question, *"When the Israelites ask who sent me, what shall I tell them is His name?"* God gave a rather lengthy answer to this seemingly simple question. Let's read the entire passage, and then we shall examine God's answer to Moses' question phrase by phrase.

> *God said to Moses,* אהיה אשר אהיה *("I AM THAT I AM"); and He said, "Thus you shall say to the sons of Israel,* אהיה *('I AM') has sent me to you.'" God, furthermore, said to Moses, "Thus you shall say to the sons of Israel, '*יהוה *(YHVH), the God of your fathers, the God of Abraham, the God of Isaac, and the God of Jacob, has sent me to you.' This is My name forever, and this is My memorial-name to all generations.*

A cursory glance at this passage reveals three names in Hebrew with their translations within parenthesis. Let's now look at each of these in turn.

In the first part of His answer God reveals His name as *"I AM THAT I AM"*.[11] In Hebrew, this phrase consists of only three words:

---

[10] Exodus 3:14-15

[11] Biblical Hebrew does not have a verb form for 'I am', thus this is not an entirely accurate translation of this phrase. Some translators render this phrase as *"I shall be as I shall be"*, but this still does not capture the nuances expressed in the Hebrew. A more accurate English rendering might be *"I shall forever be as I am"*. For the sake of convenience, I have used the traditional translation *"I AM THAT I AM"*.

אהיה אשר אהיה

ehyeh　asher　ehyeh

I AM　THAT　I AM

Notice that each word of the phrase begins with the letter *aleph* (א). Note also the pattern made by these three words. The first and last words are identical, separated by a third, dissimilar word. This is the same pattern used in the construction of the א as discussed earlier: two identical letters (י) separated by a third (ו).

Continuing, God repeats the first word of the phrase giving it as His name. He says, "*Thus you shall say to the children of Israel,* אהיה [*ehyeh* – "I AM"] *has sent me to you.*"[12]

He then alters אהיה (*ehyeh*) to יהוה (YHVH) when He says, "*Thus shall you say to the children of Israel, 'YHVH, the God of our fathers, of Abraham, Isaac, and Jacob...*'"[13] What is the purpose of this last change? And, what exactly does the name YHVH mean? Most scholars believe that YHVH is a peculiar form of the verb 'to be' (basically meaning 'I am'). It would be natural to assume that this is the case simply because יהוה closely resembles these verb forms:[14]

היה, *ha'yah* = he was
יהיה, *yi'yeh* = he will be
הוה, *ha'vah* = he is
יהוה, YHVH = ?

Others believe that the four letters of God's name were chosen for reasons known only to God and their similarity to any verb form is merely coincidental. But one thing is certain – the name YHVH means more than simply "I am". God's name is a verb. We do not pronounce it with our lips, but with our lives. God is the ultimate 'Be-er' and we are His 'be-ings'. Hence, we are not be parrots who merely mouth sounds, but we are to proclaim God's name with deeds. May God have mercy on us for taking His name in vain by using our mouths instead of our bodies to proclaim it.

A thorough discussion of God's name is too vast a subject for one chapter, so we will continue our discussion in future chapters as the Hebrew letters provide further

---

[12] Exodus 3:14
[13] Exodus 3:15
[14] Biblical Hebrew does not have a verb form for "I am".

insights into the mystery of יהוה. But I must interject one additional comment at this point. We have learned that God's name expresses His unchangeability – I AM THAT I AM. He is perfect, and perfection does not require alteration. Therefore, be careful that you never say, "It's just the way I am. I can't change." Only God can say that. You and I, on the other hand, can change ... and must change. Do not try to make yourself God's equal by claiming immutability.

א Marks the Spot

The very structure of the Torah's opening verses in the book of Genesis affirms in an amazing way the connection between *aleph* (א) and God's various names and titles. As mentioned above, יהוה has a numeric value of 26 (י + ה + ו + ה = 10 + 5 + 6 + 5 = **26**), as do the component parts of the letter *aleph* (א). Interestingly, if we start with the first letter of the Genesis 1:1 and count twenty-six letters, we arrive at another א. Also, if we take the shortened form of יהוה that is frequently used in the Bible – יה (*Yah*) – which equals fifteen (י + ה = 10 + 5 = **15**) and count fifteen letters, we once again come to an א. Verify the results for yourself by examining the passage below. (Remember to count from right to left.)

בראשית ברא אלהים את השמים ואת הארץ
והארץ היתה תהו ובהו וחשך על פני תהום ורוח
אלהים מרחפת על פני המים ויאמר אלהים יהי
אור ויהי אור וירא אלהים את האור כי טוב
ויבדל אלהים בין האור ובין החשך ויקרא
אלהים לאור יום ולחשך קרא לילה ויהי ערב
ויהי בקר יום אחד

After *Yah* (יה) and YHVH (יהוה), the two most common names for God are *El* (אל) and *Elohim* (אלהים). *El* (אל) has a numerical equivalent of 31 (א + ל = 1 + 30 = **31**), and *Elohim* (אלהים) has a numerical equivalent of 86 (א + ל + ה + י + ם = 1 + 30 + 5 + 10 + 40 = **86**). Once again, counting thirty-one letters from the beginning of Genesis, we arrive at an א. And the same result is achieved when we count to the eighty-sixth letter.

Notice also that the names *El* and *Elohim* both begin with an א. These are the earliest titles by which God is identified in the Torah. But of all His titles, the one used most by Yeshua is *Father*, which, in Hebrew, is אב (*av*). The numeric value of this word is three (א + ב = 1 + 2 = **3**), and the third letter in Genesis 1:1 is, once again, an א. The box below summarizes our discussion of these five names of God and how each one is identified with an *aleph* (א) in the Torah.

יה *Yah*,	10+5=15	The 15th letter of the Torah is א
יהוה *YHVH*	10+5+6+5=26	The 26th letter of the Torah is א
אל *El*	1+30=31	The 31st letter of the Torah is א
אלהים *Elohim*	1+30+5+10+40=86	The 86th letter of the Torah is א
אב *av*	1+2=3	The 3rd letter of the Torah is א

What about other names of God, such as *Adonai*, and "I AM THAT I AM"? Do the numerical values of these names also point to *aleph* (א)? No. However, if we investigate the numerical values of these names, they too will lead us to some amazing discoveries.

The title *Adonai* is spelled אדני and has a numerical value of 65 (א = 1, ד = 4, נ = 50, י = 10; 1+4+50+10 = **65**). Counting 65 letters from the beginning of Genesis we arrive at the letter *yad* (י). From the name אהיה אשר אהיה (*ehyeh asher ehyeh*) "I AM THAT I AM" we derive a numerical value of 543, and *hei* (ה) happens to be the 543rd letter of the Torah. The name to which these two letters point – י and ה – spell יה (*Yah*), which is a name the Bible frequently uses as a shortened form of יהוה.

The name *Yah* (יה) can be brought to completion to form יהוה only by the addition of a *vav* (ו) and another *hei* (ה). These letters are supplied by the names *Mashiach Yeshua*. *Mashiach* (משיח) has a numerical value of 358, and *Yeshua* (ישוע) equals 386.[15] The 358th letter of Genesis is a *vav* (ו), and the 386th letter is a *hei* (ה), thus bringing to completion the name יהוה as summarized below.

Adonai	אדני	= 65	The 65th letter is	י
I WILL BE...	אהיה אשר אהיה	= 543	The 543rd letter is	ה
Mashiach	משיח	= 358	The 358th letter is	ו
Yeshua	ישוע	= 386	The 386th letter is	ה

---

[15] *Mashiach*, משיח: מ = 40, ש = 300, י = 10, ח = 8; 40+300+10+8=358. *Yeshua*, ישוע: י = 10, ש = 300, ו = 6, ע = 70; 10 + 300 + 6 + 70 = 386. *Mashiach* is the Hebrew pronunciation of *Messiah* (or '*Christ*').

The unifying of the letters יה with the letters וה is a common theme in Jewish thought. The following is a standard part of the morning prayers in the *siddur* (Jewish prayer book):

> *For the sake of the unification of the Holy One, Blessed is He, and His Presence, in fear and love to unify the Name – yad-hei with vav-hei – in perfect unity, in the name of all Israel.*[16]

What does this prayer mean? The footnote in the prayer book explains:

> *The first half of the Divine name, formed of the letters yud and hei, symbolizes the Attribute of Judgment, while the second half, formed of the letters vav and hei, symbolizes the Attribute of Mercy. The blend of both attributes leads to His desired goal for Creation.*[17]

Do you grasp the significance of this? According to Jewish theology, the two halves of God's four-letter name represent His two complimentary attributes – Judgement and Mercy. It was demonstrated above that the first two letters (יה, *Yah*, a shortened form of God's name) point to the letter *aleph* (א) as do so many other of God's titles. But, the remaining two letters of His name – ו and ה – are derived by counting the numeric value of *Mashiach Yeshua*, representing God's attribute of Mercy. This reminds us of Zechariah's words that someday "*YHVH will be King over the whole earth. On that day there will be one YHVH, and His name one.*"[18] Only through the revelation of Yeshua can the character of God's name – יהוה – be known in its fullness.

The Gospel Ladder

God's purpose in drawing us unto Himself is so that we may become more like Him. He is not interested in making us gods, but in making us fit for fellowship *with* God. He created man in His own image so that fellowship with Him would not only be possible, but natural. However, when sin entered the picture fellowship with God was greatly hindered, and only through the mediation of Yeshua has fellowship been restored. This is expressed in the passage: *For there is one God, and one mediator also between God and men, the man Messiah Yeshua, who gave himself as a ransom for all…*[19]

---

[16] The Expanded Artscroll Siddur (2010), pg. 4.
[17] Ibid.
[18] Zechariah 14:9
[19] 1 Timothy 2:5-6

This, the basic message of the gospel, is also illustrated by the letter א. Jewish theologians see in *aleph*: "a ladder placed on the ground reaching heavenward... [consisting] of an upper *yud* and a lower *yud* (י), the upper one denoting the celestial and the lower one the mundane."[20] This parallels Yeshua's statement,

> "...Truly, truly, I say to you, you will see the heavens opened and the angels of God ascending and descending on the Son of Man."[21]

The picture is made complete when we realize that *yud* is not only the name of a letter but is also the word for 'hand'. Thus, the message of the gospel can be seen in the construction of *aleph* by the leaning *vav* which, like a ladder, connects the hand of God (the upper *yud*) with the hand of man (the lower *yud*).

A Holy Reversal

A truly amazing insight involving the letter *aleph* (א) is found in the story of Israel's battle with Amalek. Unlike the battle with Egypt where God did all the fighting,[22] God required Israel to do the fighting against Amalek. However, an unusual strategy was involved in this battle. Here is the story:

> *Then Amalek came and fought against Israel at Rephidim. So Moses said to Joshua, "Choose men for us and go out, fight against Amalek. Tomorrow I will station myself on the top of the hill with the staff of God in my hand." Joshua did as Moses told him, and fought against Amalek; and Moses, Aaron, and Hur went up to the top of the hill. So it came about when Moses held his hand up, that Israel prevailed, and when he let his hand down, Amalek prevailed. But Moses' hands were heavy. Then they took a stone and put it under him, and he sat on it; and Aaron and Hur supported his hands, one on one side and one on the other. Thus his hands were steady until the sun set.*[23]

Many wonderful teachings have been done on this story, but I wish to bring out something that is revealed in the Hebrew names of the three men who were on the hilltop overlooking the battle – Moses, Hur and Aaron.[24] Moses held up his staff (over

---

[20] Munk, p.54.
[21] John 1:51
[22] Exodus 14
[23] Exododus 17:8-12
[24] The correct pronunciations are *Mosheh*, *Aharon* and *Chur*.

his head, we assume) and was flanked by Hur and Aaron who helped support his hands. Here are their names in Hebrew:

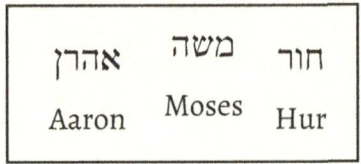

Now, notice what is revealed if we spell each of these names backward:[25]

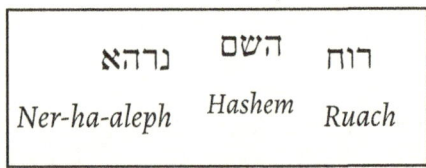

So, what do these new words mean? When Moses' name (משה, *Mosheh*) is spelled backward, it becomes השם – *Hashem* – which, you may recall is a term that means 'the Name' and is used to refer to God. Do not misunderstand. This is not to say that Moses is God! No. Moses had revealed *Hashem* to an extent that no one had done before him. But, here we are simply revealing a picture as you will see.

When Hur's name (חור, *Chur*) is spelled backward, it becomes רוח (*ruach*), which means 'spirit' as in *Ruach Hakodesh* (רוח הקדש) 'Holy Spirit'.

And, when Aaron's name (אהרן, *Aharon*) is spelled backward (נרהא) it does not create a Hebrew word. However, the first two letters – נר (*ner*) – spell the word for 'lamp'. The third letter – ה (*hei*) – is the Hebrew prefix that means 'the'. And the last letter – א (*aleph*) – is, as we have learned, the letter that represents God. Putting these together, we derive נר-ה-א (*ner-ha-'aleph'*) 'lamp of the *aleph*'.

---

[25] Though it may seem strange to reverse the spelling of a word, biblical Hebrew sometimes renders amazing insights into a name or word when this is done. For example, if we reverse the name 'Noah' – נח – it becomes חן 'grace'. And, as we know, "Noah (נח) found 'grace' (חן) in the eyes of the Lord." (Genesis 6:8)

Could the picture be more obvious? It provides a representation of God in the center, with the spirit and the Word (the lamp of God) in their supporting roles of service to Him.

But, there is a fourth character in this picture. He is the one 'on the ground' doing the fighting and leading his army in battle against Amalek. His name is Joshua (יהושע, *Yehoshua*), and he is the one in whom the efforts of Moses, Aaron and Hur find fulfillment. Joshua's name is practically the same as Yeshua's (ישוע), whose name means 'salvation', and through Yeshua the things of God find their focus in the world.

Paul wrote, *"For in Him all the fullness of 'θεοτητος (theoteitos)' dwells in Bodily form."*[26] What is *theoteitos*? This unusual Greek word is used only here in the Bible, and can be translated 'deity', 'divine nature' or 'godhead'. In other words, all the things portrayed by the reversed spelling of 'Moses', 'Aaron' and 'Hur' are encapsulated in the person of Yeshua our Messiah.

Man – Made in God's Image

The Torah states, *"God created man in His own image, in the image of God He created him..."*[27]

Though the letters of God's name – יהוה – can be arranged in descending order to produce the form of a man (see illustration), this does not mean that God looks like a man, complete with arms, legs and head. The word translated 'image' is צלם (*tzelem*), a word which refers to the essence of a thing and not just its outward appearance. God has made man *in essence* like Himself. He created us with emotions because He has emotions. He created us with a sense of humor because He has a sense of humor. And He created us with the ability to love because He *is* love.

Unfortunately, man's ability to reflect God's image has been terribly marred because of sin. Furthermore, our spiritual enemy hates us because of the One whose image we bear. Though we sometimes fail to see God's image in one another, Satan sees it clearly and hates us as a result. Because his consuming hatred drives him to destroy any reminder of his enemy, he seeks to make us suffer as he made Yeshua suffer. His intent is thwarted, however, because Yeshua was our ransom, suffering Satan's wrath in our place. And because of Messiah's resurrection, new life is

---

[26] Colossians 2:9
[27] Genesis 1:27

available to all who place their faith in Him, making it possible for God's image to be restored. This is the intended purpose of spiritual growth – growing up *"until we all attain to the unity of the faith, and of the knowledge of the Son of God, to a mature man, to the measure of the stature which belongs to the fullness of Messiah."*[28]

Though reaching the *"measure ... of the fullness of Messiah"* is a tall order, God has already laid the foundation for this work by creating man with the basic internal structure to make this objective attainable. God's essence – His personality, power, wisdom, love, character – are expressed through God's Word (which later *"became flesh and dwelt among us"*[29]) and God's spirit. So, to make man in His own image, He followed the same pattern, creating man as a soul that can express himself through his body and through his spirit.

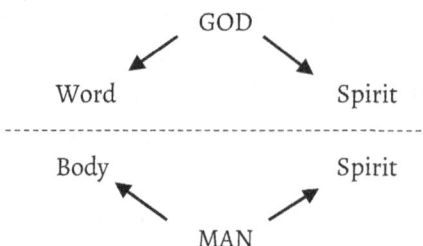

An understanding of the body, soul, and spirit is vitally important for achieving a better understanding of how God relates to the physical realm and is a subject that is rarely understood today. It is beyond the scope of this chapter (and this book) to fully explore this important subject, but a brief excursion into this topic will help us derive further insights into the letter *aleph* which will in turn provide insights into the relation of body, soul, and spirit.

In the Image of God

Since man is made in God's image, many aspects of *aleph* (א) apply to us. Before we go further with this discussion, we must first realize that God does not have a 'makeup', so to speak. God is spirit. Period. However, He manifests Himself in both the physical and spiritual realms. Likewise, the soul receives information from the physical and spiritual realms. Just as God is God, you *are* a soul. Our spirit

---

[28] Ephesians 4:13

[29] John 1:14

corresponds to God's, and our bodies correspond to the various ways God speaks into the world – through the Scriptures as well as through His Son, the Word made flesh. Nevertheless, God is one. But, we broken human beings are fragmented (a dilemma which we will discuss further in the next chapter).

The three parts of *aleph* (א) illustrate the internal relationship of man's body, soul and spirit as it reflects God's expression of Himself through the spirit and the Word – His Son. As the *vav* (ו) stretches between the upper *yud* (י) and the lower *yud*, the soul dwells between the spirit and the body. Likewise, as the *vav* is the dominant figure of the *aleph* (א), the Father is the dominate figure of the godhead and the soul is the dominant part of man.

Though each of us is a soul, we cannot see one another's souls with physical eyes. When you behold a person, you do not literally see the person himself, but only his body. The real person is inside that body looking back at you through the eyes – the windows of the soul.[30] We can think of our bodies as our 'earth suits' which allow our souls to interact with the physical world. Thus, the soul expresses itself through the body by means of words, deeds, and gestures. In other words, the flesh expresses the personality of the soul in the same way that Yeshua expressed the personality of the Father. As God's physical expression, Yeshua was literally the Word of God made flesh. His every word and action were expressions of the Father's personality, thus fulfilling Yeshua's constant desire to do the will of the Father.[31]

Since all communication between individuals takes place through the expressions of the body (speech, gestures, writing, etc.), is it any wonder that God's physical expression, Yeshua, is called 'the Word'? The writer of Hebrews expresses this as follows:

> *God, after he spoke long ago to the fathers in the prophets in many portions and in many ways, in these last days has spoken to us in his Son ...*[32]

When Yeshua spoke of Himself as the Alpha and Omega,[33] He was not merely saying that He was the First and the Last. He was also proclaiming that He *is* God's alphabet – from A to Z – through whom the Father speaks.

---

[30] Though "windows of the soul" is not a biblical phrase, it is nonetheless an accurate concept. (Compare Matthew 6:22-23 and Revelation 1:14.)
[31] John 8:28
[32] Hebrews 1:1-2
[33] Revelation 22:13-16

Not only does the soul express itself through the body, but it is through the body's five senses that the soul, in turn, experiences the surrounding world. If these senses were to somehow be turned off, the soul would be completely insulated from physical sensation. You would have no way of knowing if it were light or dark, hot or cold, or if you were alone or in a crowd.

In the same way that our bodies are sensitive to the physical realm, our spirits are sensitive to the spiritual realm...that is, they *should* be. Paul emphasized this when he wrote,

> ...Things which eye has not seen and ear has not heard, which have not entered the heart of man, all that God has prepared for those who love Him. For to us God revealed them through the spirit, for the spirit searches all things, even the depths of God.[34]

In other words, eyes and ears are incapable of perceiving things which are spiritual in nature. For perceiving those things, the spirit is necessary.

Our enemy is fearful of the believer who is mighty in spirit and has his spiritual eyes open. It has been Satan's tactic to tempt us either to ignore the spirit altogether, or to pursue spirituality by occult means or in other unhealthy ways. On the other hand, God would have us develop spiritually by means of obedience to His Word, prayer, and community.

In short, God expresses Himself in the physical realm through Yeshua (the Word made flesh) and through His spirit. Having been created in God's image, the soul of man is clothed in a body of flesh, while also having a spirit by which he may commune with God.

Let's apply what we have learned about *aleph* (א) to what we have learned about the body, soul, and spirit. As mentioned, א is constructed from a slanted *vav* (ו) surrounded by two *yuds* (י). Just as the *vav* (ו) represents the Father – the person of God Himself – so also the *vav* (ו) can be seen to depict the soul – the person of the human being. The soul (comprised of the mind, will, and emotions), is what makes you distinctly *you*. This is the essence of your personality, because the way you think (mind), the way you make choices (will), and the way you feel and respond to situations (emotions) are what make *your* soul unique from all others.

The lower *yud* (י) is the body – the lowest and earthiest part of a person wherein all physical sensations reside. The body provides the soul's contact with the physical

---

[34] 1 Corinthians 2:9-10

realm, and its five senses are five gates through which physical sensations reach the soul. Through the body we interact with others and learn many of the object lessons God has placed in nature for our instruction.

The upper *yud* (י) is the spirit – the loftiest part of a person wherein the five spiritual sensitivities reside. If you recall, the word *yud* means 'hand'. As the hand has five fingers, so the lower *yud* – the body – has five senses by which we may 'grasp' the physical realm. The upper *yud* – the spirit – also has five senses by which we may interact with the spiritual realm. Let us briefly consider each of these five spiritual senses.

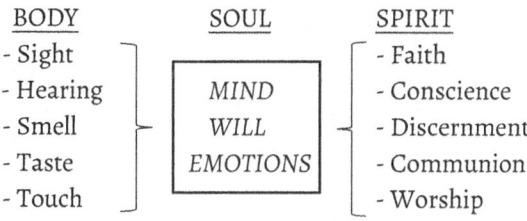

The Five Functions of the Spirit

Faith | We are to walk by faith and not by sight.[35] This does not mean that we are to go through life with our eyes closed. It means that in maneuvering through the physical realm we use our eyes (highly recommended when driving), but for those things which we cannot see God has given us faith. Like physical sight, faith allows us to *see* the spiritual realm. Faith is a gift from God[36] and the Word of God, like a pair of glasses, helps focus faith upon His truth. Faith is not wishful thinking. It is the *"assurance of things hoped for, the conviction of things not seen."*[37] In fact, faith is more dependable than physical sight, *"...For the things which are seen are temporal; but the things which are not seen are eternal."*[38] But even the eyes of faith require a light by which to see, and

---

[35] 2 Corinthians 5:7
[36] Ephesians 2:8
[37] Hebrews 11:1
[38] 2 Corinthians 4:18

Yeshua, the 'light of the world', has placed His light in a lantern called the Bible, a *"lamp unto my feet, and a light unto my path."*[39]

Conscience | The conscience is a moral alarm system located in the spirit. It goes off when we go wrong. If we heed it, we avoid a great deal of remorse and guilt. Even when unbelievers obey their consciences, they *"show the work of the Torah written in their hearts, their conscience also bearing witness."*[40] But if we violate the conscience often enough, it becomes seared as if covered with scar tissue, growing numb to things which should cause pain. Society is reaping the consequences of having taught children behaviors that run contrary to their consciences, thus making their consciences dysfunctional and insensitive to the pleadings of God's spirit.

Discernment | Yeshua commands us to be *"wise as serpents, but innocent as doves"*.[41] If we obey the conscience, we will maintain our innocence; and if we exercise discernment we will be wise as serpents. This spiritual sense complements the conscience in that while the conscience warns me of error in myself, discernment can warn me of error in others. By error I do not mean the doctrinal hairsplitting that has often plagued faith communities, but rather the discernment of the spirit and motive which underlies another's words or actions.

Satan is an accomplished deceiver and is able to counterfeit legitimate workings of the Holy Spirit. Therefore, discernment is valuable in differentiating between God's spirit and demonic spirits. John advises us to "test the spirits"[42] so that we will not easily be led astray by those who employ deception in order to appear godly. Discernment is similar to the sense of smell in that both are useful in detecting hidden rottenness.

In his comparison of the spiritual and carnal man, Paul wrote *"But the spiritual man discerns all things, yet he himself is discerned by no man."*[43] He is referring here to the ability of the spiritually perceptive person to sense what resides in the spirit of another, as well as the inability of the spiritually dead person to sense what resides in the spirit of the believer. As we grow in spiritual maturity, may we become ever more discerning so that we may more effectively minister to others, as well as protect ourselves from wolves in sheep's clothing.

---

[39] Psalm 119:105
[40] Romans 2:15
[41] Matthew 10:16
[42] 1 John 4:1
[43] 1 Corinthians 2:15

Communion | *"Oh, taste and see that the Lord is good!"*[44] Such spiritual tasting occurs only as we spend time feeding upon God's Word and conversing with Him in prayer. This is the archetype of all food and fellowship. I use the word communion instead of prayer because we tend to think of prayer as strictly one-way. We talk, God listens. Communion, on the other hand, is a two-way activity – a living relationship between man and God. Prayers can be written in a book, but communion can't. It is through communion that we intimately connect with God and He directs our paths. In communion we become prayerfully still so as to hear Him say, *"This is the way; walk in it."*[45] Communion is the attitude of prayer Paul had in mind when he said to pray without ceasing.

Worship | We tend to confuse worship with praise. Praise is a function of the soul and is expressed through the body, but worship is a function of the spirit. Yeshua said as much when He stated, *"God is spirit, and those who worship Him must worship in spirit and truth."*[46] Since God is spirit, we cannot touch Him physically. However, we can indeed touch God with that part of us that is like Him – our spirit. This occurs through worship.

Many congregations have so-called "worship teams" which can lead people in praise and singing, but only God's spirit can truly direct worship. Worship is the quiet contemplation and adoration of God born out of communion with Him. Only when we have followed His command to *"Be still and know that I am God"*[47] can we begin to worship Him in spirit and truth. Too often we work backward, attempting to arrive at worship by beginning with praise, with the result that we become spiritual cheerleaders who are attracted to praise itself instead of worshipping the One who is the object of our praise. Praise of God is the natural fruit of worshipping God. Praise should be an expression of worship, not the cause of it.

In summary, we see that *conscience* and *discernment* are especially useful in one's relationship with others, whereas *communion* and *worship* are necessary in one's relationship with God. But, all four must operate from the starting point of *faith*.

As a result of examining the distinctions which exist between the body, soul, and spirit it is easy to forget that they are closely united and that what affects one affects the other two as well. We have seen an example of this as it applies to worship: when

---

[44] Psalm 34:8
[45] Isaiah 30:21
[46] John 4:24
[47] Psalm 46:10

I worship God (spirit), I begin to rejoice in my mind and emotions (soul) and may choose to sing with my mouth, clap, or raise my hands (body). Conversely, if I accidentally drop the garage door on my toe (I speak from personal experience), my mind, will and emotions (soul) direct their full attention on the injured member (body), and I begin to call out to the Lord for help in this time of trouble (spirit).

The soul *is* the self. It is central to the body and spirit and responds fully to both. It is equally able to direct its full attention to an injured toe, or to worship of the King of Kings. This truth is reflected by the *aleph's* slanted *vav* (ו) which descends to the level of the lower *yud* (י), representing the body, and also ascends to the level of the upper *yud* (י), representing the spirit.

Keep the א in Adam

The name of the first man, *Adam* (אדם), begins with *aleph* (which again demonstrates that man is created in God's image). Realizing that the *aleph* represents God's presence, one Jewish Sage wrote that when *Adam* (אדם) sinned, the *aleph* (א) fled and only *dam* (דם, 'blood') was left.[48]

אדם - א = דם
Adam - א = 'blood'

History has repeatedly demonstrated the truth of this statement. Mankind's propensity for bloodshed has been a perpetual reminder of Adam's sin in departing from God.

The same principle can be applied to a common Hebrew word for 'man' – איש (*ish*). When the *aleph* (א) is removed from this word, we are left with *yeesh* (יש), a word meaning mere 'substance'.

איש - א = יש
'man' - א = [mere] substance

This attribute earmarks the life of the fleshly person who cannot see beyond his physical existence. He fills his life with material possessions and physical sensations

---

[48] R' Yeshayah Hurwitz (1560-1630) in <u>Shnei Luchos Habris</u>, Part Three, 13b.

in an attempt to satisfy the emptiness in his soul – an emptiness caused by the absence of God (א) in his life. However, Yeshua said, "*...not even when one has an abundance does his life consist of his possessions.*"[49]

An examination of *aleph*'s name (spelled אלף) also offers some rich insights. As we have seen, the first letter, *aleph* (א), represents God. The name of the second letter, *lamed* (ל), means 'to learn'. The last letter is *peh* (פ or ף), which means 'mouth'. Together, the three letters which spell *aleph* teach us that:

> א - We must meet *the Lord*,...
> ל - ... *learn* from Him, then ...
> ף - ... *speak* of Him.

As we learned in the last section, *vav* (ו) represents the soul. If we place a *vav* (ו) inside the word *aleph* (אלף), we form the word *aluph* (אלוף) which means 'lord' or 'master'. Do you see the picture this creates? By entrusting one's soul (ו) to God (אלף), one makes God his Lord and Master (אלוף). How much more effectively we can speak for and to our God if we have entrusted our lives to Him by making Him our Lord and Master.

In Conclusion

There is much more to be said about the letter *aleph* (א), and we will encounter it many times in chapters to come. *Aleph* (א), lord and master of the alphabet, is the first in a holy pageant of deep truths and rich insights that will be taught by the letters that follow. Although many secrets remain hidden within *aleph* which await discovery, I will end this chapter with one final insight.

In three places the Bible states that *"God is..."*, followed by something to which He can be likened. The three instances are:

> God is a consuming **Fire**   Deuteronomy 4:24   אש
> God is **Light**   1 John 1:5   אור
> God is **Love**   1 John 4:8   אהבה

---

[49] Luke 12:15

Note that each of these three words begins with the letter *aleph* (א), the letter which, more than any other, symbolizes God's nature and character.

Our God is a *consuming fire*; He is *light*; He is *love*. How can we begin to understand the magnitude of His nature? A good place to begin is by visiting God's 'house', which is the meaning of the next letter's name – *beit* (ב).

2

ב | *Beit*

God's Word, God's Dwelling

"The Word of God is in the Bible as the soul is in the body."
Peter Taylor Forsyth

The House of God

The name of the second letter of the Hebrew alphabet is *beit* (בית), which means 'house'. This word is found in several Hebrew names, such as בית-אל (*Beth-El*, 'House of God') and בית-לחם (*Bethlehem*, 'House of bread').[1] Even the shape of the letter depicts a floor, ceiling, wall and doorway of a house. Since the name and form of *beit* (ב) represent a house, we shall consider several ways in which it embodies the characteristics of a dwelling place. In this chapter we shall see how *beit* represents:

- Yeshua – in whom the fullness of the Godhead dwells
- The Bible – in which dwells God's Word to mankind

---

[1] Note that Yeshua, the 'Bread of Life', was born in a manger (literally a feed trough) in a town called *Bethlehem*, the 'House of Bread'.

- The creation – the dwelling place of mankind.[2]
- The human heart

We tend to think in terms of pictures with words serving as paintbrushes. Therefore, if we apply an inaccurate definition to a word, we create an inaccurate picture. Thus, before we proceed, it is imperative that we make a distinction between two very important words. In our discussion of the letter *beit* we will frequently encounter the terms 'Word' and 'Scriptures'. These terms are often used interchangeably, and in casual conversation this is acceptable. But the Bible uses words in precise ways because God wants us to have clear understanding, not confusion. Therefore, when the Bible uses the terms 'Word' and 'Scriptures', something specific and unique is intended by each.

The Scriptures and the Word

The Scriptures (or 'writings') are physical in nature in that they consist of ink on paper. They are God's words recorded in a physical way. Anything that can be done to a physical object can be done to the Scriptures. They can be bought, sold, burned, shredded, or stored on a bookshelf. Although we are commanded to study the Scriptures, and may even memorize them from cover to cover, it is still possible to miss their purpose and be unaffected by the spiritual light they allow us to access.

The Word, on the other hand, is spiritual and alive. You can set fire to the Scriptures, but you can't destroy the Word. You can take the Bible out of a man's hand, but you cannot take the Word out of his heart. The Scriptures are like a stained-glass window which can be admired for its intricate patterns and beautiful colors, but the Word is the light that radiates through the glass. There is an important lesson for us in this illustration: We must be careful that when we approach the Bible it is not only to admire it from a literary and intellectual viewpoint, but to also see the living God who reveals Himself through it. It is possible to study the Scriptures as did the Pharisees, thinking that by doing so we will receive eternal life.[3] But the ultimate goal of

---

[2] *Beit* has a numerical value of two, and on the second day of creation God made the oceans and the atmosphere – 'houses' for the fish and birds.

[3] John 5:39

Bible study should be to see Yeshua more clearly, for He is the living Word and the life and light of the world.

Let me illustrate this point in a different way. If you stand on the bank of a clear, quiet pond, you may admire many of the details that contribute to the pond's form and beauty. Some people read the Bible only in this way – seeing only what is on the surface. They familiarize themselves with facts and events and may even argue fine points of theology, but they never see any deeper into the heart of the Bible's message.

If you focus your eyes to look deeply into the pond, you may perceive life, like fish and aquatic plants that thrive in its depths. Likewise, looking deeper into scripture reveals a living message which can provide food for the soul. When the Bible is studied in this way, one learns life principles that will enrich one's life.

However, if you focus your eyes to gaze even deeper into the pond, it will reveal something billions of times bigger and more powerful than itself. It will reflect the sun as if it were shining up out of its depths. Similarly, if we prayerfully meditate on the Scriptures and look deeply into them, we will access the heavenly realm and behold the light of the Son – the Word of God.

Distinguishing between the Word and the Scriptures is crucial to our understanding of the letter *beit* (ב) and the lessons it holds for us, for *beit* (ב) is the house of scripture, and Yeshua – the Word – is its inhabitant. It is important to understand that in no way do I wish to diminish the importance of studying and memorizing the Scriptures. On the contrary, we are commanded, *"Be diligent to present yourself approved to God as a workman who does not need to be ashamed, accurately handling the word of truth."*[4]

The Scriptures – Home of the Word

The Apostle John wrote, *"And the Word became flesh, and dwelt among us, and we saw His glory, glory as of the only begotten from the Father, full of grace and truth."*[5] Note that John used the term 'the Word', instead of 'the Son'. The Son is called *the Word* because it is through Him that God communicated Himself to us. Take care to understand this important truth. Just as we communicate to one another by means of words, God communicates to us through *the* Word.[6] When the Word became flesh, His name became Yeshua.

---

[4] 2 Timothy 2:15
[5] John 1:14
[6] Hebrews 1:1-2

Furthermore, when the verse says *"...and dwelt among us"*, the word 'dwelt' literally means 'tabernacled'. In other words, Yeshua's body was the 'house' in which God dwelt while Yeshua was on earth. So, how does God communicate with us now that Yeshua has departed the physical realm? In what physical form does God's essence reside today? The Scriptures. They are the vehicle through which God continues to speak. Hence, we grasp the significance of the letter *beit* (ב) – the 'house' which represents both the Son (בן, *ben*) and the Scriptures since they both are the dwelling place of God and they both begin with this letter.

When I say that the Scriptures begin with *beit* (ב) I do not mean the word 'scriptures', but rather the Bible itself. Let me explain. Below is the first verse of the Bible as it appears in Hebrew.

בְּרֵאשִׁית בָּרָא אֱלֹהִים אֵת הַשָּׁמַיִם וְאֵת הָאָרֶץ׃

Notice how the ב (*beit*) which begins this verse is printed oversized – the only oversized *beit* found in the Bible. (This is just one example of the many anomalies that appear in the *Tanach* and have been faithfully reproduced by the Jewish scribes over the centuries.) The Sages see the oversize *beit* (ב) of Genesis 1:1 as a house which is closed at the top, bottom, and back, blocking from view all that comes before it. But, issuing forth from the door of this 'house' are the words of Torah in which are hidden all the secrets of God's wisdom. The remaining twenty letters of the alphabet are seen as issuing from the ב just as it, in turn, is considered as issuing forth from the א. This pictures the way that God communicates His word to the world – through the *beit* (ב) of His Son (*ben*, בן), and the *beit* which begins the Bible.

The pronunciation of *aleph* (א) and *beit* (ב) also reflect the roles of the Father and the Word. Representing the invisible God who is spirit, *aleph* (א) is silent – it makes no sound that can be voiced with a human mouth nor heard with a human ear. However, *beit* (ב) – representing both Yeshua (God's 'house' in human flesh) and the Scriptures – makes the sound of a 'B' as in "BOOM" and is the most strongly vocalized of all the letters.[7]

---

[7] There are some exceptions to this. When the ב contains a *dagesh* (a dot in the middle as in Genesis 1:1) it is pronounced like the letter B. When it lacks the *dagesh*, ב is pronounced like the letter 'V'. (Since the *dagesh* is part of the vowel system added in the Middle Ages and not part of the original Hebrew, I do not incorporate it in every *beit* where it would normally be found.)

The proclamation of the gospel is also portrayed by *beit* (ב). If we remove the ב from the first five letters of the alphabet – אבגדה – we are left with the word אגדה (*agadah*), which means 'telling' [as of a story].[8] What story is being told, and who is telling it? *Beit* (ב) – the Son – does not wish to speak about Himself (that is why it does not appear in this word), but He tells instead of the goodness and greatness of His Father. This point is also demonstrated in another way…

The Sword of the Spirit

In addition to the Scriptures being a 'home' into which God enters, it is also equated to a sword that enters us.

> *For the word of God is living and active and sharper than any two-edged sword, and piercing as far as the division of soul and spirit, of both joints and marrow, and able to judge the thoughts and intentions of the heart. And there is no creature hidden from His sight, but all things are open and laid bare to the eyes of Him with whom we have to do.*[9]

The Hebrew word for 'sword' is חרב (*cherev*). Though the Word of God has the power to unite, it must first do its work of dividing, and everything about the combination of letters in חרב screams "division" which is, after all, what a sword was created to do. This requires some explanation…

The number that the Bible uses to represent 'division' is two. The number *one* represents unity, but *two* represents division. Now consider the numerical values of the letters used to spell חרב (*cherev*) 'sword'. As you can see below, each letter of this word bears a close mathematical relationship with the number two.

2   200 2^3

---

[8] At the Passover *Seder*, participants read from a *Haggadah* (literally "the telling"), a booklet that 'tells' the story of Israel's deliverance from Egyptian bondage.
[9] Hebrews 4:12-13

To emphasize the Scripture's role as a sword we must also remember the location where God began to reveal His Word to the world – Mount Sinai. The Torah has two names for Mount Sinai. The second name is *Horeb* (חרב) – which is exactly the same word as *cherev*, 'sword'.

A Medicine and a Poison

Let's look at another word with a deep connection to the Word and a similar numerical value as *Horeb*. In fact, it is the word 'word' – דבר (*davar*).

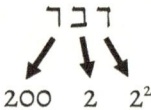

Should we be surprised that the word for 'word' and the word for 'sword' should have such a similarity? After all, the 'Word' is also the 'sword' of the spirit. But, there are two other insights that the word דבר (*davar*) illustrates for us. We shall discuss one of them now, but we will save the other one for a little later.

The word *davar* (דבר) is the root of the name Deborah (pronounced *Devorah* in Hebrew). *Devorah* (דבורה) is, more or less, a feminine form of *davar* and means 'bee'. I find this fascinating, because a bee has two qualities that are also possessed by the Word of God.

The first of these qualities is the sweetness a bee produces through its honey. Consider this verse from Psalms: *"How sweet are Your words to my taste! Yes, sweeter than honey to my mouth!"*[10] This is not the only place where God's Word is compared to honey with all of its sweetness and healthful benefits. However, the bee manifests a second, and less pleasant, quality.

Though we may rarely discuss the pain that can result from knowledge of the Word, it is likely that we have all experienced it. Like the bee, which produces honey, it can also produce a painful – and sometimes deadly – sting. This dual nature of God's Word is illustrated by the following passages from the *Talmud*:

---

[10] Psalm 119:103

R'Bana'ah used to say: *"Whoever studies Torah for its own sake, his Torah [scholarship] becomes an elixir of life to him; as it is said, 'It is a Tree of Life for those who cling to it.' ... And similarly it says elsewhere, 'For one who has found Me has found life.' But whoever studies Torah not for its own sake, his Torah [scholarship] becomes a deadly poison to him. As it is said, 'My teaching shall <u>drip down</u> [עֲרוֹף, aroph] like the rain; and the word עֲרִיפָה [ariphah] is interpreted here as nothing other than 'killing.'"*[11]

R' Yehoshua ben Levi said: *"... If one is deserving, [the Torah] becomes a drug of life to him. But if one is not deserving, it becomes a drug of death to him." And this is reflected by that which Rava said: "Where one uses [the Torah] skillfully, it is a drug of life, but where one uses it unskillfully, it is a drug of death."*[12]

These statements accord with Paul's advice to Timothy: *"Be diligent to present yourself approved to God as a workman who does not need to be ashamed, accurately handling the word of truth."*[13] And why does God's Word require careful handling? It is a sword! And an extremely sharp one at that. Sharp objects are hazardous in the hands of those who do not know how to use them.

And let us also consider Paul's warning to the Corinthians:

"... whoever eats the bread or drinks the cup of the Lord in an unworthy manner, shall be guilty of the body and the blood of the Lord. But a man must examine himself, and in so doing he is to eat of the bread and drink of the cup. For he who eats and drinks, eats and drinks judgment to himself if he does not judge the body rightly. For this reason many among you are weak and sick, and a number sleep [i.e. have died]."[14]

These warnings from the *Talmud* and the Scriptures illustrate how something that is meant for life can actually cause death. Just as a particular medicine can bring health to one individual, it can be poisonous to another. This is true as well for the Scriptures, which have been used to do both incredible good in the world and

---

[11] *b. Talmud – Taanit 7a* (Artscroll Publishers)
[12] *b. Talmud – Yoma 72b* (Artscroll Publishers)
[13] 2 Timothy 2:15
[14] 1 Corinthians 11:27-30

incredible evil. It all depends upon the integrity of the one who is using them. Satan used the Scriptures to tempt Yeshua, and Yeshua used the Scriptures to resist those same temptations.

Let us use great caution and skill in handling God's Word. And we will do so if we approach it with humility, integrity, truth and love.

"Father, You Shall Rule"

John referred to those who were spiritually mature as fathers because *"...you know Him who has been from the beginning..."*[15] The first two letters of the alphabet (א and ב) together spell the word אב (*av*, 'father'). Thus, we see in the very order of the letters the proclamation of the Father first and foremost. It is appropriate that this word is situated here at the beginning of the alphabet since all good things issue from the Father.

Since אב (*av*) is spelled using only the first two letters of the alphabet, it has a numeric value of three – the smallest of any word in the Hebrew language (א = 1, ב = 2; 1 + 2 = **3**). Considering the fact that אב (*av*) has the smallest numeric value of any word in the Torah, one may wonder what word has the highest numeric value. That distinction belongs to תשתרר (*tistareir*), which equals 1500 (ת = 400, ש = 300, ת = 400, ר = 200, ר = 200; 400 + 300 + 400 + 200 + 200 = **1500**).[16] *Tistareir* means "you shall rule."

When we combine the word having the lowest numeric value with the word having the highest, we derive "Father, You shall rule." These two Hebrew words form a phrase that is a central theme of the Bible because this simple phrase expresses both God's *love* (as a 'Father') and His *sovereignty* ("You shall rule"). Paul reflects this message in his prophecy that *"When all things are subjected to Him [Yeshua], then the Son Himself also will be subjected to the One who subjected all things to Him, so that God [i.e. the Father] may be all in all."*[17] In short, Yeshua will proclaim, "Father (אב), You shall rule (תשתרר)".

The Father's kingship is also displayed in the order of the Hebrew alphabet itself. The four middle letters of the alphabet are י-כ-ל-מ. These four letters can be arranged to make the word ימלך (*yim'loch*) "(he) shall reign". This word is first found in the phrase, *"Adonai shall reign forever and ever".*[18]

---

[15] 1 John 2:13
[16] Numbers 16:13
[17] 1 Corinthians 15:28
[18] Exodus 15:18

As we learned in Chapter 1, *aleph* (א) represents the 'Father' (אב) and His attributes. In this chapter we begin to see how *beit* (ב, which begins the word בן, *ben*, 'son') represents the attributes of Yeshua, the Son of God. And if we merge the words *Father* and *Son*, we discover something incredible…

The Rejected Cornerstone

As stated above, אב (*av*) spells 'father', and בן (*ben*) spells 'son'. Note that both words share the letter *beit* (ב). If we combine these two words so that they share the same *beit* (ב), we derive אבן (*evan*) – 'stone'. The diagram below shows this more clearly.

$$+ \quad \begin{array}{r} \text{אב} = Father \\ \text{בן} = Son \\ \hline \text{אבן} = Stone \end{array}$$

This 'stone' – the fact that the Father and the Son (Yeshua) are one – was what caused so many of the Jewish leaders to reject Yeshua's messianic claims. When He claimed that He and the Father were one, the bystanders picked up stones to stone Him.[19] Paul cited Isaiah's prophecy when he explained why so many rejected Yeshua as the Messiah –

> …but Israel, pursuing a law of righteousness, did not arrive at that law. Why? Because they did not pursue it by faith, but as though it were by works. They stumbled over the stumbling stone, just as it is written, "Behold, I lay in Aion a stone [אבן] of stumbling and a rock of offense, and he who believes in him will not be disappointed."[20]

Today, people continue to stumble over this same "stumbling stone" because they cannot accept what Yeshua claimed – that He is one with His Father. But the wise man does not stumble upon this Rock. Instead, he builds his house upon it.

---

[19] John 10:30-31
[20] Romans 9:31-33 (quoting Isaiah 28:16)

The Spirit of Prophecy

An interesting phenomenon that frequently occurs in the *Tanach* is that when a word is spelled backward, it reveals a spiritual insight into that word. (We shall discuss several of these as we make our way through the upcoming chapters.) For instance, if we take Laban's name – לבן (which means 'white') – and reverse it, we derive נבל (*naval*) which means 'fool'.[21]

If we do this with the word אבן (*evan*, 'stone') by reversing it, we derive the word נבא (*nava*) which means 'prophesy'. So, what is the connection between the 'stone' of stumbling – Yeshua – and 'prophesy'? Revelation tells us, *"For the testimony of Yeshua is the spirit of prophecy."*[22] Maybe this is just coincidence. But, I don't think so.

With the addition of the letter *yud* (י) – which we shall learn about in chapter 10 – we derive the word נביא (*navi*) 'prophet'.

In the Beginning was *"In the Beginning"*

Returning to our discussion of Yeshua as the inhabitant of the 'house' (ב), this is literally spelled out in the first word of the Bible. Let's take a closer look. Below is the first word of the Bible.

בראשית

6 5 4 3 2 1

This word is pronounced *barasheit* and means *"In the beginning"*.[23] You will notice that it is spelled with six letters (which have been numbered to simplify identification). Recall that the word for 'house' is spelled בית (*beit*). These three letters are part of the word *barasheit* (letters 1, 5 & 6). The remaining three letters (2,3,4) spell the word ראש (*rosh*), which means 'head'. Hence, we can see in *barasheit*, a 'house' containing the 'head'. Who is the head? The only one in the Bible who refers to Himself as the

---

[21] This is also the name of Abigail's husband Nabal. She spoke of him to David saying, *"Please do not let me lord pay attention to this worthless man, Nabal, for as his name is, so is he. Nabal is his name and foolishness is with him..."* (1 Samuel 25:25)

[22] Revelation 19:10

[23] When the letter ב is prefixed to a noun, it forms a preposition meaning 'in'. Example: ספר (*sefer*) means 'book', and בספר (*b'sefer*) means "in a book".

"head of the house" is Yeshua.[24] This takes on special significance when we read *"He was in the beginning with God."*[25] Not only was Messiah "in the beginning", He is also in the first word of the Bible – בראשית – which means "in the beginning". With this in mind, look at the first words of John's gospel. It begins in the same way as Genesis, *"In the beginning was the Word, and the Word was with God, and God was the Word."*[26]

Another similarity between these two verses (Genesis 1:1 and John 1:1) is found in the fourth word of each. The fourth word of John 1:1 is *ho'logos*, "the Word". The fourth word of Genesis 1:1 is את (*et*), a word consisting of the first and last letters of the Hebrew alphabet. In Revelation,[27] Yeshua refers to Himself as *"the Alpha (A) and the Omega (Ω)"*, which are the first and last letters of the Greek alphabet.

    את   *Aleph & Tuv*
    AΩ   *Alpha & Omega*

Hence, *The Word* = את = AΩ.

Correctly Cutting the Word

In his letter to Timothy, Paul made a cryptic statement that has been the object of debate ever since. He stated:

> *Be diligent to present yourself approved to God as a workman who does not need to be ashamed, accurately handling the word of truth.*[28]

This passage does not seem very complicated as it is translated above, but the Greek word translated 'handling' is literally 'cutting'. Hence, Paul is encouraging Timothy be one who is *"...accurately cutting the word of truth."* What did Paul mean by 'cutting' the Word of truth? I don't claim to know exactly what Paul had in mind, but I do know that a first century Jewish rabbi handled the Scriptures much differently that

---

[24] Matthew 10:25. The Sages point out that the letters of the word ראש (*rosh*, 'head') can be rearranged to spell אשר (*asher*, 'happiness'). From this they derive that the Torah is a "house of happiness".
[25] John 1:2
[26] John 1:1
[27] Revelation 22:13-16
[28] 2 Timothy 2:15

34 | In His Own Words

we do today. And one of the things they did was slice words open to learn what they might reveal. Let me demonstrate.

If we take the first word of Genesis – בראשית – (*barasheit*, "In the beginning") and slice it between its second and third letters, we derive the phrase – בר אשית – (*bar asheit*, "A son I shall establish").[29]

בר אשית
↙ ↘
"I shall establish" < "A Son"

This is profound. When we slice the first word of the *Torah* in this way, it reveals the seed of the gospel message concealed in the first word of the Bible.

A Door to the Son

If you recall, earlier in this chapter I said there was a second insight concerning the word דבר (*davar*) 'word'. Let's discuss this now.

You have just learned that one of the words the Torah uses for 'son' is בר (*bar*). If you look at the word for 'word' – דבר – you will notice that the last two letters spell בר (*bar*) 'son'. But, what are we to make of that first letter – the ד (*dalet*)? The name of this letter means 'door' (and we shall learn more about *dalet* in chapter 4). Now, if we put this information together, we discover that the 'Word' (דבר) provides a 'door' (ד) to the 'Son' (בר).

ד ← בר
'Son' < 'door'

How ב Came First

According to Jewish tradition, the creation of the Torah parallels the creation of the world. The *Midrash* contains a story describing how *beit* (ב) was chosen as the letter through which God would create both the world and *Torah*.

---

[29] The word אשית (*asheit*, "I shall establish") is found in Genesis 3:15, "<u>I shall put/establish</u> enmity between you and the woman..."

According to this legend, the 22 letters of the alphabet are inscribed around God's crown. When it came time to choose a letter with which to create the world, the letters leapt from God's crown to present themselves before Him to vie for this honor. Each letter, beginning with *tuv* (ת), argued its case, describing why its attributes made it the most appropriate letter for this privilege. But, as each letter stood before God in hopes of being chosen for this honor, each was rejected for one reason or another. When ב (*beit*) finally stood before God's throne it said, "Begin with me, because all creation will use me to bless You." God immediately accepted the *beit* and said, "So shall the creation begin."

The ב based its claim upon the fact that the Hebrew word for 'blessed' (ברוך, *baruch*) begins with ב. This word begins many Jewish prayer thus…

ברוך אתה יהוה אלהינו מלך העלם

Baruch atah, Adonai elohenu, Melech h'olam.

"Blessed are You, Adonai our God, King of the universe."

After *beit* (ב) was chosen, *aleph* (א) remained silent and did not contend for a right to state its claim. God asked it, "Why are you silent?", to which *aleph* responded, "I cannot compete with the other letters because they all represent plurality, and I am only one." God then said, "*Aleph*, do not fret, for you stand at the head of the alphabet like a King. You are one and I am One. It is my intention to create the world as a home for my Torah. And as I shall begin my creation with *beit*, I shall begin my Ten Commandments with *aleph*." And this, according to the *Midrash*, is why the Ten Commandments begin with the word אנכי (*anochi*, "I [am your God]").[30]

Though this fanciful story is not biblical in origin, it nevertheless expresses a Jewish idea that is very biblical. The rabbis teach that the Torah is spiritual in essence and is merely clothed in parchment and ink. This truth is illustrated even in the way Torah scrolls were once prepared. When a lamb was sacrificed, its hide was saved and used for parchment upon which God's words would be inscribed. In the same manner, the Word was clothed in skin – the flesh of Yeshua, the Lamb of God.[31] We know that Yeshua is the living Torah – the Word of God clothed in human flesh.

---

[30] Exodus 20:2

[31] There is also an important lesson here concerning our own bodies. Paul exhorted us to present our bodies as *"living sacrifices, holy and acceptable to God"* (Romans 12:1). Though we are sacrifices, our "hides" are still

Words Creative and Shocking

It is difficult for an English reader to appreciate the impact that some of Yeshua's words had on His Jewish listeners. There is no better example of this than what He said about the end of the world. Jewish theology teaches that when God spoke the world into existence, His words were not merely verbal orders that caused things to occur. Instead, His words continue to echo and pulsate like a song throughout creation, upholding the universe through the ages. It is also believed that should God ever cease to sing forth the creation, creation would cease to exist.

Indeed, there is some biblical support for this belief. The Bible states that He upholds all things *"by the word of His power..."*.[32] One rabbi explains creation this way:

> *The heaven continues to exist because not an instant goes by without God continuing to say, in effect, "Let there be a firmament" – otherwise they would return to the status that prevailed before God's will was uttered. So it is with every aspect of Creation. God's original Ten Utterances are repeated constantly in the sense that the Divine will of the original six days remains in force. Otherwise, everything would revert to the nothingness of before Creation.*[33]

When we consider this belief that God's original creative word continues to uphold the universe in its present state, we can begin to appreciate how shocking Yeshua's words must have seemed when He said, *"Heaven and earth will pass away, but My words will not pass away."*[34] In essence, He was saying that what was spoken by the Father in creation is only temporary since heaven and earth will someday pass away. But, Yeshua claimed that His own words would endure forever, indicating that His own words were more enduring than His Father's! It is obvious how one who had been trained in the oral tradition, upon hearing these words of Yeshua, was faced with the choice of either condemning Him as a blasphemer or embracing Him as the Messiah. There was no middle ground.

But, how could Yeshua's words be more powerful and enduring than His Father's? It is not that Yeshua is more powerful than God. After all, Yeshua Himself only

---

alive and intact, and they, like the parchments, should proclaim God's Torah through righteous and holy living.

[32] Hebrews 1:3 (emphasis mine)
[33] Rabbi Michael L. Munk, <u>The Wisdom of the Hebrew Alphabet</u>, Artscroll Mesorah Series, 1990.
[34] Matthew 24:35

spoke what He was told by His Father.[35] God spoke the creation into existence, but what He spoke through Yeshua were eternal, spiritual things. Thus, Yeshua's words will endure long after this current world comes to an end.

Two Points About the Beit and Two Words About the Son

Beit (ב) is always printed in Torah scrolls with two sharp points. One of these points is located at its base and points back to the *aleph* (א). The other is at the top and points upward toward God.

An old Jewish story explains these two points thus: If you should ask the *beit*, "Who made you?", it points up toward God. If you ask it, "What is His name?", it points backward toward the *aleph*. Truly, Yeshua consistently did both of these. He pointed to God and proclaimed Him as both Creator and Redeemer.

In its account of the creation, the Torah uses a unique Hebrew verb: ברא (*bara*), which means 'create'. *Bara* is used only in regard to God's ability to create, but never man's. *Bara* means to make something out of nothing, which is an impossible task for a mere human. The attributes of the great Architect and Builder, Yeshua, are proclaimed by the verb *bara* (ברא) in a stunning way.

Though the Hebrew word for 'son' is בן (*ben*), another word – בר (*bar*, the Aramaic word for 'son') – is also used frequently in the Bible.[36] By simply distancing the א (*aleph*) from the first two letters of ברא (*bara*), we derive:

ברא "create" = בר-א (*bar* א) = Son of א

Thus, we can see in *bara* the attribute of Yeshua through whom God created the heavens and the earth. As John stated in his gospel, *"All things came into being through Him, and apart from Him nothing came into being that has come into being."*[37]

---

[35] John 15:15
[36] The term *bar mitzvah* means "Son of the commandment". And Simon *bar* Jonah means "Simon, son of Jonah".
[37] John 1:3

Look again at Genesis 1:1. Do you recognize the first two words?

בְּרֵאשִׁית בָּרָא אֱלֹהִים אֵת הַשָּׁמַיִם וְאֵת הָאָרֶץ׃

The first is בראשית (*barasheit*, "In the beginning"), and the second is ברא (*bara*, 'create', or 'he created').[38] In light of the hidden meaning of *bara* as "son of א", we can read these two words as "In the beginning [was] the Son of א." John must certainly have seen this when he opened his gospel with *"In the beginning was the Word"*.[39]

בראשית   בר-א
א < the son of < In the beginning

Of Sons and Stones

While we are on the subject of 'sons', let me share a fascinating play on words that John the Immerser made in one of His teachings. When some hypocritical leaders came to be immersed by John, he sternly rebuked them saying, *"...and do not suppose that you can say to yourselves, 'We have Abraham for our father'; for I say to you that from these stones God is able to raise up sons to Abraham."*[40]

To help us appreciate John's cleverness here, let's examine the Hebrew words for 'stones' and 'sons'.

sons = בנים

stones = אבנים

At a glance, one can see that 'sons' becomes 'stones' by the simple addition of the letter *aleph* (א) to the word בנים (*banim*, 'sons'). Thus, we can see how easily בנים 'sons' can be derived from אבנים 'stones'.

---

[38] Note also that the first three letters of בראשית(*barasheit*) spell ברא (*bara*).
[39] John 1:1
[40] Matthew 3:9

The Heart – A House Divided

The Hebrew language is an onomatopoeic language. (Now there's a word you can use to impress your friends!) In case you have forgotten junior high school English class, onomatopoeia refers to a word that sounds like the thing it describes. For example, to the Greek ear a sheep does not go "ba-a-a, ba-a-a", but "bar, bar". This is why the ancient Greeks called people who could not speak Greek 'bar-bar-ians' (or, as we say, 'barbarians'). To the ancient Greeks, non-Greek speakers sounded like so many sheep going "bar-bar".

The Hebrew word for 'heart' is also an example of onomatopoeia. If you listen to a heartbeat, you hear something like 'la-bub ... la-bub'. Thus, 'heart' in Hebrew is לבב. The first letter, ל (*lamed*) always makes an 'L' sound. The letter *beit* (ב), as we have learned, makes a 'B' or a 'V' sound. Thus, לבב could be pronounced 'la-bub', just like the sound of a heartbeat. This word – לבב – is, as you may have guessed, the word for 'heart', though it is normally pronounced *levav*.

Remember how we can sometimes reverse a Hebrew word to derive a valuable insight? If we may, let's digress for a moment and use this method to see what the word for 'heart' reveals to us. If we reverse the spelling of לבב, we derive בלל (*Bavel*) which is the name 'Babel' – the place where God confused the languages of the world.[41] What is connection of 'Babel' (בבל) and the 'heart' (לבב)? The name Babel has become synonymous with confusion, and the heart is where confusion habitually finds its source as well as its home. Jeremiah wrote, *"The heart is more deceitful than all else and is desperately sick; who can understand it?"*[42] The first world religion occurred at Babel as a result of people following their hearts.

Now, back to our discussion...

You will recall that the letter *beit* (ב) means 'house'. Now, note that לבב contains two *beits* (ב), or 'houses'. This perfectly describes the human condition since our hearts, too, have two 'houses' which, unfortunately, are often at war with each other.

This internal conflict is nothing new. It has been described by philosophers and poets throughout history and has broken marriages and destroyed nations. James wrote of the man who makes a request of God but doubts that God will answer. He

---

[41] Genesis 11
[42] Jeremiah 17:9

described such a man as *"...being a double-minded man, unstable in all his ways."*[43] A more accurate translation would "double-souled".[44]

However, the Hebrew word for 'heart' is not consistently spelled the same way. (Is anything about the heart consistent?) Though it is spelled with two *beits* more than 250 times in the Bible, it is spelled with just one *beit* (לב, *lev*) more than 600 times. Thus, it would be safe to say that the preferred spelling for 'heart' is לב (*lev*), not לבב (*levav*). What are we to make of this? I think the message here is that God desires the two 'houses' in each of our hearts should be united into one and that the inner warfare should end. Our physical and spiritual desires should be in harmony, not conflict. Maybe this is what David had in mind when he wrote, *"Teach me Your way, Adonai; I will walk in Your truth. Unite my heart to fear Your name."*[45] May God grant each of us a united heart to fear His name.

The Sheepfold

Though Yeshua is the one through whom God created the world, He refers to Himself by a much humbler term – the gate of the sheep pen. John quotes Yeshua this way: *"I tell you the truth, the man who does not enter the sheep pen by the gate, but climbs in by some other way, is a thief and a robber... I tell you the truth, I am the gate for the sheep... I am the gate; whoever enters through Me will be saved. He will come in and go out, and find pasture..."*[46]

A sheep pen was an enclosure shaped very much like the letter *beit* (ב). It was used to enclose the flock at night and was just tall enough that the sheep could not jump over it. The sheep were led into the pen before dark, and the shepherd slept across the opening so as to prevent their escape.

Within the confines of the sheep pen, the flock could do as it pleased. Only when a sheep escaped from the pen, did that sheep violate the restrictions placed upon it. However, when the shepherd led the sheep out of the enclosure and they experienced freedom from the pen's confinement, another set of restrictions came into play. Though free of the sheepfold, they must now walk in obedience to the shepherd. Unlike the external limitations of the sheep pen, the shepherd was a living, breathing person who had to be followed and obeyed if the sheep were to continue enjoying

---

[43] James 1:8
[44] The Greek word used here is δίψυχος (*di-psuchos*) from δι (*di* = 'double') and ψυχη (*psuchei* = 'soul').
[45] Psalm 86:11
[46] John 10:1,7,9 (Complete Jewish Bible)

security and safety. Both the shepherd and the sheep pen provide protection and security, but following the shepherd is certainly more interesting.

The sheep pen (like all things mentioned in scripture) contains a spiritual lesson for our edification. The Torah introduced righteous restrictions to protect us from practicing sin. The enclosure of the sheep pen pictures the protection provided by the Torah regulations that restrict our behavior for our own good.[47] Yeshua demonstrated how a Torah life-style is truly lived, and He also enabled us to live it through the power of His spirit. Paul wrote that *"the righteous requirement of the Torah might be fulfilled in us, who do not walk according to the flesh but according to the spirit."*[48]

The freedom Messiah brings demands a much higher standard of righteousness than even that required by surface conformity to the Torah, because the walls of the sheep pen, like the commandments of the Torah, are an external restraint. Devotion to the shepherd's will, however, is an internal – and even more demanding – standard.

Some of the Sages taught (for whatever reasons) that the Messiah will someday close the fourth side of the letter *beit* (ב). But, I believe Messiah has already come with the purpose of opening it.

> *Therefore, Yeshua said again, "I tell you the truth, I am the gate for the sheep. All who ever came before me were thieves and robbers, but the sheep did not listen to them. I am the gate; whoever enters through me will be saved. He will come in and go out and find pasture."*[49]

Alphabetically Speaking

When preparing this chapter, I consulted my Hebrew lexicon to learn what was the first alphabetical listing for the letter ב. The first word in the lexicon to begin with *beit* (ב) is באר.[50] This word has two pronunciations, each associated with a different definition. First, it can be rendered *ba'ar*, which can mean either "to engrave, as upon a tablet [of clay or stone]", or "to expound or explain". The second way באר can be pronounced is *b'eir*, which means "a well or cistern".[51]

---

[47] Galatians 3:23-24
[48] Romans 8:4
[49] John 10:7-9
[50] Note that this word is spelled with the same letters as ברא (*bara*, 'create').
[51] For example, *Beer-Sheba* means "well of the oath".

The first rendering of באר (*ba'ar*) is illustrated by the fact that when God gave the ten commandments to Moses, they were *engraved* upon tablets of stone. And when the scriptures are *expounded* and *explained*, they become engraved upon our hearts. In this way what is external becomes internalized.

The second rendering of באר (*b'eir*) pictures the scripture's ability to quench our spiritual thirst. Yeshua said, *"...but whoever drinks of the water that I will give him shall never thirst, but the water that I will give him will become in him a well of water springing up to eternal life."*[52]

Recall also the story of when Moses struck the rock so that it brought forth water for the Israelites.[53] Look once more at the Hebrew for Genesis 1:1. Doesn't the oversized *beit* (ב) look like a rock gushing forth the words of Torah?

Destructive Stupidity

The mention of water gushing from the rock reminds me of another Hebrew word that is similar to the word באר above. Changing the middle letter from *aleph* (א) to *ayin* (ע) gives us the word בער. This word can also be pronounced two different ways. When it is pronounced *ba-ar*, it means 'stupid' or 'brutish' as in the verse *"Whoever loves discipline loves knowledge, but he who hates reproof is 'stupid'* (בער *ba-ar)."*[54]

When this same word is pronounced *bo-ar*, it describes a powerful fire as in *"For behold, the day is coming, burning* (בער *bo-ar) like a furnace; and all the arrogant and every evildoer will be chaff..."*[55]

From the way this word is used to describe both 'stupidity' and 'fire', we learn the valuable lesson about the destructiveness of stupidity. Let us not be found ignorant but wise for there is safety in wisdom. *"For wisdom is protection just as money is protection, but the advantage of knowledge is that wisdom preserves the lives of its possessors."*[56]

Two Closing Remarks

By now it should be clear that just as *aleph* (א) represents the invisible (and mostly quiet) God of the Universe, *beit* (ב) represents His words (the Scriptures) as well as

---

[52] John 4:14
[53] Numbers 20:11; Exodus 17:6
[54] Proverbs 12:1
[55] Malachi 4:1
[56] Ecclesiastes 7:12

His Son (the Word made flesh). Hebrews 1:3 says *"When He [Yeshua] had made purification of sins, he sat down at the right hand of the Majesty on high.."*[57] Isn't that exactly where the ב is located in relation to the א – on the *aleph*'s right hand?

Lastly, let us look at one more word that illustrates the relationship between *beit* (ב, the 'house') and God's Word. It is the word תיבה (*tivah*). Though not used in the Bible, it is a Hebrew word which means 'word'. However, if we reverse the order of the letters, it becomes הבית (*habeit*) 'the house'.

May God find us continuously dwelling in the house of His Word.

---

[57] Hebrews 1:3

3

ג | *Gimel*

A Voice in the Wilderness

Still with unhurrying chase, and unperturbed pace,
Deliberate speed, majestic instancy,
Came on the following Feet, and a Voice above their beat—
"Naught shelters thee, who wilt not shelter Me."

Francis Thompson - *"The Hound of Heaven"*

In chapters one and two we met *aleph* (א), which represents God the Father, and *beit* (ב), whose name means 'house' and represents Yeshua – the Word 'housed' in flesh. In this chapter we encounter the Holy Spirit which is represented by the letter *gimel* (ג). Before we examine this letter in detail, however, we must first meet a man whose identity is completely wrapped up in the *gimel*. His name is John.

Who Is John the Immerser?

John the Immerser was a remarkable man whom Yeshua described as the greatest of prophets:

> "Truly I say to you, among those born of women there has not arisen anyone greater than John the Immerser! Yet the one who is least in the kingdom of heaven is greater than he."[1]

---

[1] Matthew 11:11

What kind of prophet was John the Immerser to deserve such praise from the Messiah? What was his mission? And why did God send him at that particular time? These were the questions being asked by the Jewish leaders of the day when they sent a delegation into the desert where John was preaching. Consider their questions:

> *This is the testimony of John, when the Judeans sent to him priests and Levites from Jerusalem to ask him, "Who are you?" And he confessed and did not deny, but confessed, "I am not the Messiah."*
>
> *They asked him, "What then? Are you Elijah?"*
> *And he said, "I am not."*
> *"Are you the Prophet?"*
> *And he answered, "No."*
>
> *Then they said to him, "Who are you, so that we may give an answer to those who sent us? What do you say about yourself?"*
>
> *He said, "I am a voice of one crying in the wilderness, 'Make straight the way of Adonai.' As Isaiah the prophet said."*[2]
>
> *Now they had been sent from the Pharisees. They asked him, and said to him, "Why then are you immersing, if you are not the Messiah, nor Elijah, nor the Prophet?"*
>
> *John answered them saying, "I immerse in water, but among you stands One whom you do not know. It is He who comes after me, the thong of whose sandal I am not worthy to untie."*[3]

The Israelites of the day expectantly awaited the fulfillment of several prophecies, and these are reflected in their questions. Their first question was, *"Who are you?"*, to which John answered, *"I am not the Messiah"*. The Jewish delegation probably had hoped that he was the Messiah, the long-awaited redeemer who would deliver Israel from Roman oppression. John was exactly the fiery, bold, and radical kind of man they expected the Messiah to be, who would lead them in a revolt against their Roman oppressors. But, John was interested in the kingdom of the spirit, not a military revolt.

---

[2] Quoting Isaiah 40:3
[3] John 1:19-27 (quoting Isaiah 40:3 in verse 22)

Next, they asked him if he was Elijah. Malachi had prophesied that Elijah would come to prepare the way for the Messiah, so the delegation from Jerusalem hoped that maybe John would fulfill this prophetic role.[4] But John again answered in the negative.

Moses had prophesied that a prophet would come who would be like himself — one who would profoundly affect the Jewish nation as had Moses in the giving of the Torah.[5] If John was neither the Messiah nor the Messiah's forerunner, Elijah, then perhaps he was the prophet whose coming had been predicted by Moses. Hence, they asked him, *"Are you that prophet?"* But, again, John answered that he was not. Today we know that Moses' prophesy refers to Messiah Yeshua, who not only radically affected the Jewish nation, but the whole world. *"For the Torah was given through Moses, but grace and truth were realized by Yeshua the Messiah."*[6]

The delegation had reached the end of their list of questions and still had not discovered John's identity. If John wasn't the Messiah, or Elijah, or "the Prophet", then who was he? So, they asked him, *"Who are you, so that we may give an answer to those who sent us?"*, to which John replied, *"I am a voice of one crying in the wilderness, 'Make straight the way of Adonai.'"*[7]

They had not expected this response. John applied a prophecy to himself that was not thought to apply to a man at all. John's was a voice that rebuked sin, encouraged repentance, and proclaimed Yeshua as the Messiah – the *"Lamb of God who takes away the sin of the world"*.[8] He was God's voice dressed in camel hair, preaching in the desert. And people responded. Yeshua said that John was the greatest prophet who had ever lived. Though John had explicitly stated that he was not Elijah, Yeshua said, *"For all the Prophets and the Torah prophesied until John. And if you are willing to accept it, John himself is Elijah who was to come. He who has ears to hear, let him hear.."*[9]

But how can John be Elijah, and yet *not* be Elijah?

I want to draw your attention to something that is crucial to our understanding of John, his ministry, and the secret of *gimel* (ג). Messiah, whether He comes to a nation or to an individual heart, must have a forerunner. Even as God prepared a world in six days for the reception of man, so He commands us to prepare ourselves for the

---

[4] Malachi 4:5-6
[5] Deuteronomy 18:15
[6] John 1:17
[7] Quoting Isaiah 40:3
[8] John 1:29
[9] Matthew 11:13-15

reception of God. Whether in the Judean desert or the wilderness of the human heart, God's voice cries out, *"Prepare the way of the Lord!"* We often speak of the Lord's first and second advent, but there is also a spiritual, personal visitation He makes today to individual men and women who invite Him to reside in their heart. Man's spirit is a dry and barren wasteland without God, devoid of light and life. The voice that animated John the Immerser is the voice of God's spirit and, "if we will receive it", this voice is the Elijah that satisfies the prophecy of a forerunner for us as individuals. The name Elijah means "My God is *YaH*", and it is God's desire that we also make this our declaration.[10]

The Spirit's Threefold Work

Gimel (ג), like John the Immerser, personifies the working of the Holy Spirit in several ways. First, *gimel* (ג) equals the number three, and there are three things that God's spirit speaks to the spirit of every human being. Yeshua said that it was necessary for Him to return to the Father so that He could send the "Helper", and that:

> *And He, when He comes, will convict the world concerning* **sin** *and* **righteousness** *and* **judgment**:
> — *concerning* **sin**, *because men do not believe in Me;*
> — *and concerning* **righteousness**, *because I go to the Father and you no longer see Me;*
> — *and concerning* **judgment**, *because the ruler of this world has been judged.*[11]

Do you appreciate the implications of this statement? Here, Yeshua explains how the Holy Spirit does the work of a forerunner in every human spirit. What a comfort and encouragement it is to know that before I open my mouth to tell someone the good news of salvation in Messiah, the Holy Spirit has already been doing the work of a forerunner – preparing hearts for the reception of the gospel. The Holy Spirit is constantly convicting man that he is guilty of **sin**, that there is a standard of **righteousness** that he has failed to achieve, and that **judgment** is coming wherein he must give an account of his life.

It is remarkable that whenever missionaries have encountered a tribe or culture that has never before heard the gospel, they find that there already exists an

---

[10] *Yah* (יה) is a shortened version of *YHVH* (יהוה).
[11] John 16:8-11 (emphasis mine)

awareness in their hearts that they are guilty of sin, that there is a standard of righteousness which they have failed to achieve, and that after death there will be a calling to account for the way they have lived their lives.[12] Appropriately, the only themes of John's teaching were: sin, righteousness, and judgment to come.

John the Immerser (who came in the spirit and power of Elijah[13]) was Messiah's forerunner at His first coming. Elijah will return as the forerunner of Messiah at His second coming.[14] And the Holy Spirit is the forerunner of Messiah as He comes now, spiritually, to human hearts. Nevertheless, in all three cases the message is the same, *"Prepare the way of the Lord."*

Clothes Make the Prophet

Despite the many details the Bible gives us about the men and women found in its pages, only rarely does it describe how they dressed. However, John the Immerser is one of the exceptions in that the Scriptures tell us that he was dressed in camel's hair.[15] Why is this significant? We are provided this detail so that we will make the connection between Messiah's forerunner and the secrets of the Hebrew language.

The name of the letter *gimel* (ג) is spelled גמל (*gamal*) which means 'camel'. But, according to the Jewish Sages, the *spiritual* form of the letter is that of a man walking from the second letter *beit* (ב, the *'house'*) toward the fourth letter, *dalet* (ד).[16] In other words, the letter *gimel* represents a man dressed up like a camel emerging from the letter *beit* (ב). In fact, the second, third, and fourth letters of the alphabet spell בגד (*beged*) 'garment'.

Just as camel hair became working clothes for John the Immerser, John was the working clothes for God's spirit. John was singled out for this distinction because there is no one in the Scriptures who more clearly portrays the Holy Spirit's mission and ministry to the unbeliever. This is why Yeshua said, *"Truly I say to you, among those born of women there has not arisen anyone greater than John the Immerser! Yet the one who is least in the kingdom of heaven is greater than he."*[17]

Do you understand why Yeshua gave John such high praise? No prophet before or since has been so entirely abandoned to God's spirit as John the Immerser. Yet, in

---

[12] The author highly recommends the book *Eternity In Their Hearts*, by Don Richardson.
[13] Luke 1:17
[14] Malachi 4:5
[15] Matthew 3:4
[16] The Talmud, tractate *Shabbat* 104a.
[17] Matthew 11:11

50 | In His Own Words

the kingdom of heaven – when we will be entirely free of the hindrance of the flesh – even the least of us will be more obedient to the spirit than was John.

Another intriguing relationship between *gimel* (ג) and John is that the second and third letters of the alphabet together spell the word גב (*gav*), which means 'locust' – John's primary food source.[18]

The Gospel in Four Letters

Traditionally, *gimel*'s form – ג – is said to resemble a man, head bent, determined to make his way from the second letter to the fourth. What is the *gimel*'s mission? The Sages teach that *gimel* (ג) came from inside the ב (*beit*, the 'house') and is on an important mission to *dalet* (ד), the fourth letter.[19] The *Talmud* puts it this way:

> *Why is the leg of the gimel extended towards the dalet? Because it is indeed the manner of one who bestows kindness to run after the needy.*[20]

The Sages describe *gimel*'s mission as one of mercy to bring nourishment to *dalet* (ד). But, should *dalet* (ד) prove stubbornly closed to *gimel*, then punishment will result. (The possibility that *gimel* may bring punishment is due to the fact that *gimel*'s name may also be pronounced *g'mal*, meaning 'recompense' or 'comeuppance'.) The name of the *dalet* (ד), the letter to which *gimel* is traveling, literally means 'door'. From these four letters – א,ב,ג,ד – a story begins to unfold: The Father (אב) and His Son (ב) sent a messenger (ג) to bring nourishment to one secluded behind a closed door (ד). Aside from being a picture of a door, *dalet*'s name comes from the root word *dahl* (דל), which means 'weakness' and 'poverty'. Could an illustration of the gospel be any more explicit? It is amazing to think that when God designed the Hebrew alphabet, He did so with the message of the gospel in mind.

Regarding the statement that no one more clearly exemplified a walk in the spirit than John the Immerser, please realize that I exempt Yeshua. How could Yeshua be outdone by any man? In fact, the first four letters of the alphabet paint a very accurate picture of Yeshua as He presents Himself to the community at Laodicea, which He described as *"wretched and miserable and poor and blind and naked"*[21] – poverty-stricken,

---

[18] Matthew 3:4
[19] Osios R'Akiva, as cited by Munk, op.cit., pg. 73.
[20] *Shabbat* 104a
[21] Revelation 3:17

to be sure. He said to them: *"Behold, I stand at the door and knock; if anyone hears My voice and opens the door, I will come in to him and will dine with him, and he with Me."*²² Certainly, *gimel* (ג) must represent the spirit of Yeshua, the divine servant, coming to the aid of the needy.

In our discussion of *gimel* (ג), let us not neglect its relationship to the two letters that precede it – א and ב – which together spell אב (*Av*) 'Father'. Yeshua said, *"When the helper* (ג) *comes, which I will send to you from the Father* (אב), *that is the spirit of truth that proceeds from the Father, that will testify about Me* (ב)*."*²³

Coming After, Preferred Before

Here is another scriptural illustration of the relationship between the letters א, ב and ג. When interviewed by the Jewish leaders, John the Immerser spoke of Yeshua saying, *"He it is Who, coming after me, has come to be in front of me…"*²⁴ Think of these first three letters in light of this verse. *"He is the one who comes after me…."* This indicates that *beit* (ב), representing Yeshua, would come behind *gimel* (ג). Look at the arrangement of the letters below:

ג ב א ←

We see here that the ג (*gimel*) is walking to the left with ב (*beit*) directly behind. However, John went on to say that Yeshua *"…existed before me"*,²⁵ suggesting that ב should come *before* ג. Indeed, *beit* does precede *gimel* in the alphabetical order.

Bringer of Good Fortune

Let us consider again how the order of the first four letters depicts the Father (אב) sending His messenger (represented by ג) to the poor person (represented by ד).

ד ← ג ← ב א

---

²² Revelation 3:20
²³ John 15:26
²⁴ John 1:27 (Concordant Literal New Testament)
²⁵ John 1:15

The good news brought by ג (*gimel*) to ד (*dalet*) is good news indeed! It will bring good fortune to the poor man behind the door of *dalet* (ד). In fact, the word spelled by ג (*gimel*) and ד (*dalet*) together is גד (*gad*), which means 'good fortune'.[26]

Several centuries before John, God sent another prophet – one who disobeyed and fled in the opposite direction, got in a boat, and headed out to sea. This prophet, Jonah, was subsequently swallowed by a giant fish.[27] It just so happens that גד (*gad*, 'good fortune') spelled backward is דג (*dag*), which means 'fish'. Let's take this as a warning to always pay attention to which direction we are going.

The Kinsman Redeemer

The personality of *gimel* is beautifully depicted in the Hebrew word – גאל (*goel*) – 're-deemer'. The Torah describes the duties of a person serving in the role of a kinsman redeemer – or *goel*. A *goel* was given a unique set of duties. He was responsible to purchase back a kinsman who had been sold into slavery due to financial debt. He was also charged with redeeming a kinsman's land and avenging a kinsman's murder.[28] Two things were required for a kinsman redeemer to fulfill his responsibilities. First, he must be a kinsman. In other words, he had to be related to the one needing to be redeemed. Second, he must have the wherewithal to pay his kinsman's debts and purchase back his forfeited property.

Yeshua, our *Goel*, is the Redeemer of the entire world. He was physically born into the world as a human being so that He could be our kinsman. And, because He was sinless, He had the wherewithal to also be our Redeemer. He did not redeem the world with money but with His own sinless life. Peter describes our redemption thus:

> ... *you were not redeemed with perishable things like silver or gold from your futile way of life inherited from your forefathers, but with precious blood, as of a lamb unblemished and spotless, the blood of Messiah.*[29]

But Messiah did not merely redeem us *from* something. He redeemed us *to* something as well. He redeemed us for an ultimate purpose – to restore us, and the world, to the condition that was enjoyed by Adam and Eve before they sinned.

---

[26] *Gad* (גד) is also the name of one of Jacob's sons. (Genesis 3:11)
[27] Jonah 1:17
[28] The *Torah* describes a *goel's* duties in Leviticus 25.
[29] 1 Peter 1:18-19 (quoting Isaiah 53)

Peter goes on to describe the goal of our redemption as follows:

> ... and He Himself bore our sins in His body on the cross, so that we might die to sin and live to righteousness; for by His wounds you were healed. For you were continually straying like sheep, but now you have returned to the Shepherd and Guardian of your souls.[30]

In other words, our great *Goel*, Messiah Yeshua, redeemed us in order to restore our relationship to God. This message is beautifully depicted by the Hebrew word for *goel* – גאל. You will note that *goel* begins with *gimel* (ג) and is followed by the letters אל. These last two letters – אל – spell the word *el*, which means 'God'. So, we see in the word גאל the ג (*gimel*) boldly approaching אל, 'God'. And this is what our *Goel*, Yeshua, achieved. He approached God on our behalf. In fact, He brought us *to God*.

ג - אל

What if God Had Not Sent His messenger?

Let us take another look at the first four letters of the alphabet – א ב ג ד – and consider what would be the consequence of removing the letter representing God's messenger (ג) from the sequence. We would then have the following: אבד which forms the word *oveid*, meaning 'destruction'.[31] If we add the fifth letter of the alphabet (*hei*, ה) to the sequence we derive the word אבדה (*avudah*) which means 'a lost thing'.[32]

Needless to say, had God not sent His messenger into the world to bring us His good news, we would certainly be 'lost things' and experience 'destruction' rather than 'good fortune'. May the lessons taught by these letters inspire us to praise our Savior, who came to seek and to save those who are lost.[33]

The Sword = The Word of God

The letter *gimel* (ג) has a numerical value of three and equals the sum of the letters א (= 1) and ב (= 2), which together spell אב (*Av*, 'Father'). *Gimel*'s significance lies in the

---

[30] 1 Peter 2:24-25 (quoting Isaiah 53:5)
[31] See Numbers 24:20 for an example of אבד (*oveid*). This is also the root of the word *Abaddon* (אבדון).
[32] See Deuteronomy 22:3 for an example of אבדה (*avudah*).
[33] Luke 19:10

fact that it is a father's duty to nurture and correct his children. When *gimel*'s name is pronounced *g'mal*, it means 'to recompense'. Recompense means repayment, regardless of whether it is in the form of reward or of punishment, and no father rewards or punishes more fairly and justly than God, our Father, who both nourishes and corrects us.

The three areas in which the Holy Spirit brings conviction – sin, righteousness, and judgment to come – are the same three areas that are reflected in the structure of the Hebrew Bible, which is divided into three sections:

תורה **Torah** - Torah
נביאים **Nevi'im** - Prophets
כתובים **Chetuvim** - Writings

The Hebrew Bible is called the *Tanach*, a name derived from the first letter of each of its three parts. The *Torah* consists of the five books of Moses (Genesis, Exodus, Leviticus, Numbers, Deuteronomy) and is the first section of the *Tanach*. The *Torah* is the foundation of our faith and is read recurrently in synagogues around the world. These readings are done according to a schedule that allows the *Torah* to be read through in its entirety on an annual cycle.

Nevi'im ('Prophets') include Joshua, Judges, Samuel, Kings,[34] Isaiah, Jeremiah, Ezekiel, and the twelve minor prophets (except Daniel).

The final section, *Chetuvim* ('Writings'), contains the remainder of the Hebrew scriptures, including Daniel and Chronicles.

Yeshua referred to these three divisions of the *Tanach* when He said:

> *"These are My words which I spoke to you while I was still with you, that all things which are written about Me in the Torah of Moses and the Prophets [Nevi'im] and the Psalms [in reference to Chetuvim] must be fulfilled."*[35]

A cursory reading of the *Tanach* will reveal that these three divisions align with the three themes proclaimed by the Holy Spirit within every human heart.

The first part, *Torah*, is what awakens a true knowledge of *sin*, as Paul wrote:

---

[34] The Hebrew Bible treats 1 & 2Samuel as one book, and 1 & 2Kings as one book.
[35] Luke 24:44

... I would not have come to know sin except through the Torah; for I would not have known about coveting if the Torah had not said, 'You shall not covet.'[36]

The Writings (*Chetuvim*), on the other hand, include books such as Psalms and Proverbs, which instruct us in the ways of righteousness. These books are sometimes referred to as the Wisdom Books because they teach us how to gain wisdom and fulfill the Torah of righteousness.

The Prophets (*Nevi'im*), as the name implies, have as their central theme the judgment to come. We often think of judgment in the negative sense, as something to be feared and dreaded – and by some people it should be. In the Bible, however, the word 'judgment' is a neutral word having neither positive nor negative connotations. The Judgment is a time to reward good as well as to punish evil. The same is true of the word *g'mal*, 'recompense'.

In short, we can compare the three divisions of the *Tanach* with the three themes of the Holy Spirit as follows:

תורה	**Torah**	Torah	*Sin*
נביאים	**Nevi'im**	Prophets	*Coming Judgment*
כתובים	**Chetuvim**	Writings	*Righteousness*

Notice that the order of the *Tanach's* divisions is different than the order given by Yeshua in John 16:8-11. It may be that God places judgment in the center to emphasize that at the time of the Judgment the righteous and the wicked will be separated as depicted in the chart above.

The Heart of Scripture

To conclude our discussion of the letter *gimel* (ג), let us look at the only place in scripture where *gimel* is printed oversize. It is found in the middle verse of the Torah – Leviticus 13:33. Here is the verse as it appears in a Hebrew Bible. (The word in the small rectangle is והתגלח (*v'hit'galach*), and you will notice that the fourth letter is an enlarged ג.)

---

[36] Romans 7:7

> לֹא פָשָׂה הַנֶּתֶק וְלֹא הָיָה בוֹ שֵׂעָר צָהֹב וּמַרְאֵה
> הַנֶּתֶק אֵין עָמֹק מִן הָעוֹר וְהִתְגַּלָּח וְאֶת הַנֶּתֶק לֹא
> יְגַלֵּחַ וְהִסְגִּיר הַכֹּהֵן אֶת הַנֶּתֶק שִׁבְעַת יָמִים שֵׁנִית

As we have seen, the ג is a spiritual man dressed like a camel. I believe, however, that God wants to remove the camel hair so as to reveal the one hidden within – the Holy Spirit which John the Immerser depicts. So, what does *v'hit'galach* mean? It means, *"And he shall be shaved"*.

And some people think God has no sense of humor.

4

ד | *Dalet*

A Witness at the Door

Behold a stranger at the door!
He gently knocks, has knocked before;
Hath waited long, is waiting still;
You treat no other friend so ill.

Rise, touched with gratitude divine;
Turn out his enemy and thine,
That soul-destroying monster, sin,
And let the heavenly stranger in.

Admit him, ere his anger burn;
His feet departed, ne'er return;
Admit him, or the hour's at hand
You'll at his door rejected stand.

— Anonymous

In the previous chapter we learned that *gimel* (ג) pictures the Holy Spirit in pursuit of one who is in need, knocking at his heart's door, represented by *dalet* (ד) which means 'door'. Thus, in the context of the Hebrew alphabet *dalet* symbolizes a person's heart which, like a door, can be either closed or open to God. A door is an obstacle that can either separate or allow entrance, and this is illustrated by the fact that the first appearance of ד is in the word ויבדל (*vayav'deil*) *"and He separated"*.[1]

A Testimony of God's Sovereignty

Much of our discussion about *dalet* (ד) will center around the meaning of its numeric value, which is four. In short, the Bible used the number four to represent testimony and witness, especially between the spiritual and physical realms. Throughout the Bible this number symbolizes God's testimony to the world – testimony concerning His sovereignty and character. One might think that *two* would be a more suitable number for this purpose, since the *Torah* commands that every matter should be established by the mouth of at least two witnesses.[2] But, that is an example of human testimony, and not the kind of testimony four represents. When it comes to God's testimony to us, the representative number is 2x2, or 2^2.

This aspect of the number four is pictured by what transpired on the fourth day of creation. On the fourth day God established the sun, moon, and stars *"to give light on the earth"*, and to serve as *"signs"*. The sun was given to rule over the day and the moon to rule over the night.[3] Likewise, we see the four aspects of Yeshua, the Light of the world, portrayed in the four gospels as a picture of God's love and forgiveness toward mankind. Without this light we remain in spiritual darkness.

One of the most graphic displays of God's power and sovereignty was on Mount Carmel when Elijah challenged the priests of Baal to a showdown. The pagan priests prayed for Baal to send down fire from heaven to consume their sacrifice, but without success. However, when Elijah prayed to YHVH to do the same for his sacrifice, the fire immediately came down and consumed the altar and its sacrifice. To make this miracle an even greater challenge and thus magnify God's glory, Elijah used four barrels of water to repeatedly douse the altar and sacrifice. Here again we see the number four used to display God's power and sovereignty.

Since four is the number of testimony from God to the world, the Bible contains four accounts of Messiah's life in which we discover four aspects of Messiah's character and ministry. If we wish to know the Messiah portrayed in the Scriptures, we must understand His four 'faces' as they are depicted in the four Gospels.

---

[1] Genesis 1:4
[2] Deuteronomy 17:6; 19:15
[3] Genesis 1:14-19

Matthew | *Messiah the King*

Matthew's gospel portrays Yeshua as King and refers to Him as the "Son of [King] David" more than the other three gospel writers combined. Matthew also quotes the *Tanach* more than the other gospels (93 times) demonstrating how Yeshua had fulfilled its messianic prophecies. Matthew also uses the word king nearly twice as often as the other writers and frequently stresses that Yeshua is the "King of the Jews". To support this, he opens his gospel with Yeshua's genealogy tracing it from Abraham through David to Joseph, Yeshua's foster father. Matthew did this in order to show that Yeshua was of the royal lineage of David and thus in direct line to inherit the throne of Israel. He also groups Yeshua's ancestors in groups of 14 since this is the numerical value of David's name – דוד.[4]

At the time of Yeshua's birth, Israel was a province of the Roman empire and was ruled as a Roman protectorate. This became an important factor at His trial. Yeshua's detractors, testifying that He claimed to be a king, said, *"We have no king but Caesar."*[5] In truth, Yeshua has the lawful claim as King and will someday take His rightful place upon the throne of David in a kingdom yet to come.

Mark | *Messiah the Servant*

Mark portrays Yeshua in His role as servant in a gospel which is brief and action-packed, filled with accounts of His miracles and acts of service. This gospel begins with neither a family tree nor an account of Yeshua's birth. Mark's gospel rushes right into the thick of the action as illustrated by the fact that in the first chapter alone Yeshua proclaims His message, calls disciples, casts out demons, visits numerous cities and synagogues, and heals all who come to Him. One of Mark's favorite words is 'immediately', which he uses as much as the other three gospel writers combined. Forty times he says, *"And immediately Yeshua…"* Immediate action is the hallmark of an effective servant.

When translators begin the work of translating the Apostolic scriptures into a new language, they usually begin with Mark's gospel because of its brevity and crisp narrative style. It lacks many of the finer details found in Matthew and Luke and does not focus on deep spiritual insights as does John's gospel, but it accomplishes the purpose for which God inspired it – to portray the servant's heart that beats within

---

[4] Matthew 1:17 (ד = 4, ו = 6, ד = 4; 4 + 6 + 4 = **14**.)
[5] John 19:15

Yeshua's breast and the devotion with which He ministered to all whom He encountered.

Luke | *Messiah the Man*

Luke was an educated doctor who portrayed Yeshua in His humanness. Luke's is the longest of the gospel accounts, and with a physician's trained eye he describes in greater detail the conception, birth and crucifixion of Yeshua. Luke records a family tree, but it differs from Matthew's in several ways.[6] First, instead of recording Yeshua's lineage through Joseph, he records it through His mother, Mary.[7] Second, Luke traces this lineage backward from Mary instead of forwards through Abraham. Third (and this is very important to our discussion), he traces it not merely back to Abraham, but all the way back to Adam, emphasizing once again that Yeshua was the Son of Man, a term Luke uses 25 times.

Luke did not end his record of Yeshua's works with the last verse of his gospel but continued to describe the birth and growth of the redeemed community during its early history in his second book, *The Acts of the Apostles*.[8] Luke refers to his gospel as an account of *"all that Yeshua began to do and to teach"*,[9] indicating that he considered Acts as an extension of that account. We might say that Luke's is the longest of the gospels because it consists of two books – Luke *and* Acts.

John | *The Divine Messiah*

The fourth gospel is different from the other three in many ways. Unlike Matthew and Luke, John did not begin his gospel with a genealogical record. However, he did not altogether omit an account of Messiah's roots. John opens his gospel with the immortal words, *"In the beginning was the Word, and the Word was with God, and the Word was God"*,[10] followed by the assertion that *"...the Word became flesh and dwelt among us..."*[11]

---

[6] Luke 3

[7] Hence, Yeshua had not only a legal right to the throne through his foster father Joseph, but also a blood right to the throne through His mother Mary.

[8] If you read the opening verses of these two books, you will notice that they are both dedicated to a man named *Theophilus*.

[9] Acts 1:1

[10] John 1:1

[11] John 1:14

It is widely held that John's gospel was the last book of the Apostolic Scriptures to be written. Historical data indicates that after his exile on the Isle of Patmos (where he penned the book of Revelation), John returned to the city of Ephesus where he wrote his gospel. John's knowledge of the visions of Revelation gave him incredible insight when writing his gospel. The Gospel according to John establishes the divinity of Yeshua in a striking and emphatic way, for it displays the essence of Yeshua's character in the light of the *shekinah* glory of God.

The Four Heavenly Creatures

I have briefly described the character of each of the gospels as they picture the four aspects of Messiah's character and ministry. These same four aspects are displayed in several passages of scripture, but we shall examine one in particular – the heavenly throne room described by John in the book of Revelation.

In the fourth chapter of Revelation John is transported to the heavenly throne room where he beholds God's glory and majesty. Among the many details he describes four creatures stationed around God's throne. He writes, *"The first creature was like a lion, and the second creature like a calf, and the third creature had a face like that of a man, and the fourth creature was like a flying eagle."*[12] Can you see the similarities between these four creatures and the characteristics of Messiah depicted in the four gospels? I compare them in the chart below.

Gospel	Emphasis	Creature
MATTHEW	Messiah as KING	The LION
MARK	Messiah as SERVANT	The OX
LUKE	Messiah as MAN	The MAN
JOHN	Messiah as DIVINE	The EAGLE

By surrounding Himself with these four creatures, God portrays four aspects of His own character that are, in turn, reflected by Yeshua. Our problem is that we are prone to embrace only one or two of Yeshua's characteristics instead of all four. Our failure to know Him in His fullness results in theological and spiritual error which negatively impacts our lives. When, for instance, we focus exclusively on Messiah's

---

[12] Revelation 4:7

kingship, we will view Him as a tyrant to be feared, not loved. Focusing only on His servanthood reduces Him to a slave who must obey our whims. Focusing only on Messiah's humanity is to make Him a demigod fashioned in our own image – an object of casual familiarity and devoid of authority. By focusing only on His divinity apart from His other attributes, we characterize Him as untouchable and unsympathetic to our needs.

We must learn to seek God's face, and we must seek to know Messiah as He is and not as we wish Him to be. Paul understood this when he wrote, *"Therefore from now on we recognize no one according to the flesh; even though we have known Messiah according to the flesh, yet now we know Him in this way no longer."*[13]

The "worldly point of view" is a very narrow one, whereas Messiah embraces the fullness of truth. This is one reason He calls Himself *"the Alpha and the Omega (AΩ), the first and the last, the beginning and the end"*[14] – or, as it would appear in Hebrew, the *Aleph* and *Tuv* (את). Regarding the number four as the number that witnesses to Yeshua, it is interesting to note that the fourth word of the Bible is the word את (*et*) – a word spelled using only the first and last letters of the alphabet.

We have learned that *aleph* (א) – the first letter of the alphabet – is also the letter which best represents the invisible God. Accordingly, the names of the first three of the creatures surrounding God's throne begin with this same letter.

Lion	ארי	*ari*
Ox	אלף	*aleph*[15]
Man	איש[16]	*ish*

The Hebrew word for 'eagle', on the other hand, does not begin with *aleph* (א). Why does the fourth creature – the eagle – break the pattern? The Hebrew scriptures made it clear that Messiah would be a *king* (the Lion of the tribe of Judah), and that He would be a *servant* and a *man* (represented by the ox- and man-like creatures), but although the *Tanach* hinted at Messiah's divinity, it took Israel completely by surprise when Yeshua claimed to be the "Son of God" (represented by the *flying* eagle). Even

---

[13] 2 Corinthians 5:16
[14] Revelation 22:13
[15] The structure of the א is described by linguists as depicting the head of an ox. Even its name – *aleph* – means "ox".
[16] I could also have opted for the word אדם (*adam*) which also begins with *aleph* (א).

today if you ask most Jewish people why they do not believe Yeshua is the Messiah, one of the responses you are likely to hear is that Yeshua claimed to be God by calling Himself God's Son.

Yeshua never claimed to *be* God, and Paul stated that He *"did not regard equality with God a thing to be grasped"*.[17] Nevertheless, Yeshua was divine in a way that is beyond our ability to understand, and this truth is revealed in the Apostolic Scriptures, especially in John's gospel. Accordingly, if we look up the Greek word for 'eagle', we discover that it is αετος (*aetos*) which begins with *aleph's* Greek counterpart – *alpha* (A) – the first letter of the Greek alphabet.

Lion	ארי	*ari*
Ox	אלף	*aleph*
Man	איש	*aish*
Flying Eagle	Αετος	*aetos*

These four characteristics of the Master are pictured in other passages of scripture as well. For example, Zechariah prophesied:

> *From [Judah] will come the **cornerstone**,*
> *from them the **tent peg**,*
> *from them the **bow of battle**,*
> *from them every **ruler**…*[18]

Consider how each of these four objects parallels one of the four characteristics of the Messiah. Every building begins with the placement of the **cornerstone**, which in turn determines the position of every other stone in the building. Yeshua is the cornerstone *"which the builders rejected"*, the *"stone of stumbling"* and *"rock of offense"*.[19] As explained in chapter 2, Yeshua's claim to be one with the Father was highly offensive to the leaders of His generation and was the primary reason they rejected Him. The cornerstone in Zechariah's prophecy symbolizes the divinity of Messiah as portrayed in John's gospel.

The **tent peg**, like the cornerstone, is also part of a building. But, unlike the cornerstone, it is a small and humble object that is not given a place of distinction and

---

[17] Philippians 2:6
[18] Zechariah 10:4 (emphasis mine)
[19] 1 Peter 2:7-8.

prominence. The tent peg serves the tent by being beaten into the ground and kept under constant strain. Hence, the tent peg represents Messiah the Servant as portrayed in Mark's gospel.

The **bow of battle** is a picture of Messiah the Man as portrayed in Luke's gospel. This is not apparent at first glance, since what does a 'battle bow' have to do with Messiah's being a human? The answer is found in Hebrews:

> *Therefore, since the children share in flesh and blood, He Himself likewise also partook of the same, that through death He might render powerless him who had the power of death, that is, the devil.*[20]

The battle bow is the only weapon listed among the four objects. It is an instrument of death, and Yeshua had to become a man in order to destroy our enemy. Therefore, the battle bow represents Messiah the Man as depicted in Luke's gospel.

And finally, the **ruler** represents Messiah the King as portrayed in the Gospel of Matthew.

Let us examine one concluding passage that depicts the four aspects of Messiah's character and ministry. At Passover we drink four cups of wine, each one commemorating an aspect of Israel's deliverance from Egyptian bondage. This tradition is rooted in the Torah's description of the four facets of their deliverance. I have divided this passage into its four statements alongside the appropriate Passover cup.

"I am Adonai, and...

Cup 1— "***I will bring you out*** *from under the burdens of the Egyptians, and ...*

Cup 2— "***I will deliver you*** *from their bondage.*

Cup 3— "***I will also redeem you*** *with an outstretched arm and great judgments. Then...*

Cup 4— "***I will take you for My people****, and I will be your God; and you shall know that I am Adonai your God, who brought you out from under the burdens of the Egyptians."*[21]

It is apparent how each of these statements parallels its gospel counterpart. The first statement – *"I will bring you out from under the burdens of the Egyptians"* – parallels the message of Matthew, the gospel of the King. In essence He is saying that instead of serving king Pharaoh, you will serve Me as your King. Instead of Pharaoh's yoke, you will wear Mine, *"For My yoke is easy and My burden is light."*[22] In Jewish thought, a

---

[20] Hebrews 2:14
[21] Exodus 6:6-7
[22] Matthew 11:30

person is 'yoked' to the person he serves, and a student is likewise 'yoked' to his teacher. If we serve King Yeshua, then we bear His yoke.

The second statement refers to slavery in bondage and parallels the gospel of Mark who portrays Yeshua as Messiah the Servant.

The third statement parallels Luke's gospel, which portrays Yeshua as the Son of Man. This is significant especially in light of what has just been said concerning the battle bow, since Yeshua came as a man to destroy the one who held us in bondage. The cup representing this statement is referred to as the "Cup of Redemption" and is drunk after the *Seder* meal is eaten. This, the third cup, is the one Yeshua gave to His disciples after His last *Seder* meal saying, *"This cup is the new covenant in My blood"*.[23] It was soon after this that Yeshua was crucified. In that single act He redeemed us by destroying the one who held us in bondage to sin.

The fourth statement, *"...you shall know that I am Adonai your God..."* obviously parallels the message of the gospel of John, who emphasizes the divine nature of Messiah Yeshua.

The Heart of the Matter

The responsibility of a witness is to share that which he has seen and heard. However, it is not the witness's responsibility to force the listener to act upon the testimony. That is the listener's responsibility alone. Likewise, there are sometimes false witnesses in spiritual matters, and it is up to each individual to discern the validity of a matter by examining it in light of the Scriptures. Paul praised the believers at Berea calling them "noble-minded ... *for they received the word with great eagerness, examining the Scriptures daily to see whether these things were so."*[24] Do you see the balance here? The Bereans had the rare quality of possessing both openness of mind to receive and skepticism enough to search the Scriptures in order to establish the validity of the message.

We should delight to search out the heart of an issue, for God is delighted when we do. This is indicated by a pair of words located at the very heart of the Torah. I mention them here because they both begin with *dalet* (ד). The Torah contains an even number of words, hence there are two words that reside at its center. These two words (found in Leviticus 10:16) are דרש דרש (*darosh darash*). Though they are spelled

---

[23] 1 Corinthians 11:25
[24] Acts 17:11

identically, they are pronounced differently. The first word ends the first half of the Torah, and the second word begins the second half. The words *darosh darash* literally mean *"searching, he searched"*, or *"he diligently searched"*.

It would appear that God purposefully placed these two words at the heart of His Torah because He desires every person to come and reason together with Him, to think, to inquire, and to search.[25] Both of these central words begin with *dalet* (ד), the 'door', because inquiry opens the door to the deep things of God contained in the Scriptures. We need not fear that God's Word will fail under close scrutiny. As powerful microscopes have allowed us to look deeply into the design of God's physical world, diligent inquiry into the Scriptures will allow us to discover the secrets residing there that He delights to reveal.

Now that we have discussed at some length the fourfold witness that the *gimel* (ג) brings to the *dalet* (ד), let us continue our study and see what *dalet*'s response should be to *gimel*'s (ג) message.

The One Who Dwells in Poverty

Again, the name of the letter *dalet* literally means 'door'. The order of the letters thus far depicts the Father (אב) sending His messenger (ג) to approach it. What will be the outcome of this divine encounter? The structure of the *dalet* (ד) shows it to be top-heavy and about to fall to the left – away from the approaching *gimel* (ג). But, as pointed out by the Jewish sages, *gimel* (ג) with its two legs will easily catch *dalet* (ד) with its single leg.

The imbalance, or indecisiveness, of *dalet* (ד) is also depicted by the way it is printed in Torah scrolls. If you examine the details of a *dalet* found in a Torah scroll, you will discover a sharp vertical point at each end of the horizontal stroke, as shown below.

The Sages refer to these vertical points as *dalet*'s 'ears'. One ear listens for the steps of the approaching ג, and the other inclines in the opposite direction. The corresponding human condition is accurately described by Paul when he wrote, *"For the*

---

[25] Isaiah 1:18

flesh sets its desire against the spirit, and the spirit against the flesh; for these are in opposition to one another..."[26] What is the remedy to this situation? The passage continues to explain that the cross of Messiah must be applied to the sinful desires of our fallen natures. *"Now those who belong to Messiah Yeshua have crucified the flesh with its passions and desires."*[27]

At the risk of jumping ahead, I will give you a glimpse of one of the most important insights contained in this book. The last letter of the Hebrew alphabet – *tuv* (ת) – means 'cross'. Yes, you read that correctly. Keep this in mind as you read the chapters to come and pay close attention to how this letter (ת) affects the words in which it is found. We will look at one example as we close this chapter.

The word 'door' (דלת, *dalet*) is constructed of the word דל (*dal*) with the letter *tuv* (ת) affixed to the end. *Dal* means 'pauper' or 'poverty' – which describes our spiritual condition before we met Yeshua. But, when we encounter the 'cross' (ת), it provides us with a door (דלת) of faith through which we can begin to experience the freedom and joy of real living.

> *I have been crucified with Messiah, and it's no longer I who live, but Messiah lives in me; and the life which I now live in the flesh I live by faith in the Son of God, who loved me and gave Himself for me.*[28]

Though death is neither a popular nor pleasant subject, it is nevertheless one of the most important things we could discuss. As we shall see, death is necessary in order for us to complete the work God has assigned us.

The Door of Death

Read the following familiar passage and see if you notice something missing:

> *Then God said, "Let Us make man in Our image, according to Our likeness; and let them rule over the fish of the sea and over the birds of the sky and over the cattle and over all the earth, and over every creeping thing that creeps on the earth." God*

---

[26] Galatians 5:17
[27] Galatians 5:24
[28] Galatians 2:20

created man in His own image, in the image of God He created him; male and female He created them.[29]

Okay, did you figure it out? Look again if you must. Pay attention to the use of the words 'image' and 'likeness'. God said, *"Let us make man in our image, after our likeness..."* Then it says, *"So God created man in His own image, in the image of God he created him..."* What happened to the word 'likeness'? God set out to create man according to two qualities – God's *image* and *likeness* – but only God's *image* is mentioned at the time of man's actual creation. This is extremely significant.

The two words employed here are *tzelem* (צלם) and *damut* (דמות). *Tzelem* means 'copy' or 'image'. This word is derived from *tzel* (צל) 'shadow', as in the name *Betzalel* (בצלאל) "in the shadow of El".[30] Similarly, *tzalam* is the modern Hebrew word for 'photographer'. It is not the purpose of this book to explore how a human being can be made in the *image* of God when God is spiritual, not physical.[31] But, there are endless insights to be gained by meditating on how the human body reflects God's invisible attributes. Just as an artist's personality is seen through his style and techniques, God's personality and wisdom are displayed in every detail of our makeup from our cells to our bones to our brains. But let's now turn our attention to *damut*.

Damut (דמות) is usually translated 'likeness' and, unlike *tzelem*, *damut* involves choice. All human beings are born in God's *tzelem*, but to be in God's *damut* requires an act of the will. To be in God's *damut* means I willingly align my soul with His in such a way as to reflect His character and personality. Our likes and dislikes become the same as His. His motivations become my motivations. I love what He loves, and my desires reflect His. But, note again that though God made man according to his *tzelem*, it does not state that man was made according to His *damut*. How is this second phase of development accomplished? The answer is hidden in the Hebrew. Take another look at the word *damut*:

דמות

Remember how we sliced *barasheit* (בראשית) to reveal hidden insights? If we divide *damut* between the first and second letters, we derive:

---

[29] Genesis 1:26-27
[30] Exodus 36:1
[31] For a fuller treatment, see the author's commentary on Genesis.

ד|מות

The name of the first letter – *dalet* (ד) – means 'door'. The remaining three letters spell the word *mut* (מות) which means 'death'. Together, we see that *damut* (דמות) expresses the message 'door of death'. This begs the question, what does a 'door of death' have to do with being made after God's likeness? However, to answer this question, we must ask another. What *is* death?

Normally, when we think of death, we conjure pictures of a lifeless body, a funeral, a life over and done. However, this is a very narrow understanding of death. When a person dies, he or she does not cease to exist. What actually occurs is the separation of the soul from the body. The body returns to dust and the soul returns to its source. When we think of death, we must think 'separation'. In fact, we often use the word 'death' and 'die' in exactly this context. We speak of a friendship 'dying' or a marriage 'dying' or the light 'dying' as the sun goes down. In each instance, the entities described do not cease to exist, they merely separate from one another.

With this understanding of death, we ask again why is a door of death necessary for a person to achieve God's 'likeness'? The answer provides insight into one of the most foundational principles of God's Word – the principle of the cross – a principle by which every follower of Yeshua is called to live. The principle of the cross is absolutely necessary for anyone who chooses to follow Messiah. He said:

> *"And he who does not take his cross and follow after Me is not worthy of me ... If anyone wishes to come after Me, he must deny himself, and take up his cross, and follow Me."*[32]

This is the principle by which Yeshua lived His life, and it is the principle by which we, too, are to live our lives in the world. But, by definition, living according to the principle of the cross requires a daily dying to one's own impulses. We simply cannot continue to do things our way. To be made after God's likeness (*damut*) we must willingly walk through this "door of death". This is the cost of following God. But, it is worth it. Yeshua continues:

---

[32] Matthew 10:38 and 16:24

"For whoever wishes to save his life shall lose it, but whoever loses his life for My sake will find it." [33]

Having been made in God's *tzelem* (צלם), we are capable of love and compassion. But will we make that choice? If we wish to be made in his *damut* (דמות), we must exercise our wills, say 'no' to our own comfort, and do what is pleasing to Him and what is best for others. This is the essence of the two great commandments – to love God with all of our heart, soul, and strength and to love others as ourselves. After all, this is how God first loved us, and this is the "door of death" we are invited to enter.

Again, when Yeshua extended His invitation *"to come after Me"*, what else could "come after Me" mean than "be like Me"? This is what following Yeshua is all about – making our lives more like His. And how do we achieve this likeness to Yeshua? By entering the door of death – by taking up our cross and following Him.

Yeshua Himself walked through this "door of death" for our sakes. But, before he could do that, He had to enter the world through a different door – the door provided by the tribe of Judah.

Judah Provides the Door

Yeshua was born into the tribe of Judah. The name Judah – יהודה – is the only name in the Bible to contain all of the letters of God's name – יהוה. Only one other letter is added – *dalet* (ד), the 'door'. Through Judah, God provides the door through which we can have access to Him. As we have seen, four is the number of witness and, significantly, the name Judah (יהודה) features a *dalet* as the fourth letter.

יהוה = YHVH

יהודה = Judah

In the next chapter we shall discover what happens to the *dalet* (ד) when it admits the truth brought by the *gimel* (ג), because the next letter – *hei* (ה) – is simply a *dalet* (ד) with a little something added inside.

---

[33] Matthew 16:25

5

ה | *Hei*

The Breath of God

The dreadful joy Thy Son has sent
Is heavier than any care;
We find, as Cain his punishment,
Our pardon more than we can bear.
G.K. CHESTERTON

We have begun to discover the unfolding of a story through the names, shapes, sounds, and meanings of the Hebrew letters. In the first three letters we encountered the unique oneness of God and learned how א pictures the Father, ב pictures the Son, and ג pictures the ministry of the Holy Spirit. Next, we observed *gimel* (ג) approaching *dalet* (ד) the 'door' of the 'poor' man – and heard the fourfold message he brought to him. Now, in the letter *hei* (ה) we encounter *dalet* once again, but this time *dalet* contains an additional small pen stroke thus creating the letter *hei* (ה). In Torah scrolls this added stroke appears as an inverted י (*yud*).

We will learn more about *yud* (י) in Chapter 10, but recall that it was introduced as a component of the letter *aleph* (א - which represents the one invisible almighty God and has a numerical value of one). One could almost say that a *yud* (י) left the *aleph* (א) and went to dwell inside the *dalet* (ד). The presence of the י (*yud*) inside the ד (*dalet*) pictures God's spirit indwelling the believer.

The Creative Power of ה

When God's spirit resides within a person's life, that life takes on an entirely new identity, and the change that transpires can be dramatic. We will better appreciate this change as we examine *hei* (ה) and discover the lessons it holds for us. *Hei* (ה) is a mysterious and many-faceted letter, full of insights and applications. It is a letter of meekness as well as of power: of hushed expectancy and creative dynamism. According to the *Talmud*, it was with the letter *hei* (ה) that God created the present world.[1] The Sages derive this from two sources. The first is found in Psalms.

> *By the word of Adonai the heavens were made,*
> *And by the breath of His mouth all their host.*[2]

The first phrase, "*By the word of Adonai the heavens were made...*" refers to the creative action of the letter ב (which, as we learned in chapter 2, pictures Yeshua the Word – the One by whom creation came into being[3]). The second phrase, "*...by the breath of His mouth all their host*", refers to the letter *hei* (ה) because the sound made by *hei* (ה) is nothing more than a breathing outward – a mere exhalation of breath without movement of the lips or tongue. As ב (*beit*, the 'house') was the letter by which God is said to have made the physical universe, *hei* (ה) – the out-breathing of His spirit – is the letter by which that universe was animated. The same may be said of man. We were created by the Son of God, but we are made new creations by the spirit of God.

The belief that God used *hei* (ה) to create the universe is also based on a small ה found in Genesis 2:4 as shown below.

אֵלֶּה תוֹלְדוֹת הַשָּׁמַיִם וְהָאָרֶץ בְּהִבָּרְאָם בְּיוֹם עֲשׂוֹת
יְהוָה אֱלֹהִים אֶרֶץ וְשָׁמָיִם: וְכֹל ׀ שִׂיחַ הַשָּׂדֶה טֶרֶם יִהְיֶה

---

[1] *Menachot 29b.*
[2] Psalms 33:6
[3] John 1:3

The word in the smaller box is בהבראם (*b'hibar'am*, "when they were created", or "*in their creation*"). The second letter of this word is a small *hei* (ה). The Sages say that the *hei* (ה) is printed in this way so as to set it apart from the rest of the word thus rendering it: ב-ה-בראם. This allows the word to be translated: "*With* ה *they [the heavens and earth] were created.*"[4]

ב - ה - בראם

they were created. < ה < With

There is a second interpretation that may be rendered by this arrangement. Let's look at the word בהבראם again. As stated above, *beit* (ב) represents the living Word – Yeshua, the Son of God. Following (*beit*) ב is a small *hei* (ה) as if just breathed forth by the ב. (In fact, the ה is almost small enough to fit inside the ב.) In other words, בהבראם could be interpreted: "*The Son* (ב) *breathed forth* (ה) *creation* (בראם)." This would agree with the verse we just read from Psalms, "*By the word of Adonai [Yeshua being the Word] the heavens were made, and by the breath of His mouth all their host.*"

Spiritual Breathing

This is not the only example of the creative force of God's breath. God also breathed life into Adam.[5] When we consider that by His breath God created the vast expanse of the heavens, then we must stand in awe as we consider that this same God also stooped to breath into man's nostrils the breath of His own life. This must have been David's thought when he penned the words:

> *When I consider Your heavens, the work of Your fingers, the moon and the stars, which You have ordained; what is man that You take thought of him, and the son of man that You care for him?*[6]

Could there be a more powerful demonstration of God's desire for intimacy with mankind than by the sharing of His own breath? God's breath is still available today to bring life to our weak and faltering spirits. God's breath is constantly available through His Word exactly as Paul wrote, "*All Scripture is breathed out by God…*"[7] Just as

---

[4] Osios R' Akiva, as cited by Munk, op.cit., pg. 86.
[5] Genesis 2:7
[6] Psalms 8:3-4
[7] 2 Timothy 3:16 (ESV)

we continue to inhale and exhale air so as to sustain biological life, let us also continue to inhale the breath of God through the words of scripture so as to insure the daily maintenance of our spiritual life. It is my prayer that you will discover something of God's breath even in the study of His alphabet.

Not only is God's breath available to us, but there is a way that our breath – i.e. our spirit – is available to Him. In other words, we can commune with Him in a deeply spiritual way. This is reflected in the word הגה (*hagah*). Before we consider the definition of this word, look at the letters themselves and recall what they mean. The word begins and ends with ה (*hei*), and in the middle is a ג (*gimel*) which pictures a man walking from one ה to the other. So, what does this word mean? It is the word 'meditate', as in...

> *"This book of the Torah shall not depart from your mouth, but you shall* meditate *on it day and night, so that you may be careful to do according to all that is written in it; for then you will make your way prosperous, and then you will have success."*[8]

As a person meditates in God's Torah, their spiritual essences mingle together just like the breath of two people in conversation. Meditation on God's Word should be our daily practice. This is the practice of the righteous man, for *"... his delight is in the Torah of Adonai, and in His Torah he* meditates *day and night."*[9]

God's love for mankind is on record throughout the Scriptures, but the enemy's tactic is to convince us that God is more or less in a permanent state of anger with us. Satan insists that we must somehow work to merit God's love. The Bible, to the contrary, emphatically states that God *is* love and that He is slow to anger,[10] even though He sometimes is provoked to the point that anger is necessary. Paul put it best when he wrote:

> *But God demonstrates His own love for us, in that while we were yet sinners, Messiah died for us. Much more then, having now been justified by his blood, we shall be saved from the wrath of God through Him. For is while we were enemies we were reconciled to God through the death of His Son, much more, having been reconciled, we shall be saved by His life.*[11]

---

[8] Joshua 1:8
[9] Psalm 1:2
[10] 2 Peter 3:9
[11] Romans 5:8-10

God's Sigh

If you are a parent, you know how disappointing it is when your child misbehaves, and discipline must be employed. This is exactly how our heavenly Father sometimes feels. Shortly before his death, Moses appealed to the Israelites to obey God by recalling the rebelliousness of the previous generation. He pleads...

> *"Do you thus repay Adonai, O foolish and unwise people? Is not He your Father who has bought you? He has made you and established you."*[12]

This verse is part of a long poem called *The Song of Moses*[13] which is printed in Torah scrolls in two columns (as is sometimes done with poetic material in the *Tanach*). If you examine this passage in a Torah scroll, you will notice something interesting. This verse is preceded by an oversized ה as shown below.

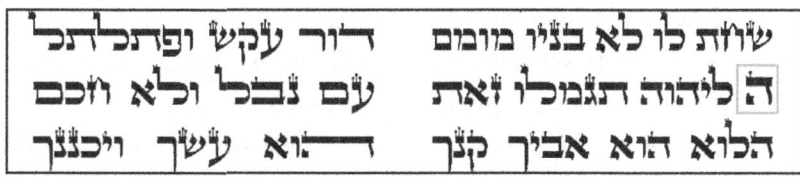

This enlarged ה is not part of a word. It stands entirely alone. Translators are baffled as to how to translate this lone letter. However, the Sages suggest that this letter represents God's "sigh" as He begins to recount His people's checkered history of faithlessness. Remember that ה (*hei*) makes the sound of breath or, in this case, a sigh.

The Blood Covenant

One of the most fascinating uses of the letter *hei* (ה) as a symbol of God's gracious and loving attitude toward man is found in the story of the blood covenant which God made with Abraham. To fully appreciate the significance of what transpired between God and Abraham, we must understand something of what a blood covenant meant in ancient Middle Eastern culture. Then, as now, the world was a dangerous place, and it was wise to have a trustworthy friend should disaster strike. Having such a friend in a time of crisis could make the difference between life and death. Hence, a

---

[12] Deuteronomy 32:6
[13] Deuteronomy 32:1-43

blood covenant was established in order to publicly and legally bind two friends together for life. This formal procedure generally followed the outline described below.

When two men who fully respected and trusted each other chose to enter into a formal pact in order to secure mutual protection for themselves and their families, they called their family members, friends, and neighbors to gather and witness the making of a blood covenant. In the presence of those gathered, these two men documented the stipulations of the covenant in the form of a contract outlining the duties and responsibilities of each party. This contract described the purpose of the covenant, its rules, and the blessings for keeping – and the curses for violating – its stipulations. Two copies of the contract were made, and these were signed with blood drawn from the veins of the two covenant partners. To draw blood for the signing a wound was made, usually in the right forearm. This wound was kept open in order to form a scar as a living sign of the covenant – a sign made in the bodies of the men themselves. The men would also join these wounds temporarily, allowing their blood to flow together so as to symbolize the sharing of a common blood and, thus, a common life. The contracts were then folded and sewn into small leather packets which the men wore either around the neck or upper arm.

In the presence of the witnesses, the men then exchanged a portion of their armor, property, flocks and names. This last bit was accomplished by adding to each man's own name a letter or syllable from the name of the other. For example, if I were to enter into a covenant with a person named John Smith, he might take the 't-o-n' from the end of my name (Luton) and add it to his own, thus changing it from Smith to Smithton. This practice is reflected to this day in the tradition of a bride taking her husband's last name when they marry.

After these exchanges were concluded, an animal (usually a bull or ox) was killed and cut entirely in two. The halves were laid side by side and the two men walked between the two halves as a sign that they walked 'in one blood'. To conclude, a feast was prepared for all of the family members and guests.

From that day forward each man was responsible to protect and avenge the other should the need arise. Should one of the men die, the other took the responsibility of caring for the dead partner's wife and children. This was an irrevocable part of the covenant.[14] Being in a covenant relationship with another person provided many benefits as well as many responsibilities.

---

[14] For a fuller treatment of this subject, the author recommends The Blood Covenant, by H. Clay Trumbull (Impact Books).

From this brief explanation of the blood covenant we can begin to appreciate what a shock it must have been to Abraham when one day God unexpectedly announced...

> I will establish My covenant between Me and you and your descendants after you throughout their generations for an everlasting covenant, to be God to you and to your descendants after you.[15]

Think for a moment how incredible it is that God – the Creator – would choose to make a blood covenant with a mere man. Yet, this is exactly what God did. A careful reading of the account in Genesis reveals that all of the elements of a blood covenant were executed between God and Abraham except for one detail – the most important detail of all. How could God, who is spirit, share His blood with Abraham? Through the act of circumcision Abraham shed his own blood as a seal of the covenant, but how could God shed His own blood when He had none to shed? The answer came almost 2,000 years later when God "was in Messiah".[16] Yeshua sat with His disciples at the Passover Seder and said, *"This cup is the 'new covenant' in My blood…"*[17] Just as Abraham had offered his own son to God as a sacrifice, God also offered His Son at Golgotha as a sacrifice for us.

A Change of Names

Having discussed all this, what does the blood covenant have to do with *hei* (ה)? As mentioned, one of the traditions in a blood covenant was the partial exchange of names, and God did this with Abraham. Though Abraham's name was originally Abram, God changed his name from Abram to Abraham by the addition of the letter *hei* (ה). *Abram* (אברם), with the addition of the ה, became אברהם (*Abraham*).

God did the same thing for Abraham's wife Sarai by adding a ה to her name, thus making it שרה (*Sarah*). In other words, God shared the two *hei*'s (ה) of His own name יהוה (YHVH) by placing one of them in Abram's name and the other in Sarai's. Just imagine – God gave half of His holy name to this elderly couple because He chose to establish a covenant with Abraham. Such a display of grace had never been seen before. But, it is the kind of grace upon which the redeemed community of Messiah is

---

[15] Genesis 17:7. The entire account of the covenant established between God and Abraham may be found in Genesis 15-17.
[16] 2 Corinthians 5:19
[17] 1 Corinthians 11:25

established. What God sealed with the letter ה in the lives of Abraham and Sarah, Yeshua seals with the Holy Spirit - the breath of God - today. *"... having also believed, you were sealed in Him with the Holy Spirit of promise"*.[18]

There is a common notion among Christians that the Jewish people in biblical times did not enjoy close intimacy with God. This is not only a common notion, but a false one, as well. Men and women throughout the *Tanach* enjoyed an intimate relationship with God as much, or more, than many Christians do today. Gentile Christians must be careful that they do not "look down their noses" at the righteous people who lived before Messiah came. They knew God, and they knew Him well.

ה at the Front

Adam's body came to life only after the breath of God was breathed into him. Instead of remaining a body of inanimate dirt, Adam rose up and walked as a man made in God's image. *Hei* (ה) does a similar thing linguistically by giving definiteness to any word to which it is prefixed. When *hei* (ה) is attached to the front of a word it is equivalent to prefixing the word 'the'. For example: עץ (*etz*) "a tree" becomes העץ (*ha'etz*) "the tree" and איש (*ish*) "a man" becomes האיש (*ha'ish*) "the man". It could be said that when *hei* (ה) is prefixed to the front of a word, that word derives an individuality that was lacking before its arrival.

The ability of *hei* (ה) to add individuality and character to a word is indicative of what also happens to any person when the Holy Spirit is breathed into his or her life. When God saves a man, God begins to make him into the individual He intends him to be. He progresses from being just *"a"* man to being *"the"* man whom God has made in His own image.

ה at the Back

Though a word gains definiteness when *hei* (ה) is prefixed to it, something else unique occurs when *hei* (ה) is affixed to the end of a word. As with many languages (but not English), Hebrew nouns have gender - every noun is identified as either feminine or masculine. These feminine nouns can generally be recognized because they end with the letter *hei* (ה). Even the shape of *hei* is described by some Sages as representing the womb - the symbol of creation and birth. In fact, it was after the addition of the ה to the names of Abraham and Sarah that they finally conceived and bore a child.

---

[18] Ephesians 1:13

In a similar way, it is the indwelling of the Holy Spirit that equips a person with the ability to reproduce spiritually. For example, it is only after the filling of the Holy Spirit that one begins to produce the spirit's fruit. Paul wrote, *"But the fruit of the spirit is love, joy, peace, patience, kindness, goodness, faithfulness, gentleness, self-control; against such things there is no law."*[19] This fruit is attractive and delicious, satisfying the needs of those in hunger. But, at its center, as with most fruit, seed is found. In this case, the seed is that incorruptible seed by which one is reborn. That seed is the truth of the Word.[20]

From what we have seen thus far, it is obvious that *hei* (ה) represents the presence of the Holy Spirit in a believer's life, equipping us to bring forth new life in others. Truly, this powerful concept is at the heart of the gospel of grace. *"For I am not ashamed of the gospel, for it is the power of God for salvation to everyone who believes, to the Jew first and also to the Greek."*[21]

The Hebrew word for 'gospel' – בשורה (*besorah*)[22] – contains a powerful lesson for those who wish to share it with others. Sometime this word is spelled without the *vav* (ו), thus rendering it בשרה.[23] Note that בשרה ends with the letter ה (*hei*). We have learned that *hei* (ה) represents God's spirit, so what happens to בשרה – 'gospel' – if we remove the *hei* (ה) from the word? *Besorah* (בשרה) 'gospel' becomes *besor* (בשר) 'flesh'.

$$בשרה = \text{'gospel'}$$
$$-ה$$
$$בשר = \text{'flesh'}$$

The Seal of the Holy Spirit

When God's spirit indwells a person, that person becomes an entirely new creation – a new species as it were.[24] This is illustrated brilliantly in the same word we examined earlier – בהבראם (*b'hibar'am*, *"when they were created"* or *"in their creation"*). We learned how this word can also be read ב-ה-בראם, *"with* ה *they were created"*. But, there is

---

[19] Galatians 5:22-23
[20] 1 Peter 1:23
[21] Romans 1:16
[22] *Besorah* (בשורה) literally means "good news" and is a common word in the *Tanach*. (Example: 2 Samuel 18:25.)
[23] See 2 Samuel 4:10 and 2 Kings 7:9 for examples.
[24] 2 Corinthians 5:17

another possible reading: *'The Son (ב) breathed the hei (ה) into....*" Before we continue, look closely at the remaining four letters (בראם) and notice that they are the same letters that comprise the name אברם (*Abram*). The transformation is made simply by moving the א to the front of the other three letters.[25]

In other words, the ב breathed – ה into אברם (*Abram*) – and 'creation' (בהבראם) occurred. What kind of creation? Once again, when God's breath (His spirit) enters a man, that man becomes a *new* creation.

We have learned that with the arrival of the י (*yud*), ד (*dalet*, 'door') becomes a ה (*hei*). According to most linguists, the form of the letter ה depicts a window. Unlike a door, which is used to bar entrance to intruders, a window allows light and air to enter the house. Hence, we could say that with the arrival of the י (*yud*), the ד (*dalet*) – 'door' – becomes a ה (*hei*) – 'window'. When the spirit of God indwells us, it develops within us a transparency and openness that allow the mutual exchange of light and life. Thus, the window of the soul allows our entire being to be filled with light.[26]

Keep in mind that the character of the letter *hei* (ה) is derived from the presence of *yud* (י) within the *dalet* (ד). As the world was created with the *beit* (ב), the *Talmud* teaches that *yud* (י) was the letter used to create the World to Come[27] – a world of spiritual light and sanctity. This is the message of the letter ה. God has commanded us *"Be holy for I am holy"*[28] – a tall order indeed, and an impossible one without the help of the indwelling spirit of God. He calls us to set ourselves aside for His holy purpose whatever it may be. Only then will we become the unique people God desires us to be.

A Lesson in Brokenness

Turning from sin to God and to His holiness is the essence of repentance. This is pictured beautifully in Hebrew. The Sages teach that the word for repentance – תשובה (*teshuva*) – can be read תשוב-ה (*tishuv-hei*) – "return to ה". Every appearance of this letter is an invitation to return to God while the *window* of opportunity is open. It is

---

[25] Likewise, whenever God breathes His Spirit into our lives, א 'moves to the front'.
[26] Matthew 6:22
[27] Menachot 29b
[28] Leviticus 11:44-45; 1 Peter 1:16

also taught that the small opening in the upper left side of the ה indicates that there is always room for people to return to God.[29] Could this tiny opening be the "eye of the needle" Yeshua referred to when He described how difficult it is for a rich man to enter the kingdom of God?[30]

As we conclude this chapter, I have yet to share what the name of the letter *hei* (ה) means. To appreciate its meaning, we must go back to the story of Jacob, Abraham's grandson, whose name means 'usurper' or 'supplanter'. He was named this because he emerged from his mother's womb grasping his twin brother Esau by the heel.[31]

For most of his life Jacob was grasping for something ... and paying the consequences. When he managed to finagle his way into getting Esau's blessing, he had to flee his brother's wrath. After many years of separation from his family, Jacob decided to return home and make amends with Esau. In preparation for this meeting he sent his family, servants, and cattle ahead to appease his brother's anger. When Jacob was finally alone, God came to him, wrestled with him, and dislocated Jacob's hip. But, He also blessed him and changed his name from *Jacob* ('supplanter') to *Israel* ('prince of God').[32] Jacob would no longer have to grasp and supplant someone else to get what he wanted. There was no need because he was now a 'prince' who no longer needed to 'grasp' for what he wanted.

One of the ways God accomplished this in his life was to use Jacob's fear of his twin brother Esau. When Jacob was told that Esau was riding toward him with 400 men, Jacob was terrified and began to strategize how he could save his household from destruction. But note again the number of people coming toward Jacob – Esau plus 400 men.[33] A total of 401 men were riding toward him. If we convert this number into its Hebrew letter equivalent, it becomes את (א = 1; ת = 400), which are the first and last letters of the alphabet – the equivalent of Alpha and Omega (ΑΩ). This provides insight into the fact that what Jacob imagined to be an enemy, was actually God in disguise.

Similarly, while Jacob waited alone all night preparing to meet his brother, someone jumped him in the dark and wrestled with all night. The Torah states, *"Then*

---

[29] Munk, op.cit., pg. 87.
[30] Matthew 19:24
[31] The name יעקב (*Jacob*) is a play on words. It's most literal meaning is "heel", but it is closely related to a word of uncertain definition used in relation to Jacob in Genesis 27:36, which could possibly be "outwitter", "cheater", or "deceiver", but is most frequently translated "supplanter".
[32] *Israel* can also be translated 'straight to God'.
[33] Genesis 32:6

Jacob was left alone, and a man wrestled with him until daybreak."[34] Who else could this be but Esau! Certainly, this is what was in Jacob's mind. Imagine Jacob's predicament. He knew that Esau wanted to kill him, but he did not want to kill Esau.

At sunrise Jacob realized the truth – what he imagined in the dark to be his enemy, he discovered in the light to be God. God blessed him and changed his name from Jacob to Israel. Jacob arose a different man. The Torah states

> "... Jacob named the place Peniel [פניאל, "face of El"], for he said, 'I have seen God face to face, yet my life has been preserved.' Now the sun rose upon him just as he crossed over Penuel, and he was limping on his thigh."[35]

God is always in the midst of those things we fear. So, why do we fear anything other than God! The Scriptures make it clear that fear is illegal for the believer. We are to fear God alone, and nothing else. Our fear is to belong only to God. But, when we give it to anyone or anything else, it is actually a form of idolatry. *Fear of Adonai is the beginning of wisdom.*[36] Hence, fear of anything else is foolishness.

For Jacob, blessing came at the price of brokenness. To become usable, we need God's blessing. But, we also need Him to break us of our self-will, pride, and fear of things that do not deserve our fear. This is what God did with Jacob and many other men and women in scripture. This is the same principle by which Yeshua fed the multitudes. He took what was given to Him, blessed it, then broke it and fed 5,000 families with it.[37]

Look again at the ה and notice its two legs. Do you see how one of them is 'out of joint'? This letter always reminds me of Jacob, who became *Israel* and the father of the twelve tribes. The definition of the word *hei* (הא) is 'to break'. May God (as He did with Jacob) bless us, break us, and use us for the advancement of His kingdom ... and may God also fill us with the breath of His spirit.

---

[34] Genesis 32:24
[35] Genesis 32:30-31
[36] Proverbs 9:10
[37] Matthew 14:21

6

ו | *Vav*

A Man of the Word

In a place where there are no men, strive to be a man.
PIRKEI AVOT 2:6

A Tabernacle in the Torah

If you had the opportunity to examine a random selection of Torah scrolls like the thousands used in synagogues around the world, you would notice that they all bear similar features. For example, each scroll is comprised of roughly 245 precisely ruled columns, each normally forty-two lines in length. You would see no chapter or verse markings, nor any punctuation or capitalization to indicate the end of one sentence and the beginning of the next. In fact, the only indication you would have that you had reached the end of a book is four blank lines that appear between the end of one book and the beginning of the next.

Upon further examination, you would notice that almost every column of a Torah scroll begins with the same letter.[1] Torah scribes employ great skill and planning so that each column begins with a word whose first letter is ו (*vav*). Torah scribes have practiced this tradition for many centuries based upon a passage from the Torah which states:

---

[1] There are only five exceptions to this rule. For a list of these exceptions see This Is the Torah, Alfred J. Kolatch; Jonathan David Publishers, Inc., pg. 109.

> "You shall make the court of the tabernacle. On the south side there shall be hangings for the court of fine twisted linen one hundred cubits long for one side; and its pillars shall be twenty, with their twenty sockets of bronze; the hooks of the pillars and their bands shall be of silver."[2]

Though it is not so obvious to the non-Hebrew reader, there is much about this description of the tabernacle that also applies to a Torah scroll. The tabernacle was the habitation of God's *shekinah* glory while the Israelites traveled in the wilderness, hence it is appropriate that the Torah, the habitation for His Word, should be fashioned similarly. For instance, the Hebrew word for 'curtain' (יריעה, *yeri'ah*)[3] is the same word used for a sheet of parchment. And עמוד (*amud*, 'post' or 'pillar') is the same word used for a column of print. Each curtain of the tabernacle was fastened to its post by means of a 'hook' (ו, *vav*), which is the name of the letter under discussion in this chapter.

For centuries scribes would begin each column of the Torah with the letter *vav* (ו) because its form depicts a hook fastened to a post. In this way, each column of print depicts a curtain of the tabernacle, and the *vav* (ו) *hooks* each column of print to a sheet of parchment. It is a challenging task for a scribe to position words so accurately as to ensure that each column begins with a word whose initial letter is *vav* (ו), but this task is made easier by the fact that more Hebrew words begin with *vav* (ו) than with any other letter.

The reason for this is that *vav* (ו), when prefixed to a word, means 'and'. For example, the addition of a ו (*vav*) changes עץ (*etz*) from 'a tree' to ועץ (*v'etz*) 'and a tree'. *Vav* – the 'hook' – literally hooks words together. This is, after all, the purpose of the word 'and' – to bring two things into relationship with each other. *Vav* (ו), which is spelled ואו has a numerical value of 13, which just so happens to be the same value as the word אחד (*echad*) 'one'.[4] *Vav* makes two things one. *Vav*, which has a numerical value of six, first appears in the sixth word of the Bible. There it is used as a prefix meaning 'and' in the phrase *"the heavens* and *the earth"*.

---

[2] Exodus 27:9-10
[3] Exodus 26:1. The word used in 27:9 is a more general term meaning 'hangings'.
[4] ו = 6, א = 1, ו = 6; 6 + 1 + 6 = 13. א = 1, ח = 8, ד = 4; 1 + 8 + 4 = 13.

The Center of the Torah

Vav has the distinction of being the middle letter of the Torah. One could say that it *hooks* the first half of the Torah to the second. The *vav* located at the center of the Torah is printed oversize as indicated below.

The word containing the oversized *vav* in this passage is, appropriately, the word *gachon* (גחון), which means 'belly'. I say 'appropriately' because the large *vav* (ו) exists in the very 'belly' of the Torah.[5] This is the only occurrence of an oversized *vav* (ו) in the Torah, but there exists an even stranger form of this letter in the book of Numbers where the ו is broken entirely in half.

The Broken ו

The book of Numbers contains a story that is shocking yet full of meaning and insight for those who study it. In this story we read of how God's anger was stirred up against Israel because they had become involved in the paganism and immorality of the Moabites. God's anger was finally appeased when a young priest named Phinehas took decisive action. Here is the story as it appears in the Torah:

> Then behold, one of the sons of Israel came and brought to his relatives a Midianite woman, in the sight of Moses and in the sight of all the congregation of the sons of Israel, while they were weeping at the doorway of the tent of meeting. When Phinehas the son of Eleazar, the son of Aaron the priest, saw it, he arose from the midst of the congregation and took a spear in his hand, and he went after the man of Israel into the tent and pierced both of them through, the man of Israel and the woman, through the body. So the plague on the sons of Israel was checked. Those who died by the plague were 24,000.
>
> Then Adonai spoke to Moses, saying, "Phinehas the son of Eleazar, the son of Aaron the priest, has turned away My wrath from the sons of Israel in that he was jealous

---

[5] Leviticus 11:42

with My jealousy among them, so that I did not destroy the sons of Israel in My jealousy. Therefore say, 'Behold, I give him My covenant of peace.'"[6]

In this story we encounter two men and witness the effect that their opposing actions had on the Israelite nation. The lustful behavior of the first man contributed to the deadly plague which God unleashed upon the Israelites. In contrast, the righteous actions of Phinehas brought an immediate halt to the plague. Because Phinehas was zealous for God's honor, God said, *"I give him My covenant of peace."* The word 'peace' in Hebrew is *shalom* (שלום). The illustration below shows the word in this passage as it appears in a Torah scroll.[7] Notice that the *vav* (ו) contained in the word *shalom* is broken in two.

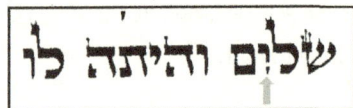

The broken *vav* (ו) in this passage appears exactly this way in all Torah scrolls. For centuries the Sages have conjectured as to why this tradition was established. We shall examine three possible answers as to why God broke the *vav* (ו) in this word. The first of these is merely interesting, but the other two teach important lessons about ourselves and about our God.

Look closely at the broken *vav* (ו) and notice that it forms a letter which we have encountered several times in previous chapters. The broken *vav* forms the letter *yud* (י) with a vertical line directly beneath it. The name of the letter *yud* means 'hand' and, according to the story, Phinehas took a spear in his hand and ran it through the bodies of the sinning couple. Thus, the broken *vav* forms a picture of a hand with a spear extending down from it.

ו = Man

To appreciate the next two insights, we must understand the significance of *vav*'s numerical value. Though *vav*'s name means 'hook', its numerical value represents man. And what number is that? The book of Revelation states that the identifier of the Anti-Messiah *"... is that of a man ...666"*.[8] The fact that six represents mankind was not news

---

[6] Numbers 25:6-12
[7] Numbers 25:12
[8] Revelation 13:18.

to John's Jewish readers because they had known this for centuries based upon this number's use in the Bible. For example:

- Man was created on the sixth day.[9]
- Man is limited to six degrees of freedom (forward, backward, left, right, up, down).
- Man is to work six days out of the week.[10]
- Six millennia are appointed for the duration of man's history before the coming of Messiah.[11]

There are many other Biblical examples which indicate that the number six is closely linked to the things of man. The *hook*, the "and", and the 6 are all brought together in *vav* (ו) because this letter represents the essence of mankind. For instance, the nature of the 'and' is perfectly illustrated in man because he is the 'and' of God's creation – made of spirit *and* flesh. And through Yeshua – the Son of Man – are the spiritual and physical dimensions *hooked* together in an eternal bond.

With these things in mind, let us consider again the broken *vav* (ו) in the word *shalom*. If the ו there represents a man, then who could this broken man be? Isaiah wrote of Messiah: *"The chastening that brought us peace [shalom] fell upon Him."*[12] Our peace with God was purchased by means of Messiah being broken. Instead of running His spear of judgment through his sinning creatures, God allowed his Son, Yeshua, to take our punishment upon Himself. It was through Messiah's brokenness that we are made whole, and it was by the spear driven into His side that we were spared the punishment we deserve.

However, there is a brokenness of another kind that is required of us. We discussed this briefly at the end of the previous chapter in the context of the story of Jacob. But, here in the broken *vav* (ו) we see brokenness illustrated in a different and more detailed way. To understand what I mean, let us look at this broken ו exactly as it appears in a Torah scroll.

---

[9] Genesis 1:22-31
[10] Exodus 20:9
[11] This is a Jewish insight gleaned from the fact that there are six *alephs* (א) in the first verse of the Bible. One of the definitions for the word *aleph* is '1,000'. Thus, 6 x 1,000 = 6,000.
[12] Isaiah 53:5

Here we can see the individual parts of the broken ו – the thin vertical stroke at the bottom and the *yud* (י) formed above the break.[13] But also note the tiny stroke extending above the *yud*.[14] Thus, we can see that this *vav* (ו) is actually comprised of three parts rather than two as it appears in printed Hebrew Bibles. We saw how *aleph* (א) – the letter which represents God – is comprised of three components. Likewise, in this letter the three components of man are perfectly illustrated.

The central *yud* portion of the ו (above the break) corresponds to man's soul, which is what we essentially are. The soul is comprised of our mind, will and emotions – the attributes that form our personality, or self. Protruding downward is a line that connects the *yud* to the earth. It is this thin, fragile line that represents the body. One can see how tentative it is and how easily it could be snapped and our connection to this physical world broken. The small upward-pointing crown protruding from the *yud* represents man's spirit as an extension of his soul in its attempt to reach toward God. But the difference between the average man of the world and the man who is at peace with God is that the spiritual man has been 'broken'. His soul finds its identity not in the flesh, but in the 'crown' of his spirit. Only by becoming a "broken *vav*" do we come into God's covenant of peace and experience the *shalom* of God. And only through brokenness do we change from a *Jacob* ('supplanter') to an *Israel* ('prince of God').

Let us not hinder God's loving hand as He would bring us into peace by way of brokenness. May He make us like Phinehas who was zealous for God and saved many from death, and not like the lustful man whose physical passions brought death and shame to himself and to his people.

The Mystery of the Five *Vavs*

Malachi prophesied that Elijah would return immediately prior to the arrival of the Messiah. We discussed previously how John the Immerser is the fulfillment of this prophecy for believers today, but the literal fulfillment has yet to occur. Elijah's name

---

[13] The illustration shown here is from a *Sephardic* Torah scroll. *Ashkenazic* Torah scrolls do not always include the full complement of *tagin* ('crowns') and thus do not normally have a crown at the top of the *vav*.
[14] The KJV calls these flourishes 'tittles' (Matthew 5:18), but in Hebrew they are called *tagin* – 'crowns'.

in Hebrew is אליהו (note the *vav* – ו – at the end). But, five times in the *Tanach*, Elijah's name is spelled defectively by the omission of the *vav* (ו), rendering it as אליה.[15]

Jacob's name is spelled יעקב. But, five times in the *Tanach* his name is spelled defectively by the *addition* of the letter *vav* (ו) rendering it as יעקוב instead of יעקב.[16] In other words, five times in the *Tanach* a *vav* (ו) is missing from Elijah's name and five times it is added to Jacob's. What is God seeking to teach us here? Since the *vav* (ו) is transferred from Elijah's to Jacob's name five times, it is obvious that there is something 'Elijah' has that 'Jacob' normally doesn't. This transferal occurs exactly five times – the numerical value of the letter *hei* (ה), which, you may recall, represents the breath of God. Might this entire scenario be a picture of the day when God will breathe His spirit – the spirit that animated and inspired the prophet Elijah – into 'Jacob' (i.e. the nation of Israel)? It certainly is consistent with the many prophecies concerning the revival awaiting the Jewish nation. Isaiah wrote, *"And I will give them one heart, and put a new spirit within them. And I will take the heart of stone out of their flesh and give them a heart of flesh."*[17]

The day is coming when Israel will be given both a new heart and a new spirit like Elijah's that they may recognize Yeshua as Savior and Messiah. Their hearts will be turned to their father Jacob who became a "Prince of God" (*Israel*) when he wrestled with and yielded his life to God. May the day come quickly when that which was Elijah's will be given to Jacob in order that his children may become the true Israel of God.

The Star of David

Having observed *vav*'s association with the number six, I would like to close with a note concerning the Star of David, Israel's national symbol.[18] I discuss it here because six is the number of man, and the six-pointed Star of David brilliantly illustrates the proper relationship of a man to God.

As you can readily see, this star is constructed of two triangles – one pointed downward, and the other upward.

---

[15] 2 Kings 1:3,4,8,12/ Malachi 3:23
[16] Leviticus 26:42/Jeremiah 30:18/33:26/46:27/51:9
[17] Ezekiel 11:19
[18] Also called *Mogen* ["shield of"] *David*.

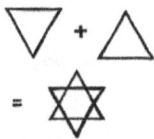

The downward-pointing triangle is an apt representation of the body, soul, and spirit of man. The upward-pointing triangle is an apt representation of the Father, Son, and Holy Spirit. When the two come into a proper relationship, they form a star – a source of light in the darkness. Anyone who is in a right relationship with God becomes a light-bearer in a dark world. In this way, the Star of David is also a symbol of the coming Messiah. As Isaiah prophesied:

> And now says Adonai –
>   Who formed Me from the womb to be His Servant,
> To bring Jacob back to Him
>   So that Israel might be gathered to Him,
>   (For I am honored in the sight of Adonai,
>   And my God is My strength),
> He says, "It is too small a thing that You should be My Servant
> To raise up the tribes of Jacob
>   and to restore the preserved ones of Israel;
> I will also make You a light for the nations,
>   So that My salvation may reach to the end of the earth."[19]

---

[19] Isaiah 49:5-6. The word "salvation" in this passage is ישוע, *Yeshua*.

7

ז | *Zayin*

The Sword and the Seed

What makes the difference is not how many times you have been through the Bible, but how many times and how thoroughly the Bible has been through you.
                    — Gypsy Smith

Since *zayin* concludes our first series of letters portraying the story of the gospel, let's review briefly what we have learned so far. *Aleph* (א) represents the one, almighty, invisible God who reveals Himself through the Scriptures (ב). God's plea to mankind goes forth from *beit* (ב), carried by the Holy Spirit (ג) to the poor man who lives behind the closed 'door' (ד). Having received the truth of the gospel, the spirit of God enters him and the *dalet* (ד) becomes a *hei* (ה). One who has been filled with God's spirit and begins to grow in the righteousness of Messiah becomes a new creation – a true man (ו).[1]

---

[1] Interestingly, the second, third, and fourth letters of the alphabet spell the word בגד (*be'ged*) 'garment', suggesting that the one who has received the Holy Spirit has begun to weave a garment of righteousness as described in Revelation 19:7-8.

In this chapter we witness the equipping of the new man with the sword of the spirit, the Word of God, because the name of the letter *zayin* means 'weapon', and its form (ז) represents a sword.

A Word About Swords

Paul brilliantly describes the believer's spiritual armor using specific first-century military terms. He was familiar with these since Roman soldiers, with their armor and weapons, would have been a common sight in his day. Note how he assigns to each piece of armor a spiritual counterpart:

> *Therefore, take up the full armor of God, so that you will be able to resist in the evil day, and having done everything, to stand firm. Stand firm therefore, having girded your loins with truth, and having put on the breastplate of righteousness, and having shod your feet with the preparation of the gospel of peace; in addition to all, taking up the shield of faith with which you will be able to extinguish all the flaming arrows of the evil one. And take the helmet of salvation, and the sword of the spirit, which is the Word of God.*[2]

Though volumes have been written about this spiritual armor, our primary interest is the sword, which is the only weapon on this list. *Zayin*'s name means 'weapon' and its form is that of a sword (ז) with its grip at the top and its blade pointing downward. In Paul's description of spiritual armor he refers to *"the sword of the spirit"* and uses a specific Greek word for 'sword', a word that perfectly illustrates the power of the sword of the spirit – God's Word. But, before we look at the kind of sword Paul refers to, let's consider the swords he did not mention.

In Paul's day the sword was the military weapon of choice, and several varieties were in use. One type was the *romphia* (ρομφια), a long, curved, single-edged, scimitar-like weapon which was effective for felling the enemy by sweeping it in a wide arc. Unfortunately, if one missed on the first swing, an opening was left for the enemy to deliver a fatal thrust during the time it took to reverse the direction of the heavy blade for a return sweep. Consequently, this weapon – the *romphia* – was not the sword Paul referred to as the *"sword of the spirit"*.

---

[2] Ephesians 6:13-17

Another common variety of sword used in Paul's day was the *xiphos* (χιφος), a long, straight sword used mainly for thrusting. It had a very sharp point and could damage the enemy from a more comfortable distance, but it lacked the mass and strength required to deliver the hacking blow required to cut through armor and limbs. Understandably, the *xiphos* was not the weapon referred to as the *"sword of the spirit"*.

The term Paul did use in Ephesians was *machaira* (μαχαιρα), better known as the Roman short sword. Few people in the modern world appreciate the effect this innovative Roman weapon had upon history, for the *machaira* was a deadly and effective instrument which contributed greatly to Rome's successful conquest of the world. Compared to the massive swords commonly used by Rome's enemies, the *machaira* looked puny and almost laughable. But Rome had the last laugh. With the *machaira*, Rome conquered an empire.

The *machaira* owed its effectiveness to several features. It had two sharp edges which allowed both forehand and backhand swings. It was short enough that it could be maneuvered quickly and accurately, and its strong broad blade had a very sharp point which allowed for a deadly thrust.

Machaira is the term Paul used to describe God's Word as the *"sword of the spirit"*, because God's Word also has two sharp edges – the Hebrew Scriptures (the *Tanach*) and the Greek (or 'Apostolic') Scriptures – both of which lead to the Word's one inescapable theme – Messiah Yeshua. He is the central point to which both the Hebrew and Greek Scriptures point. And, unlike the *romphia* or the *xiphos*, God's Word is not cumbersome or unwieldy. According to the writer of Hebrews, God's Word is:

> ... *living and active and Sharper than any two-edged sword* [machaira], *and piercing as far as the division of soul and spirit, of both joints and marrow, and able to judge the thoughts and intentions of the heart*.[3]

Just as the soldiers of Rome conquered the world using the *machaira*, may God grant us skill in the use of its spiritual counterpart – the most powerful of all weapons. In Chapter 2 we examined *beit* (ב), the 'house' which represents the Scriptures, as the habitation of God's Word. Now, in the letter *zayin* (ז), we encounter the Word itself in its power and authority.

---

[3] Hebrews 4:12

The Sword of Truth

Yeshua prayed to the Father saying, *"Your word is truth"*.[4] He also spoke of Himself saying, *"I am the way and the truth and the life."*[5] Comparing these two statements, we see that Yeshua *is* the Word of truth. The Hebrew word for truth is אמת (*emet*) and is spelled using the first, middle, and last letters of the alphabet, as shown in the illustration below.[6]

אבג דהוזחטיכך ל מ מסנןסעצץפףק רשת

This illustrates that truth is not confined. It encompasses everything from the beginning to the end. This is also demonstrated by the fact that the first two letters of אמת (*emet*) spell אם (*eem*) 'mother', and the last two letters of אמת spell מת (*mut*) 'death'. In other words, it requires a lifetime – from 'mother' (i.e. 'birth') to 'death' – to grasp the full scope of truth.

If we compare the words 'truth' (אמת) and 'falsehood' (שקר, *sheker*), we notice a profound physical difference between the two. The letters forming אמת 'truth' have broad stable bottoms, but the letters forming שקר 'falsehood' have pointy unstable bottoms. Similarly, truth is stable and stands on its own whereas falsehood is easily toppled by truth.

We have seen that 'truth' (אמת) is spelled with the first, middle and last letters of the alphabet, but where do find the letters of 'falsehood' (שקר)? They are clustered together in a jumble near the end of the alphabet as you can see below.

אבג דהוזחטיכךלמסנןסעצץפףק רשת

You will also notice that the three letters that spell 'falsehood' (שקר) are out of order. Thus it is with falsehood. Unlike אמת ('truth'), falsehoods are small, disorderly and unstable. How perfectly Hebrew illustrates the truth about falsehood.

---

[4] John 17:17

[5] John 14:6

[6] One may wonder how *mem* (מ/ם) can be the middle letter of the alphabet when the Hebrew alphabet contains an even number of letters. As explained in the Introduction, five of the letters have two forms – the regular form (used at the beginning and middle of a word), and the final form (used only at the end of a word). When the alphabet includes these final forms (as in the illustration), the total number of letters is brought to 27, thus making *mem* (מ) the middle (14th) letter.

Seeing that אמת (*truth*) is formed from the first, middle, and last letters of the alphabet prompts us to ask what word is similarly produced from the Greek alphabet. Combining the first, middle, and last letters of the Greek alphabet, we derive the word ανω (*ano*), which means 'upward' or 'above'.

α β γ δ ε ζ η θ ι κ λ μ ν ξ ο π ρ σ ς⁷ τ υ φ χ ψ ω

We can see from this that when we 'lift up' (ανω, *ano*) God's Word, we lift up 'truth' (אמת, *emet*). As Yeshua said, *"But I [the Truth], if I am lifted up from the earth, will draw all men to Myself."*[8] Yeshua, who is the alphabet through whom God speaks, draws men to Himself when truth is proclaimed.

These insights can be summed up in a diagram of a *machaira*:

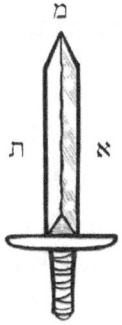

The א represents the *Tanach* (or, Hebrew Scriptures) which pointed forward to Messiah. The ת represents the Apostolic (or Greek) Scriptures which point back at Messiah. The *mem* (מ) stands for משיח (*Mashiach*) – the Messiah who came and lived in between the writing of the Hebrew and Greek Scriptures and to whom they both point. Once again, these three letters spell אמת (*emet*, 'truth').

Psalm 91

As we consider the power of God's Word as the sword of the spirit, we must appreciate that this is not merely a figure of speech. The weapon which God has provided us

---

[7] As with Hebrew, Greek also incorporates final forms but only with one letter – *sigma* (σ/ς) – included in the illustration.
[8] John 12:32

is powerful and effective. Paul stressed this when he wrote, *"... the weapons of our warfare are not of the flesh, but divinely powerful for the destruction of fortresses."*[9]

This truth is reinforced in a passage from Malachi where God commands us to *"remember the Torah of Moses My servant"*.[10] Here, the word 'remember' is זִכְרוּ (zicru), spelled with an oversize *zayin*. The oversize ז ('weapon') found in the word 'remember' reminds us that God has given us a formidable weapon which is highly effective against both our accuser, Satan, and his only weapon – the lie. Hence, we understand that our spiritual sword is wielded with the mind. So, let us be careful to *"remember the Torah of Moses"*.

The form of the *zayin* (ז) is identical to the flourishes found on many of the letters in a Torah scroll. The letters which most frequently have these decorations (called *tagin*) are: ש,ע,ט,נ,ז,ג,צ. They typically appear in Torah scrolls as shown below.

שׁ עׁ טׁ נׁ זׁ גׁ צׁ

Yeshua said, *"For truly I say to you, until heaven and earth pass away, not the smallest letter ['yud'] or stroke ['tagin'], shall pass from the Torah until all is accomplished."*[11] In saying this, Yeshua signified that even the tiny decorations on the letters are not trivial. How could these tiny *zayin*-shaped decorations have any significance for us today? Scholars are uncertain of the purpose for these decorations[12], but a Jewish tradition concerning one of the Psalms provides an amazing insight into these decorations.

Whenever rabbis perform an exorcism they quote Psalm 91. This Psalm contains many references to God's protecting power and ability to deliver from the oppression of the enemy. It also describes how God is a refuge and a fortress to those who trust in Him. It comforts those in trouble with the promise that, *"You will not be afraid of the terror by night, or of the arrow that flies by day, of the pestilence that stalks in the darkness, or the destruction that lays waste at noon."*[13] This is a favorite Psalm that has provided great comfort to those who embrace its truths.

However, there is something very unusual about this psalm that is unapparent to English readers: none of its sixteen verses contains a *zayin* (ז). *Zayin* is a commonly

---

[9] 2 Corinthians 10:4
[10] Malachi 4:4
[11] Matthew 5:18
[12] One theory is that they are a form of musical notation.
[13] Psalm 91:5-6

used letter in the *Tanach*, so it is unusual that it should be entirely absent from a Psalm of this length. On the other hand, this psalm contains many *zayins* in the form of *tagin* decorations. When rabbis read this psalm aloud, they believe that the many *zayins* that appear as decorations on its letters find their voice in the spiritual realm where they bring destruction to demonic forces. It is believed that the *zayins* – the Psalm's weapons – are released into the spiritual realm to do battle against the forces of darkness.

Of Bread and War

The name of the letter *zayin* (ז) may be spelled in two ways. When it is spelled זין it means 'weapon'. But, when it is spelled זן (without the י) it means 'to nourish' or 'sustain'. These two concepts – 'weapon' and 'nourishment' – seem worlds apart until one learns that *bread* and *war* are closely related in both the Hebrew language and Jewish thought. The Hebrew word for 'bread' is לחם (*lechem*) and the word for 'war' is מלחמה (*mil'chamah*). Note that the word for *bread* is in the center of the word for *war*. In Hebraic thought, success in battle is measured by how much land is won since land is the source of sustenance. Therefore, to win land is to win bread.

These two meanings of *zayin*'s name illustrate two benefits we derive from God's Word – spiritual nourishment and spiritual protection. Yeshua emphasized the first when He quoted the Torah saying, *"Man shall not live on bread alone, but on every word that proceeds out of the mouth of God."*[14] God's principal intention for His Word is the spiritual nourishment of His people. (After all, Yeshua refers to Himself as the "Bread of Life", not as the "Sword"). This is further illustrated by the first two appearances of *zayin* (ז) in the *Torah* – מצריע זרע (*matzriah zerah*, "yielding seed").[15]

It is only due to Adam's fall and the place thus given to our spiritual enemy in this world that the Word of God must double as our spiritual food and our spiritual weapon. The day is coming, however, when our spiritual enemies will no longer be a nuisance to us and we will no longer need to use God's Word as a sword. Isaiah foresaw that day and wrote of the time when warfare will cease – *"They will hammer their swords into plowshares and their spears into pruning hooks."*[16] Just as swords and spears (instruments of warfare) will be transformed into plows and pruning hooks

---

[14] Matthew 4:4 (quoting Deuteronomy 8:3)
[15] Genesis 1:11
[16] Isaiah 2:4

(instruments of nourishment), so the day is coming when God's Word will no longer be used for spiritual warfare. But, it will remain our source of spiritual nourishment.

The Letter With Two Faces

In keeping with the above, the Sages claim that *zayin* (ז) has two faces – one to the left and one to the right. The two faces of *zayin* (ז) – warfare and nourishment – are pictured also in the letter *gimel* (ג). If we examine a *gimel* (ג) as it appears in a Torah scroll, we notice that it is actually a *zayin* (ז) with a *yud* (י) for a foot.

You may recall that *gimel* (ג) represents the Holy Spirit as hurrying to the door of the poor man pictured by *dalet* (ד). As the ג approaches the ד, which face of the ז will be presented? Is he coming to warn of punishment or to appeal in gentleness? God desires repentance one way or another.

In his letter to the Romans, Paul appealed to them on the basis of God's goodness, saying, *"Or do you think lightly of the riches of His kindness and tolerance and patience, not knowing that the kindness of God leads you to repentance?"*[17] But, in regard to the Corinthians Paul reminded them that they came to God because of the sorrow that God had sent them, *"… for you were made sorrowful according to the will of God, so that you might not suffer loss in anything through us. For the sorrow that is according to the will of God produces a repentance without regret …"*[18] *Zayin*'s two faces remind us to consider both *"the kindness and severity of God."*[19] God's severity and God's kindness both lead to repentance. Thus, the two faces of *zayin* (ז) are the two faces of scripture. One person reads the Bible and experiences conviction while another reads the Bible and experiences comfort. To the one, Yeshua appears as a lion, and to the other as a lamb.

Nowhere are these two faces of our Master seen more clearly than in His words to the community at Laodicea. As a lion, Yeshua threatens this lukewarm congregation with the sword – *"Those whom I love, I reprove and discipline; therefore be zealous and repent."*[20] As a lamb, He also pleads with them, offering nourishment – *"Behold, I stand*

---

[17] Romans 2:4
[18] 2 Corinthians 7:9b-10a
[19] Romans 11:22
[20] Revelation 3:19

at the door and knock; if anyone hears My voice and opens the door, I will come in to him and will dine with him, and he with Me."[21] The image of Yeshua as *zayin* (ז) coming to knock at the door reminds us once again of the *gimel* (ג) approaching *dalet* (ד, the 'door').

As Yeshua approaches the door of your heart, which face of the *zayin* does He offer? Does He come as a lamb, or as a lion? Does He come to nourish? Or, does he come wielding a sword? Kindness and sorrow can each provoke repentance, but the decision as to which one it shall be is chiefly yours.

A Slice of Time

Zayin's numerical value is seven, which is a number with special significance in scripture. The *Midrash* says that all sevens are blessed, since seven is frequently used in the Bible in the context of blessing, completeness, fullness, and rest.[22] The Hebrew word for 'seven' is שבה (*shevah*). When this same word is pronounced *savah* it means 'to be full' or 'satisfied', as illustrated by the fact that God rested on the seventh day from His six-day work of creation. The word 'Sabbath' (שבת) is taken from this same root.

Though the Bible contains many occurrences of the number seven, each with a special spiritual significance, this number is used most often in reference to divisions of time, as in the example of the seven-day week. Since the seventh letter is a 'sword', it is appropriate that it should be used to *slice* time into its component parts. Some examples include:

> *Week of Days* | Six days of work followed by a Sabbath day of rest
> *Week of Weeks* | The day of *Shavuot* (Pentecost) always falls 49 days (7 x 7) after the day of First Fruits[23]
> *Week of Months* | The seven biblical Feast Days all fall within a period of seven months[24]
> *Week of Years* | Six years of sowing and reaping are followed by a year of Sabbath rest wherein the ground lies fallow[25]
> *Week of Weeks of Years* | Forty-nine (7 x 7) years followed by the Year of Jubilee

---

[21] Revelation 3:20
[22] *VaYikra Rabbah* 29:10
[23] Leviticus 23:15-21
[24] Leviticus 23:1-44
[25] Leviticus 25:1-5

> wherein all debts are canceled, and all slaves are freed.[26]
>
> *Week of Millenniums* | Six thousand years of human history followed by a thousand years of Messiah's kingdom.[27]

Another outstanding example that we must consider is found in the ninth chapter of Daniel – one of the most extraordinary prophetic passages in the Bible. There we read how Daniel received an angelic visitation concerning Israel's future history. Gabriel told Daniel:

> *Seventy sevens have been decreed for your people and your holy city, to finish transgression, to make an end of sin, to make atonement for iniquity, to bring in everlasting righteousness, to seal up vision and prophecy and to anoint the most holy place.*[28]

The 'sevens' referred to are weeks of years, producing a total of "seventy sevens", or 490 years.

Daniel was also told exactly when this 490-year period would begin, and at what point during that period the Messiah would come and die. We know historically that Yeshua was crucified in the 483rd year of this time span. But, since many of the Jewish leaders still refused to acknowledge Yeshua as the Messiah, God postponed the commencement of the final seven-year period. The final 'seven' that is yet to come is described in detail in the book of Revelation. There it is referred to as the Great Tribulation.

The Number of Perfection

These examples indicate that with the number seven comes finality. However, it is the kind of finality that results in *Sabbath*. It is God's goal to bring us into His rest, as stated in Hebrews:

---

[26] Leviticus 25:8

[27] From Adam to Abraham was approximately 2,000 years. From Abraham to Messiah was approximately 2,000 years. From Messiah's first coming until His return will be approximately 2,000 years. This makes a total of 6,000 years which will be followed by Messiah's 1,000-year rule. (Revelation 20)

[28] Daniel 9:24. For a thorough analysis of the seventy weeks of Daniel 9, the author recommends the book, The Coming Prince, by Sir Robert Anderson (Kregel Publishers).

There remains a Sabbath rest for the people of God. For the one who has entered His rest has himself also rested from his works, as God did from His. Therefore let us be diligent to enter that rest ...[29]

We have seen from these examples that this finality is often merely the conclusion of one cycle which heralds the beginning of another. (The greatest example of this is when Yeshua arose from the dead on the first day of the week.) The Hebrew alphabet itself is constructed along these lines because with the letter *zayin* (ז) we end one cycle, and with the letter *chet* (ח) – which symbolizes 'life' – we begin a new cycle of Hebrew letters.

---

[29] Hebrews 4:9-11a

Series Two

The Spiritual Walk

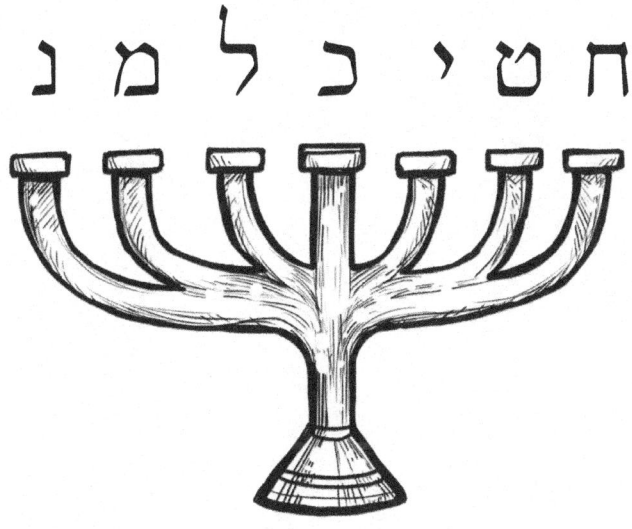

8

ח | *Chet*

Life Abundant

Teach me to live that I may dread
The grave as little as my bed.
Thomas Ken — *"Evening Prayer"*

A Sign of Life

It is a popular Jewish fashion to wear a silver or gold pendant shaped either like the letter ח (*chet*) or the word חי (*chai*) – short for חיים (*chaim*, 'life'). The tradition of wearing these symbols as a necklace may be based on the verse, *"...they will be life to your soul and adornment to your neck."*[1]

When the blood of the Passover lamb was applied to the doorposts and lintel of each Hebrew home, it formed the shape of the letter *chet* (ח), the letter which is synonymous in the Jewish mind with *life*. The spiritual walk is a walk of faith that is both abundant and gratifying, available only by resting in what Messiah accomplished on the cross while simultaneously walking in obedience to God's Word. As we study our second cycle of Hebrew letters, we will gain insight into this walk of faith.

The words *life*, *grace*, and *rest* are closely related in scripture. By God's *grace* we receive the gift of eternal *life* and are invited to enter His *rest*. The relationship of these

---
[1] Proverbs 3:22

three words is illustrated by beginning with the word חי (*chai*, 'life') and lengthening the י (*yud*) so that it becomes a ן (final *nun*) thus forming חן (*chen*, 'grace'). *Yud* (י) is symbolic of the Holy Spirit, and *grace* is demonstrated when the Holy Spirit reaches down (ן) into the depths of our being and brings life and salvation. But this occurs only through faith, which requires that we rest in God's grace.[2]

The fourth chapter of Hebrews repeatedly stresses that the evidence of faith is resting from one's own works and resting instead in the finished work of God.[3] This principle is also illustrated by the Hebrew word for 'grace'. If we reverse the letter order of חן (*chen*, 'grace'), we get נח (*noach*, 'rest').

To clarify, the word for 'life' is חי (*chai*). Lengthening the י so that it becomes a ן renders the word חן (*chen*, 'grace'). Reversing the letters of חן renders נח (*noach*), which means 'rest'. *Noach* is the same as the name *Noah* who "...*found grace in the eyes of Adonai*".[4] As a result of this grace, Noah and his family lived. We must follow the same pattern.

	חי	= *Life*
Lengthen the *yud* —	חן	= *Grace*
Reverse the letters —	נח	= *Rest*

Another example of *chet*'s (ח) association with life is found in the story of the birth of Isaac. Isaac's name – יצחק – comes from the root צחק (*tz'chak*), which means 'to laugh'. Looking carefully at the word צחק we can see that it begins with צ (= 90), which was the age of Sarah at the time of Isaac's birth. Notice also that this word ends with ק (= 100), which was Abraham's age at Isaac's birth. Between these two letters is *chet* (ח), the letter of life. The lesson here is clear: though Abraham was 100 (ק) and Sarah was 90 (צ), God kept His promise that between the two of them would come forth a new life (ח) – Isaac, whose name means 'laughter' (יצחק).[5]

---

[2] Ephesians 2:8-9

[3] The faith whose proof is *rest* applies only to one's individual needs. But, James (2:15-17) clearly shows that in the context of the needs of another immediate action is imperative since "*faith without works is dead.*"

[4] Genesis 6:8

[5] This story is supported another way in that *tzaddi* (צ) is the eighteenth letter of the alphabet, and 18 = חי (*chai*, 'life'). [ח = 8, י = 10; 8+10 = 18]

The Number of New Beginnings

One of the most dramatic illustrations of God's salvation is the story of Noah and the ark. Only eight passengers were aboard the ark and were consequently saved from the great flood, and eight is the numerical value of *chet* (ח). Just as these eight souls were given a new beginning after the flood waters subsided, many other examples in scripture can be found where the number eight represents new beginnings. The first example we shall look at is found in the ceremony of *Brit Milah* – the covenant of circumcision.

When God established His covenant with Abraham, He said, *"And every male among you who is eight days old shall be circumcised throughout your generations ..."*[6] At the *Brit Milah* ceremony, the eight-day-old male enters a covenant relationship with God's people and is given his Hebrew name – a name which is kept secret until the moment of circumcision.[7] The *Brit Milah* is so important in Judaism that only after circumcision is the male child considered to be fully human.

Another notable example of eight as the number of new beginnings is illustrated by the fact that God made a covenant with Abraham on eight occasions, thus establishing Abraham as the father of the Jewish nation. Also, David, the great king of Israel, was the eighth son of his father Jesse.[8] When the temple was restored after the Babylonian exile, the outer area was consecrated for eight days, and another eight days were spent consecrating the inner area.[9] The Feast of Tabernacles, which anticipates the beginning of the Messianic Age, is the only biblical holy day observed for eight days.[10] Aeneas was healed after eight years of paralysis.[11] On the eighth day of preparation Aaron was called by Moses to serve as High Priest.[12]

The greatest new beginning of all, however, was Yeshua's resurrection on the first day of the week. What does this have to do with the number eight? Recall from the previous chapter that seven represents completeness. Thus, eight is the number of new beginnings as it commences a new cycle. Since Yeshua's resurrection occurred

---

[6] Genesis 17:12. It is believed that the number eight was chosen so that the child would have experienced at least one Sabbath before undergoing *Brit Milah*.

[7] Luke 1:21

[8] 1 Samuel 17:12

[9] 2 Chronicles 29:17

[10] Though the Torah originally assigns seven days for the Feast of Tabernacles, it then adds an eighth day – *Shemini Atzeret*. (Numbers 29:35)

[11] Acts 9:33-34

[12] Leviticus 9:1,8

on the first day of the week, we could say that He arose on the first day of a new cycle – the eighth day.[13]

The Hebrew alphabet is arranged in a similar fashion. Having completed our examination of the first seven letters which introduced the story of the gospel, we arrive at the eighth letter – the beginning of a new cycle which introduces the walk of faith. The illustration below shows the seven letters of the first cycle and their relation to the seven letters of the second cycle.

The first two letters of the alphabet spell the word אב (*av*, 'father'). This is appropriate since all things proceed from the Father, and the first cycle of letters introduces the gospel that brings us into a restored relationship with the Father. But the walk of faith, represented by the cycle of letters beginning with ח, reveals a new kind of relationship with Yeshua, who becomes our Brother.[14] The writer of Hebrews described this new relationship when he wrote, *"For both He who sanctifies and those who are sanctified are all from one Father; for which reason He is not ashamed to call them brothers."*[15]

Though it may seem strange to think of Yeshua as a brother, it shouldn't. Especially when we consider that *His* Father has become *our* Father as well. This is exactly how Yeshua would have us think of Him as we walk yoked together shoulder-to-shoulder in this present world. This is illustrated in the arrangement of letters shown above. The vertical rectangle encloses the word אח (*ach*, 'brother'), a word that also means 'relative', 'fellow countryman', and 'friend'. Yeshua is all of these to the one who walks yoked together with Him.[16] As brothers, we share the same Father whose character traits we will emulate if we remain yoked to His Son, Yeshua, our elder

---

[13] Interestingly, the gematria of Yeshua's name in the Greek (Ἰησους) equals 888. (I = 10, η =8, σ = 200, o = 70, υ = 400, ς = 200; 10 + 8 + 200 + 70 + 400 + 200 = 888)

[14] This is somewhat similar to the arrangement of the Ten Commandments. The first five deal with our relationship with God, while the last five deal with our relationship with man.

[15] Hebrews 2:11

[16] John 15:15

Brother. Paul wrote, *"For those whom He foreknew, He also predestined to become conformed to the image of His Son, that He would be the firstborn among many brothers."*[17]

Three Ways to Say 'Life'

To grasp the lessons that are contained in this multi-faceted letter, remember that *chet* stands out from the rest of the letters as the one which represents life. If we bear in mind that we are comprised of three parts (with physical life, soul life, and spiritual life), we can begin to probe the mysteries of the letter *chet*.

Chet (ח) has three forms. The most common form is the one I have been using – ח – and is the one used in everyday printed text. But, there are two other forms that are found in Torah scrolls. Every Torah scroll will use one or the other of these. In the author's fanciful view, these three forms (the printed, plus the two used in Torah scrolls) beautifully illustrate the *spiritual*, *soulish* and *physical* life of an individual. The chart below will help to illustrate this relationship. (And, again, this is merely my own imaginative insight.)

Secular Form	Torah Scroll Forms	
BODY	SOUL	SPIRIT
ח	ח	ח
Physical Life	Soulish Life	Spiritual Life

It is obvious at a glance that the everyday form of *chet* which is used in conventional printed Hebrew is quite different from the forms used in Torah scrolls. This commonplace form of *chet* I imagine as representing the physical body.

The two forms that are used for holy purposes are much more elaborate. I imagine these as corresponding to the spirit and soul – areas where God has begun His redeeming work in the believer. God always works with us from the inside out. He begins by taking up residence in the spirit the moment a person extends an invitation to Him, and from there He begins work on the soul. The form representing the body

---

[17] Romans 8:29

is rather plain compared to these other two. But there is a day coming when our physical bodies will undergo a marvelous transformation. Let me explain.

From the Inside Out

All of the scriptures which discuss our salvation can be divided into three groups: those in the past tense (*"have been"* saved), those in the present tense (*"are being"* saved), and those in the future tense (*"shall be"* saved). If we examine biblical passages carefully, we discover that those in the past tense describe the salvation of the spirit; those in the present tense describe the salvation of the soul; and those in the future tense describe the salvation of the body. Salvation is a process that begins when we acknowledge Yeshua as our Lord. But, the *salvation of the soul* (the mind, will and emotions) occurs over a period of a lifetime.

Because God *has* changed our spirits, and *is* in the process of changing our souls, the forms of *chet* (ח) representing these two areas are more fully developed and ornate than the simple and plain form representing the physical. But the day is coming when these bodies of flesh will also be redeemed just as Paul described, *"And not only this, but also we ourselves, having the first fruits of the spirit, even we ourselves groan within ourselves, waiting eagerly for our adoption as sons, the redemption of our body."*[18] Until then, our bodies remain more or less the same as they were before we met the Savior.

The soul, therefore, has become a battleground that stands between the spirit (which *has* been redeemed by God) and the flesh (which is still unregenerate). These two are constantly at war, and so we are faced with the daily choice between walking in the spirit or walking in the flesh.[19]

This is why the forms of *chet* (ח) representing spirit and soul are so ornate and the form representing the body is so plain. What God *has* done, and *is* doing in the believer's life is, for the most part, an internal work. The *shekinah* glory that dwells within the true believer is hidden from the eyes of the world because the believer's soul and spirit are like the inner chambers of the tabernacle – hidden from view yet filled with light and beauty. The body, however, is like the outer court – open to the world's view but subject to age and natural forces.

---

[18] Romans 8:23
[19] Galatians 5:16; Romans 8:10-12

Yoked to God

Most modern forms of the Hebrew letters are not significantly different from their counterparts found in Torah scrolls. But, as stated earlier, *chet* (ח) is a distinct exception. As you can see this in the illustration below.

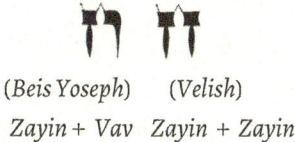

(*Beis Yoseph*)   (*Velish*)
Zayin + Vav   Zayin + Zayin

There are two traditional letter styles used in Torah scrolls: *Velish* and *Beis Yoseph*. These two styles are nearly identical for most letters. In the case of *chet* (ח), however, there is a profound difference between the *Velish* and the *Beis Yoseph* styles. One form is created by combining a *zayin* (ז) and a *vav* (ו). The other is formed by yoking two *zayins* together. Let's examine first the form comprised of two *zayins*.

Recall that *zayin* (ז) represents the sword of the spirit – the Word of God – providing both protection and nourishment. It is called the sword of the spirit because it is itself spiritual and the tool of God's spirit at work in our lives. We could say that the sword of the spirit (represented by *zayin*) is the Holy Spirit doing its sharp and effective work in the depth of our being. *Zayin* (ז) also has a numerical value of seven, which is the number of completion. Consequently, the salvation that has been established by the presence of God's spirit in our own spirit is a complete and finished act. The Holy Spirit is the seal of that salvation,[20] and the two *zayins* we see yoked together are a picture of the believer's spirit *yoked* to the Holy Spirit. The two *zayins* that form *chet* (ח) are indistinguishable except that one of them is adorned with a crown.

The second ornate form of *chet* (ח) found in Torah scrolls is formed by the combination of a *zayin* (ז) and a *vav* (ו). Recall that *vav* (ו) equals six and represents man. Here you can see the *vav* (ו) turned toward a *zayin* (ז) to which it is yoked. This arrangement provides an accurate illustration of what Yeshua said when He invited us to...

> Take My yoke upon you and learn from Me, for I am gentle and humble in heart, and you will find rest for your souls. For My yoke is easy and My burden is light.[21]

---

[20] Ephesians 1:13-14
[21] Matthew 11:29-30

Who else could this *zayin* (ז) possibly represent but Yeshua in His roles of protector and nourisher – the Word made flesh? And could His "easy" yoke be more aptly represented than by the light and simple yoke which joins these two letters into one? Interestingly, the numerical values of ו and ז added together equal thirteen (ו = 6, ז = 7), which is the same value as the words *ahavah* (אהבה) 'love' and *echad* (אחד) 'one'. Hence, we catch a glimpse of the character and purpose of Messiah's yoke. By His love we become one with Him.

Do not let the truth and beauty of this reality escape you, that God has done (and is doing) a great and glorious work in your soul and spirit. Though the earthly container, your body, may grow old and feeble, His presence within you is growing ever stronger and clearer. Paul expressed it best:

> *For God, who said, "Light shall shine out of darkness," is the One who has shone in our hearts to give the light of the knowledge of the glory of God in the face of Messiah. But we have this treasure in earthen vessels, so that the surpassing greatness of the power will be of God and not from ourselves; we are afflicted in every way, but not crushed; perplexed, but not despairing; persecuted, but not forsaken; struck down, but not destroyed; always carrying about in the body the dying of Yeshua, so that the life of Yeshua also may be manifested in our body.*[22]

As we continue with this series of letters dealing with the walk of faith, let us not forget the letter with which this series begins – *chet* (ח), the letter of life. The only way to experience the abundant life of which Yeshua spoke is to walk daily in faith and obedience to His Word.

---

[22] 2 Corinthians 4:6-10

9

ט | *Tet*

A Matter of Life and Death

"You will be dead so long as you refuse to die."
George MacDonald – *Lilith*

In order for us to appreciate the truths contained in the letter *tet* (ט), it is necessary to lay some groundwork concerning our enemy, Satan. The necessity for this will, I trust, become evident as we proceed. Though not a pleasant subject, it is nevertheless a crucial one for any believer who strives to be successful in his or her spiritual walk. Therefore, we shall begin our discussion with a consideration of Satan's primary target – the mind.

The Battle for the Mind

It is often said that if you don't believe in the devil before following God, you will certainly believe in him after. The moment we choose to live for Messiah we become a threat to Satan and he will do what he can to prevent us from maturing in our faith. The Bible clearly states that we do have an ancient and malicious enemy who despises us. But *nowhere* in scripture are we told to fear him. On the contrary, it assures us that our enemy is now defeated and can cause us no real harm. Following are a few passages that confirm this truth:

> *When He had disarmed the rulers and authorities, He made a public display of them, having triumphed over them through Him.*[1]

> *Therefore, since the children share in flesh and blood, He Himself likewise also partook of the same, that through death He might render powerless him who had the power of death, that is, the devil, and might free those who through fear of death were subject to slavery all their lives.*[2]

> *We know that no one who is born of God continues to sin; but he who was born of God keeps him safe, and the evil one does not touch him.*[3]

Satan's only weapon is the lie. He is a liar and the inventor of the lie. The lie is the only original idea Satan ever had,[4] and he has used it effectively throughout history. Since our enemy is armed with the lie, God has supplied us with weapons of truth which are particularly effective against it. Paul describes their effectiveness thus:

> *For the weapons of our warfare are not of the flesh, but divinely powerful for the destruction of fortresses. We are destroying ...*
> *...speculations and every...*
> *...lofty thing raised up against the knowledge of God, and we take every...*
> *...thought captive to the obedience of Messiah.*[5]

Notice that each of the three things our spiritual weapons are designed to combat – arguments, ungodly pretensions, and disobedient thoughts – have to do with the mind. The mind is the battleground upon which spiritual warfare is waged because it is there alone that our enemy's sole weapon can have effect.[6]

Though Satan's target is the mind, this does not mean that he is imaginary. He is real but has been stripped of his power and thus cannot *make* us do anything, that is unless we yield control of our minds to him by believing his lies. Paul states it clearly when he writes...

---

[1] Colossians 2:15
[2] Hebrews 2:14-15
[3] 1 John 5:18
[4] John 8:44
[5] 2 Corinthians 10:4-5
[6] For an insightful study of this subject, the author highly recommends Neil T. Anderson's book, <u>The Bondage Breakers</u> (Harvest House Publishers, 1993).

For the mind set on the flesh is death, but the mind set on the spirit is life and peace, because the mind set on the flesh is hostile toward God; for it does not subject itself to the Torah of God, for it is not even able to do so.[7]

The battle for the mind is a matter of life and death. This is why true change in a person's life requires a change of mind. Paul once again describes it best when he writes...

And do not be conformed to this world, but be transformed by the renewing of your mind, so that you may prove what the will of God is, that which is good and acceptable and perfect.[8]

Transformation comes about by the *renewing* of the mind, and this occurs only when it is set free by truth. Yeshua said...

"If you continue in My word, then you are truly disciples of Mine; and you will know the truth, and the truth will make you free."[9]

"If you continue in My word" can only mean study and obedience to what Yeshua commands us through His word. Though it sounds strange to modern ears, freedom comes only through obedience, and obedience requires discipline. The same principle applies to any endeavor, whether it is music, art, or sports. The freedom of expression displayed by an accomplished figure skater, painter, or pianist is the result of discipline and dedicated obedience to a coach or teacher. Anyone who is in serious training must learn to submit to the one who is in authority over him. The trainee may not understand why a certain command is given or why a particular exercise is assigned, but the instruction must be obeyed if he desires to make progress.

If we desire the true freedom and transformation of a redeemed life, we too must practice discipline and obedience toward the supreme coach and teacher – Yeshua. Only afterwards will the disciple fully understand and appreciate the wisdom of the one in authority.

---

[7] Romans 8:6-7
[8] Romans 12:2
[9] John 8:31-32

The Walk of Faith

The walk of faith is also a form of training under a coach whose ways we may not thoroughly understand. God said:

> *"For My thoughts are not your thoughts, nor are your ways My ways", declares Adonai. "For as the heavens are higher than the earth, so are My ways higher than your ways and My thoughts than your thoughts."*[10]

Because God's ways and thoughts are so much loftier and different from ours, the things He may ask of us can seem unusual or impractical to our way of thinking. For example, the message of the Gospel seems foolish to the non-believer. Paul said, *"the message of the cross is foolishness to those who are perishing"*.[11] Furthermore, Paul stated that God purposefully operates in this way so as to require humility and faith on our part:

> *Where is the wise man? Where is the scholar? Where is the debater of this age? Has not God made foolish the wisdom of the world? For since in the wisdom of God the world through its wisdom did not know Him, God was well-pleased through the foolishness of the message proclaimed to save those who believe. For indeed Jews ask for signs and Greeks search for wisdom, but we proclaim Messiah crucified, to Jews a stumbling block and to Gentiles foolishness, but to those who are called, both Jews and Greeks, Messiah the power of God and the wisdom of God. Because the foolishness of God is wiser than men, and the weakness of God is stronger than men.*[12]

God's ways, however unusual, are never illogical. He is the author of logic and order, not of confusion.[13] Everything God does is established upon flawless logic and common sense though it rarely appears so at first. This is why we are instructed not to lean upon our own understanding.[14] The understanding that God has given us is like a caboose on a train: the caboose does not pull the train but trails behind. Neither did God give us understanding to direct our destinies. (He has given us faith for that.) Our understanding, like the caboose, follows behind faith so that we may understand

---

[10] Isaiah 55:8-9
[11] 1 Corinthians 1:18
[12] 1 Corinthians 1:20-25 (emphasis mine)
[13] 1 Corinthians 14:33
[14] Proverbs 3:5 / 2 Corinthians 5:7

what God *has already done*, not try to figure out what He is *going to do*. If we choose to live by faith in God, we will gain the wisdom and guidance we need to live lives that are pleasing to Him. Understanding will follow.

Satan's suggestions, on the other hand, always seem to make good sense at first, which is why Adam and Eve led the world into the mess in which we now find it. Proverbs says, *"There is a way that seems right to a man, but its end is the way of death"*.[15] Even when Satan tempted Yeshua, he tempted Him to do things that seemed perfectly logical. However, Yeshua did not succumb to these satanic suggestions, but countered each suggestion with the Word of God.[16] Yielding to the enemy's temptations is the same as obedience to the enemy. And, if we obey our enemy, the resulting consequences will reveal the foolishness of our decision. Likewise, if we obey the Master, the resulting consequences will eventually confirm the wisdom of our decision, for *"wisdom is vindicated by all her children"*[17]

I have begun this chapter with a discussion concerning the walk of faith because our success in this walk depends upon our ability to discern wisdom from foolishness. The lessons of *tet* (ט) will help us toward this goal.

The Two Faces of *Tet*

Tet (ט) has a dual nature because it represents objective good as well as hidden evil.[18] Only when we have been yoked to Yeshua (as depicted by ח), can we be sure to distinguish between truth and falsehood. We shall examine several examples of *tet*'s dual nature representing both the goodness of God and the deceitfulness of Satan. Though *tet* (ט) may often represent something evil, remember that our God is sovereign, and *"... God causes all things to work together for good to those who love God, to those who are called according to His purpose"*.[19] This is why *tet* (ט) is such an important member of the cycle of letters dealing with the walk of faith.

Faith requires us to act upon the basis of God's assessment of a situation instead of relying upon our own human reasoning. Some things which appear good are actually evil; while other things which truly are good may often be quite unpleasant and uncomfortable. We must therefore exercise faith in God's verdict on every issue. The construction of this letter depicts this kind of faithful submission.

---

[15] Proverbs 14:12
[16] Matthew 4:1-11
[17] Luke 7:35
[18] For instance, the words 'purity' (טהור, *t'hor*) and 'impurity' (טמא, *t'mah*) both begin with *tet*.
[19] Romans 8:28

Most Torah scrolls depict both *chet* (ח) and *tet* (ט) as constructed from the combination of a ו (*vav*) and a ז (*zayin*). *Chet* (ח) is comprised of a ו and ז yoked together as equals, but in *tet* (ט) we see the ו on the right bowing in submission to the ז on the left. The illustration below shows *chet* and *tet* as they appear in a Torah scroll.[20]

Not only are ח and ט comprised of the same two component letters, but *tet* (ט) reveals a secret contained in the letter *chet* (ח). As a yoke of oxen pulls a plow, it appears that each ox does fifty percent of the work, which is indeed the case for a matched pair of experienced oxen. But, in order to train a young ox to pull a plow effectively, it is yoked to an older and more experienced animal so that the younger may learn from the older. The farmer in this case does not expect the young ox to do fifty percent of the work. His only purpose is for the young ox to learn.

The same is true in the walk of faith. Yeshua said, *"Take My yoke upon you and learn from Me..."*[21] Messiah's yoke is not given to us so that we can perform an equal amount of work. His yoke is given that we may *learn* His ways. This is the secret of *chet* (ח). Recall that *chet* (ח) represents the life that results from our union with Yeshua. *Tet* (ט) represents 'death'. It represents death to everything outside the yoke of Yeshua and death to self and to our way of doing things. This death to self is a vital part of submitting to His lordship over us. In fact, it was once the custom of kings to mark the burial place of their dead with the letter *tet* (ט), which in the Jewish mind symbolizes death, because the name *tet* closely resembles the word טיט (*tyit*, 'mud') – the stuff from which our bodies are made and to which they shall return.

Death is an ugly thing, so ugly, in fact, that it caused Yeshua to weep for His friend Lazarus at his grave.[22] But since Yeshua has conquered death, and we have passed from death to life, it no longer holds any threat or fear for the believer. The only things in us that will die are those things that need to die so that God's resurrection life may be displayed in us. These are the truths taught by the dual nature of this letter. *Tet* (ט) is basically a ח (*chet*) that has been turned upside down. Though death

---

[20] Though the *tet* may look more like it was comprised of a *zayin* (ז) and a *kaf* (כ), tradition teaches that it is actually comprised of a *zayin* (ז) and a bent *vav* (ו).
[21] Matthew 11:29
[22] John 11:35

and life are opposites, our Messiah is ruler of both, and through death He imparts abundant life.

It may come as a surprise to discover that the letters ח and ט spell the root of the word חטא (*cheit*, 'sin').[23] However, it actually makes perfect sense. The power of sin (חטא) is effectively dealt with in our lives when we have experienced both life in Messiah (symbolized by ח) and death to self (symbolized by ט). The following passage demonstrates this principle.

> *Therefore I urge you, brothers, by the mercies of God, to present your bodies a living and holy sacrifice, acceptable to God, which is your spiritual service of worship. And do not be conformed to this world, but be transformed by the renewing of your mind, so that you may approve what the will of God is, that which is good and acceptable and perfect.*[24]

Offering our bodies as living sacrifices is a prerequisite for the renewing of our minds. It is vitally important that we realize this because denying physical lusts enhances the perceptibility of the mind and spirit. It has been said that the problem with living sacrifices is that they keep crawling off the altar. But, the yoke of Yeshua will prevent this from happening because living sacrifices are not placed upon an altar. They are placed in a yoke. When we have experienced life in Yeshua (ח) and death to self (ט), then the way is made clear for us to demonstrate God's *"good and acceptable and perfect will."*

What's in a Picture?

According to tradition, *tet* (ט) signifies a serpent. Its left side forms the head and its right side forms the tail. Throughout scripture the serpent is a symbol of mankind's enemy – Satan.[25] Yet how can this letter depict a man (ו) bowing in submission to Yeshua (ו) and at the same time depict Satan and death?

Because of his pride, Satan rebelled against his Creator and sought to establish himself as a god. There is a tendency in each of us to do the same. As long as we occupy these bodies of flesh, the kind of pride and rebellion which motivated Satan can also manipulate us if we allow it. This is why Paul invites us to present our bodies as

---

[23] Interestingly, it is thought that because *chet*(ח) and *tet*(ט) spell this shortened form of 'sin', that is the reason these two letters appear nowhere in the names of the twelve tribes.
[24] Romans 12:1-2
[25] In fact, ט (the serpent) is found at the core of Satan's name (שטן).

living sacrifices and thus die to the built-in tendency to live according to our selfish urges. This is the conflict pictured by ט, the symbol of the serpent and of death.

We must make a choice. We can choose to die *in* our sins and thus remain separated from God. Or, we can die *to* our sins and thus be eternally joined with Him. The latter is what is pictured by the ט of the Torah scroll – a man bowing in submission to the Lord Yeshua. Dietrich Bonhoeffer wrote, "When Christ calls a man, He bids him come and die."[26] To be yoked to Yeshua is to be committed to His goals and to walk in His path; but to do so one must die to one's own ambitions and abandon one's own path. This is exactly what Yeshua meant when He said, *"If anyone wishes to come after Me, he must deny himself, and take up his cross daily and follow Me."*[27]

When we submit our dreams, our ways, and ourselves to God, He exposes the subtle serpent hidden within. Often, in my experience, God requires that I give up something in which I see no harm. Only after wrestling with the issue and conceding my will in the matter did God then reveal the hidden danger that lay within. Occasionally, when God asks us to surrender something to Him, He returns it to us – but only after He has dealt with it. These lessons, and their connection to the letter *tet* (ט), are graphically illustrated by what occurred with Moses when God called to him from the burning bush.

Moses spent the first forty years of his life in Pharaoh's court living as a prince of Egypt. After a failed attempt to deliver an Israelite by killing his Egyptian oppressor, Moses fled into the wilderness where he spent the next forty years of his life as a shepherd. Only then, at the age of eighty, was Moses called by God to return to Egypt, this time to deliver *all* the Israelites from slavery. Though Moses considered himself retired from the delivery business, God wanted him re-fired with a holy commission to return to the calling God had in mind for him from the beginning.

When Moses asked what evidence he could give the Israelites so they would believe that God sent him, he received this reply:

> *Adonai said to him, "What is that in your hand?"*
> *And he said, "A staff."*
> *Then He said, "Throw it on the ground."*
> *So he threw it on the ground, and it became a serpent, and Moses fled from it.*

---

[26] The Cost of Discipleship, pg. 99.
[27] Luke 9:23

> *Then Adonai said to Moses, "Stretch out your hand and grasp it by its tail" – so he stretched out his hand and caught it, and it became a staff in his hand – "that they may believe that Adonai, the God of their fathers, the God of Abraham, the God of Isaac, and the God of Jacob, has appeared to you."*[28]

Moses' staff was a symbol of his livelihood and a source of protection and security as he led sheep in the wilderness. At this point in his life, it is likely that if it came to a showdown between Moses trusting in God for his security or in his staff, Moses would have chosen his staff. This is why God required that it be submitted to Him by being cast to the ground. When Moses did so, the true nature of the staff was revealed.

There was nothing inherently evil about Moses' staff. It was just a piece of wood. But when we put our trust in anything apart from God, it becomes an idol. And when anything becomes an idol, it also becomes an instrument of Satan in our lives. The account tells us that when Moses saw the staff turn into a serpent, he ran from it. What he had embraced for forty years suddenly became a source of terror to him. But, when he obeyed God and took it up again, it returned to an ordinary staff – but not so very ordinary, for with this staff Moses would proceed to turn the Nile to blood, part the Red Sea, bring water from a rock, and secure Israel's victory in battle. The staff of Moses had now become the staff of God.

These truths are illustrated by the Hebrew letters used in the story, such as the word for 'staff' which is מטה (*mateh*). Notice the letter *tet* (ט) – the 'serpent' – nestled in the center of this word. The two letters surrounding *tet* (ט) spell *mah* (מה), which means "what?". So, if we ask what (מה) is in Moses' staff (מטה), the answer is a 'serpent' (ט).

We need to ask ourselves: "What is the *staff* I am clinging to which God would have me relinquish? *What* is that thing in my life that I look to for security and identity that has not been submitted to God's lordship?" If we will submit that thing, God will reveal the *serpent* within it. If we do not, then we reveal the serpent's nature within us.

Maybe it is because *tet* resembles a serpent that it is the least-used letter in the *Tanach*. In fact, it appears nowhere on the stone tablets Moses brought down from Mount Sinai. However, *tet* does appear in Moses' repetition of the ten commandments many years later. Just before he died, Moses reviewed the Israelites' history

---

[28] Exodus 4:2-5

since they left Egypt. He reminded them of their past failures and of God's grace and warned them about the days ahead as they prepared to cross into Canaan. But, as he repeated the ten commandments, he inserted a phrase that did not appear on the original tablets. When reciting the fourth commandment he inserted the following words:

> "You shall remember that you were a slave in the land of Egypt, and Adonai your God brought you out of there by a mighty hand and by an outstretched arm; therefore Adonai your God commanded you to observe the Sabbath day."[29]

This verse includes the only *tet* (ט) in the ten commandments. It is found in the word נטויה (*ne'tuyah*), which means 'outstretched'. Was Moses recalling his own outstretched arm when he picked up the serpent 40 years ago?

The Serpent Revealed

The mythical gods of the Egyptians were counterfeits – not gods at all. And it is well known that the plagues God sent against Egypt were specifically designed to expose the impotent sham of each so-called Egyptian god. For instance, they worshipped the Nile River. God turned it to blood. They worshipped a frog-god. God sent them so many frogs they became utterly disgusted with them. They worshipped the sun-god and the moon-god. God made it dark for three entire days and nights. You get the idea.

If you outline the sequence of plagues, you will discover that they occur in sets of three. The first, fourth, and seventh plagues were announced to Pharaoh in the morning. The second, fifth, and eight plagues were announced in Pharaoh's palace. The third, sixth, and ninth plagues occurred without warning.

A close look will reveal other details of the three cycles of plagues, but here I wish for us to look at the last plague of each cycle – the third, sixth, and ninth plagues. They appear in the chart below.

#3 – Lice	כנם	*kinim*
#6 – Boils	שחין	*shechin*
#9 – Darkness	חשך	*choshek*

---

[29] Deuteronomy 5:15

Note the second letter of each of these plagues and that will reveal the true object of the Egyptians' worship and the cause of their misery. These three letters spell the word נחש (*nachash*) 'serpent'.

The Serpent's Tail

One of the reasons Satan hates us (aside from the fact that we are made in God's image) is that his dominion over the earth was taken from him and given to man. The *Talmud* suggests that the serpent was originally intended to be a servant of man.[30] However, following the serpent's rebellion, dominion of the world was transferred to Adam – a creature made of dirt. How humiliating this must have been for our enemy, the *"Star of the Morning"*[31] – the brightest of all God's creation.

In the 28th chapter of Ezekiel (one of the most peculiar chapters in the Bible), God speaks against the *"king of Tyre"*. As in so many prophetic passages, this prophecy has a dual purpose. God never does just one thing at a time, and when He speaks we can be certain that more is being said than may at first appear. (As the Psalmist wrote, *"One thing God has spoken, two things have I heard"*.[32]) Though addressed to the King of Tyre, the larger message of this passage actually has to do with Satan himself. We see Satan described as a stunning creature more closely resembling a jewel-bedecked dragon than a loathsome serpent:

> *"You were in Eden, the garden of God. Every precious stone was your covering: the ruby, the topaz and the diamond; the beryl, the onyx and the jasper; the lapis lazuli, the turquoise and the emerald; and the gold, the workmanship of your settings and sockets, was in you. On the day that you were created they were prepared."*[33]

Note that nine stones are mentioned, which is also the numerical value of *tet* (ט). The breastplate worn by the High Priest was also adorned with precious stones upon which were inscribed the names of the twelve tribes of Israel. The high priest wore the breastplate when he went before God to intercede for the nation of Israel. It appears that this would have originally been Satan's assignment as the *"covering*

---

[30] b.*Talmud*: Sanhedrin 59b
[31] Isaiah 14:12
[32] Psalm 62:11
[33] Ezekiel 28:13

cherub".³⁴ In fact, the word for breastplate (חשן, *choshan*) is comprised of the same letters which spell 'serpent' (נחש, *nachash*).

But instead of serving God, Satan coveted to *be like* God.³⁵ Consequently, his dominion was taken from him and given to newly-created man. There is a profound lesson for us here. Satan rebelled against God because he did not want to accept a position of humility. Unfortunately, we are prone to follow his example. When we resist our God-given responsibilities because they seem too small and insignificant for us, then we align our attitudes with Satan's. Once again, Yeshua said, *"Take my yoke upon you and learn from Me, for I am gentle and humble in heart…"*³⁶

The character of the serpent resides in each of us just as it did in Moses' staff, and when we are "cast down" is when it will most likely reveal itself. We indulge it whenever we choose to walk in the flesh (our way) rather than in the spirit (God's way). By so doing we feed the sinful tendency to usurp God's authority and rebel against Him. When Satan was cursed, God doomed him to *"crawl on [his] belly"* and *"eat dust all the days of [his] life".*³⁷ When we follow Satan's example of rebellion, his fate also becomes ours. We too will crawl upon our bellies in the sense that we will cease to walk in the dignity to which God has called us, and our only satisfaction will come from feeding on 'dust' – the substance of which our flesh is made. We were created for better things than this. We were created to perform good works in Messiah Yeshua,³⁸ and He made of us a kingdom of priests for this very purpose.³⁹

As Adam was given dominion over the earth, God has given us dominion over our passions. In *chet* (ח) we beheld the life that is ours in Messiah Yeshua, but in *tet* (ט) we are faced with the choice of life or death: a deeper kind of life and a deeper kind of death. We may either die to self so as to live for the One who died for us or live for the self at the cost of the high calling in Messiah Yeshua.⁴⁰ If Satan, through his subtlety, cannot prevent us from becoming believers, he will certainly do his utmost to prevent us from becoming effective ones.

Tet (ט) first appears in the Bible at the beginning of the word טוב (*tov*) when God proclaimed that the light was "good". Maybe you have seen the light of God's truth and moved toward it. But, have you seen just how astonishingly good that light is? If

---

[34] See Chapter 1.
[35] Isaiah 14:12-14
[36] Matthew 11:29
[37] Genesis 3:14
[38] Ephesians 2:10
[39] Revelation 1:6
[40] Philippians 3:14

you have, then, like *vav* (ו) you will bow in submission to *zayin* (ז) – the One who is the living Word. Only then will you become truly fruitful in your walk of faith. And if you count the kinds of spiritual fruit which you shall produce – love, joy, peace, longsuffering, gentleness, goodness, faith, meekness, and temperance – you will discover that they are nine in number – the equivalent of the letter *tet* (ט).[41]

Recall that ג (*gimel*) represents a man sent from the 'Father' (אב, *Av*) to take a message to the 'door' (ד) of the 'poor man' (דל, *dal*). But, what does the ג have to say to ט (*tet*) the 'serpent'? The Vilna Gaon[42] observed that "in the entire *Torah* the two letters ג and ט are nowhere next to one another – neither within one word nor even as the last and first letters of adjacent words."[43] Why are these two letters always kept separated? They spell the word גט (*get*), which is a divorce document, and divorce is something that God hates.[44]

The Serpent's Head

After the serpent enticed Adam and Eve to sin, God appeared on the scene to pronounce His judgment. Though He did not curse Adam and Eve, He did curse the serpent and the earth. Here is what He proclaimed to the serpent:

> *Adonai Elohim said to the serpent, "Because you have done this, cursed are you more than all cattle, and more than every beast of the field. On your belly you will go, and dust you will eat all the days of your life. And I will put enmity between you and the woman, and between your seed and her seed. He shall crush your head, and you shall crush His heel."*[45]

What a sovereign God we have that at the outset He would prophecy that a seed from the woman would someday crush the head of the serpent. This prophecy points to Yeshua who is the promised 'seed'. In the process of crushing the serpent's head, the 'heel' was also crushed. These happened simultaneously. When a person takes a step, the heel is the part of the body that first comes in contact with the ground.

---

[41] Galatians 5:22
[42] Elijah ben Solomon Zalman (1720-1797)
[43] Munk, Michael L., The Wisdom in the Hebrew Alphabet, p.124.
[44] Malachi 2:16
[45] Genesis 3:14-15

Yeshua is the 'heel' by which God stepped into the world.[46] And at the cross we see the heel of the "seed" crushing the head of the serpent.

Messiah's defeat of our enemy is illustrated in many of the stories found in the *Tanach* – David slaying Goliath, God drowning the Egyptians, and Elijah defeating the priests of Baal, to name a few. But a story that contains a unique insight into the letter *tet* (ט) is that of Noah and the ark. Let me explain.

When God cursed the serpent, He used the verb ארר (*arar*) 'curse'. When God saved Noah and his family via the ark, it came to rest on a mountain named *Ararat* (ארט), which is comprised of ארר 'curse' and ט (*tet*) the 'serpent'. Do you see the picture? By means of the flood, God destroyed Satan's handiwork on the earth while at the same time saving Noah and his family. When the ark came to rest, it was atop *Ararat* – a picture of the 'curse' on the 'serpent'.

As we leave this chapter and move to the next, we leave the least used letter in the *Tanach* (ט) and move on to the smallest yet most used letter – *yud* (י).

---

[46] As Paul wrote: "... *God was in Messiah reconciling the world to Himself...*" (2 Corinthians 5:19)

10

י | *Yud*

The Hand of God

"When we ask for the Holy Spirit, we receive the very nature of God."
Oswald Chambers

"The Very Nature of God"

Yud (י) should be familiar to us since we have encountered it as a component in several of the previous letters.[1] It is found twice in the *aleph* (א), provides a foot for the *gimel* (ג), and resides within the *dalet* to form the letter *hei* (ה).

Since it is suspended in space, it can be said that *yud* (י) has no earthly foundation but is instead anchored in heaven. This is one reason why י is so closely associated with spiritual things. Due to these attributes (and others which we shall soon discover) *yud* (י), more than any other letter, represents the Holy Spirit. Although *gimel* (ג) represents the mission of the Holy Spirit in the world, and *hei* (ה) represents the work of the Holy Spirit in the life of the believer, *yud* (י) represents the spirit as the very life and essence of God.

---

[1] *Yud* can also be pronounce *yod*.

Yud (י) is formed simply by placing pen against parchment. In which case, one could say that every letter begins with *yud*. As one noted rabbi observed, "...each letter can be seen as the tracing of the pathway of a *yud* in motion".[2]

Yud's small size has also made it a symbol of humility and, as the only letter which is suspended in air, it illustrates the words of James, *"Humble yourselves in the presence of the Lord, and he will exalt you."*[3] God's concern for the small and seemingly insignificant is also reflected in the words of Yeshua: *"...not so much as a yud or a stroke [tagiin] will pass from the Torah – not until everything that must happen has happened."*[4]

A striking example of the power of *yud* is the effect it has on the word שמם (*shameim*) 'desolation'. With the addition of a simple י (*yud*), שמים (*shameim*) 'desolation' becomes שמים (*shamaim*) 'Heaven'. Though small and humble, the presence of *yud* (י) can have a powerful impact.

Yud's (י) significance is also demonstrated by the fact that each letter which follows it is a multiple of its numeric value of ten. Thus, *yud* is a factor of all the remaining letters, which in turn reflect *yud*'s characteristics:

>   Spirituality | the י is elevated above the line
>   Humility | the י is the smallest letter
>   Maturity & Order | י's numeric value is 10
>   Strength | the word *yud* means 'hand'

Yud, God's Initial

One example of how *yud* (י) represents the Holy Spirit is found in the changing of the name Hoshea (הושע, *Hoshea*) to Joshua (יהושע, *Yehoshua*) by the addition of a י.[5] When Moses laid his hands on *Hoshea*, he imparted his spirit and authority to him. *Hoshea*'s name was then changed to *Joshua* by the addition of the letter *yud* (י).[6] This changed his name from *"Salvation"* (*Hoshea*) to *"YH will save"* (*Yehoshua*, or "Joshua").

>   הושע = Hosea (*Hoshea*)
>   יהושע = Joshua (*Yehoshua*)

---

[2] Ginsburgh, Rabbi Yitzchak, The Alef-Beit, pg. 158 (Aronson, 1995).
[3] James 4:10
[4] Matthew 5:18 (*Jewish New Testament*)
[5] Numbers 13:16
[6] Numbers 13:16; 27:22-23; Deuteronomy 34:9

Yud is also the letter most frequently used to begin the names of important people and places in the *Tanach*. A partial list includes the following.

Isaac	יצחק
Jacob	יעקב
Joseph	יוסף
Isaiah	ישעיה
Jeremiah	ירמיה
Israel	ישראל
Jerusalem	ירושלים
Yeshua	ישוע

Yud is also the letter most closely related to the name of the nation of Israel. Israel is identified in the *Tanach* by four different names, each beginning with *Yud*.

Israel	ישראל
Jacob	יעקב
Judah	יהודה
Jeshurun[7]	ישרון

The Hand of God

The name of the letter *yud* is spelled יוד. Though this word is not found in the *Tanach*, neither are the names of many of the other letters of the Hebrew alphabet. However, Rabbi Akiva comments on this word in his famous *midrash*: "Do not read *yud* (יוד) but *yad* (יד) – 'hand'."[8] Rabbi Akiva is indicating by this that the name of this letter is closely related to the Hebrew word for 'hand' – יד (*yad*).

The letters which spell yud's name – יוד – also represent the work of the Holy Spirit. Examining these three letters reveals that each one is an expansion of the one preceding. The first letter – yud (י) – is little more than a point. The second letter – vav (ו) – develops the point into a vertical stroke. The final letter – dalet (ד) – develops

---

[7] Deuteronomy 32:15; 33:5; 33:26; Isaiah 44:2
[8] Shulman, Yaacov Dovid, The Aleph Beit of Rebbi Akiva (Power Sefer Press, 2018).

the one-dimensional vertical line into a two-dimensional figure having length and width.

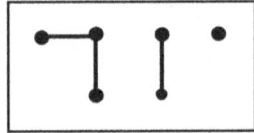

The Sages saw this as representing the Holy Spirit speaking forth the truth of Torah from the spiritual dimension into the width and breadth of the physical realm.[9] The sequence of these three letters is a reminder that everything which comes from God's hand is alive and growing. Conversely, when we break fellowship with God our life tends to weaken and shrink, reversing our progress with God. This is illustrated by reading these letters in reverse, in which case they spell יוד (dawway) 'faint'. The forward and backward spelling of *Yud's* name should remind us of Isaiah's words:

> Yet those who wait for Adonai will gain new strength. They mount up with wings like eagles. They will run and not get tired. They will walk and not become weary.[10]

Looking at the spelling of יוד (*yud*) in a third way, we can see an abbreviated gospel message. The word יוד gives us a picture of the Holy Spirit (י) being incarnated in flesh as a man (ו)[11] who calls Himself the 'Door' (ד).[12]

Yud (י) occurs in an unusual form twice in the Torah. The first occurrence is a *yud* that is oversize, while the second is a *yud* that is undersize. In the passage "*But now ... let the power of the Lord be great, just as You declared*",[13] the word *"be great"* is spelled with an enlarged *yud*: יגדל (*yigdol*). These words are part of Moses' plea for God to have mercy upon the Israelites in spite of their refusal to enter the land of Canaan. In the passage "*You neglected the Rock who begot you, and forgot the God who gave you birth*,"[14] a small *yud* is found in the phrase "*you neglected*" (תשי, *t'shi*).

---

[9] The Alef-Beit, pgs. 154, 411.
[10] Isaiah 40:31
[11] Colossians 2:9
[12] John 10:9
[13] Numbers 14:17
[14] Deuteronomy 32:18

Thus, in the verse dealing with God's greatness, the י is very large. But, in the verse describing how Israel forsook their God, the י is quite small.

Large *Yud*: יגדל (*yigdol*) = "displayed"
Small *Yud*: תשי (*t'shi*) = "forgot" or "forsaken"

These two passages illustrate how the presence of the Holy Spirit can be strengthened (enlarged) within us when we magnify God's name or reduced when we forsake Him through disobedience or complaining.

The Hand of Man

The first occurrence of the word 'hand' in the Torah is found in the unhappy story of Adam and Eve. After they had sinned, God expelled them from Eden. Concerned that they might cause additional damage to themselves, we are told:

> Then Adonai Elohim said, "Behold, the man has become like one of us, knowing good and evil; and now, he might stretch out his hand (יד, yad) and take also from the tree of life, and eat, and live forever..."[15]

Why did God not want Adam and Eve to eat from the tree of life? Wouldn't eternal life be a good thing for them?

There is a deep principle at work here that we discussed in chapter 4. However, the short answer to our question is that had Adam and Eve eaten from the tree of life while in a state of sin, they *would* have lived forever in this fallen state without hope of restoration. Only through death could they be released from the grip of sin.

The second place the word 'hand' (יד, *yad*) occurs is in the story of Cain and Abel wherein Cain used his hand to murder his brother.[16] And, the third occurrence of 'hand' is in reference to man's toil in the cursed soil.[17] The hand of man has a very checkered history. Man first used his hand to steal, then to murder, then to toil against the curse. Compare these deeds to those Yeshua did with His hands. He used His hands to give, to heal and to bless. Then we nailed them to a cross.

All the world's sins arose from that first act of taking in the garden of Eden. Ever since, all sins have been a form taking. We must learn to never take, but to receive. The difference between taking and receiving is the difference between heaven and hell. When we have truly learned to receive instead of take, then we can learn the

---

[15] Genesis 3:22
[16] Genesis 4:11
[17] Genesis 5:29

difference between giving and merely selling, which is giving for the sake of receiving. The Master said, *"Freely you received, freely give."*[8]

Yud (י) is used to represent a hand in several Hebrew words. Here are two examples: Jacob was born grasping the heel of his twin brother Esau.[19] This event is pictured in the spelling of Jacob's name – יעקב. In these four letters we see the hand (י) grasping onto the 'heel' (עקב, *ackov*) of Esau. Also, the Hebrew word for 'close friend' is ידיד (*yadid*). Here we see the root of the word 'hand' (יד) used twice in succession, representing two hands interlocked in friendship.

The Orderly Work of God

Having a numerical value of ten, *yud* is considered to represent order, completion, and logic. Ten is the base upon which universal counting systems are established. We also find this number frequently used in the *Tanach* to represent sets of completed items. In chapter 7 we discussed how the number seven represents cycles. That is different from the completed sequences of things represented by the number 10. Cycles are meant to be repeated. The sequences listed here are not. Here are a few examples:

- There were 10 generations from Adam to Noah.
- There were 10 generations from Noah to Abraham.
- God created the world with 10 utterances.
- God gave 10 commandments.
- God delivered Israel from Egypt by decreeing 10 plagues.
- A *minyan* (a group of 10) is required for prayer in the synagogue.
- The Israelites tested God ten times in the wilderness.
- 10 men in the *Tanach* are called "man of God".

The Letter of Masculinity

The word יה (*yah*) – the shortened form of God's name יהוה (YHVH) – is described by the Sages as possessing a unique representation of God's creation of the heavens and the earth. They taught that with י (the letter of order and logic) God created the World-to-Come, and with ה (the letter of femininity and grace) He created the present world.

---

[18] Matthew 10:8
[19] Genesis 25:26

The characteristics of these two letters are also reflected in the Hebrew words for 'man' (איש, *ish*) and 'woman' (אשה, *ishah*). As we learned in Chapter 5, *hei* (ה) has the softest sound of all of the letters – a mere exhalation of breath. It is affixed to the end of a word to form the feminine ending. Even its shape is said to denote a womb. This is the letter found at the end of אשה (*ishah*, 'woman'). But *yud* (י) – 'hand' – represents the work of forming things into useful items. This is graphically seen in the story of God creating Adam. The *Torah* states, *"The Adonai Elohim formed man from the ground..."*[20] Here the word וייצר (*va'yitzer*) *"and He formed"* is unusual in that it contains two *yuds* (י). The Sages teach that these two *yuds* represent the "two *hands*" of God used to form man from the dust of the earth. In other words, God handmade Adam out of the dust.

The Sages also teach that when God made man and woman, He placed the *yud* (י) in man and the *hei* (ה) in woman thus causing them to display the corresponding characteristics of God in their natures. This is depicted in the diagram below.

Yah

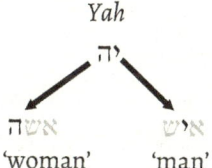

'woman'   'man'

One without the other is incomplete – an important reason why it is not good for man (or woman) to be alone through life.[21] Equally important (especially in the marriage relationship) is that a man *be* a man, and a woman *be* a woman. One sometimes meets men who are ashamed to be men and women who are ashamed to be women. Such individuals often try to *transition*, but ultimately do a sorry job of it. We don't need a hybrid gender wherein all distinctions are lost. Whether you are a man or a woman, you belong to a very honorable gender and need not be ashamed of it. The *yud* (י) of the male and the *hei* (ה) of the female come directly from the name of God – יה (*Yah*). When man (איש) loses the characteristic of the י (representing his masculinity) and the woman (אשה) loses the characteristic of the ה (representing her

---

[20] Genesis 2:7
[21] Genesis 2:18

femininity), then all that is left is אש (*aish*) 'fire' which will consume them in their desire to live apart from God's pattern for mankind.[22]

Observe also that man's representative letter (י) is found at the very center of his name (איש), and that woman's representative letter (ה) is found on the outside of her name (אשה). This supports the observation that men tend to be more closed or "bottled up" in keeping their thoughts and feelings to themselves, while women tend to be more relational and sensitive to others as well as more expressive of their feelings. This is another reason why a man and a woman need one another. Each brings balance to the other in a way that produces strength and equilibrium to the marriage.

When I entered into marriage almost forty years ago, I immediately began to experience a greater sensitivity to others through my wife's emotional perceptions. Likewise, my wife discovered that in other situations there was a new ability to see logical progress without emotional confusion. Together we have found a balance and maturity that has been a continuous blessing in our lives together. This is a part of the glue that keeps two people united for a lifetime and makes of the two, one.

The Filling of the Holy Spirit

In the series of letters representing the walk of faith, we have encountered in *yud* the one letter that most perfectly depicts the Holy Spirit. To walk by faith is to walk by the leading of the Holy Spirit. This does not mean that we sacrifice common sense and wisdom to the control of fanciful whims, but that we sacrifice *our* goals and methods to the lordship of our God. God does not contradict Himself. What He prompts us to do through His spirit He will also verify through the teaching and principles found in scripture. When we have died to self (as depicted by the letter *tet* - ט) then we will be filled with the Holy Spirit (י). The pictures formed by these letters are truly amazing when one considers the filling of the Holy Spirit.

Rabbi Aaron Raskin writes, "The design of the *tes* [sic] is like a pot, a vessel with an inverted rim, representing hidden or inverted good."[23] One can see the ט as an empty vessel and the י above it as God's spirit being "poured" in. This is exactly what the *tet* (ט) needs for it to become truly טוב (*tov*) 'good'.

---

[22] 1 Corinthians 6:9,10
[23] Raskin, Aaron L., <u>Letters of Light</u>, pg. 93.

י
↓
ט

Though we were created by God to contain His spirit, we tend to fill ourselves instead with inappropriate things. As we empty ourselves of accumulated worldly debris, we create a capacity for something far better. As new wine skins, God will fill us with the new wine of His spirit and we will be stretched to new limits. In fact, the letters יט spell the word *yat*, which means to 'stretch' or 'extend'. Let us allow God to fill us with Himself and thus stretch us so that we may fulfill His purpose during the short and precious time we have been allotted here on earth.

As we shall learn in the next chapter, God's purpose for filling us with His spirit is not only that we may experience a full life with Him, but also that we may accomplish useful work for His kingdom.

11

כ, ך | Kaf

Good Works in Messiah Yeshua

He who labors as he prays lifts his heart to God with his hands.
St. Bernard of Clairvoux

The Work of the Palms

Kaf's name means 'palm' as in the palm of the hand.[1] The *Tanach* frequently refers to the toil, labor, or power of one's *palms* and not just the work of one's *hands*. Hence, in Hebraic thought, כ – the letter whose name means 'palm' – symbolizes, among other things, productive labor. Just as כ (*kaf*) follows directly after י (*yud* – the letter whose name means 'hand'), so our hands should be put to use doing the productive labor for which God has prepared us. This is the message of the letter *kaf* (כ).

You may have noted that *kaf*'s (כ) appearance is similar to that of *beit* (ב). This similarity is not merely cosmetic. *Kaf*'s (כ) theme of work is reflected in the letter *beit* (ב) because both of these letters represent construction and production. They are also similar numerically. *Beit* (ב) equals 2 and *kaf* (כ) equals 20.

But, the most profound bond between *kaf* and *beit* is a spiritual one. You may recall from Chapter 2 that *beit* (ב) represents the Word of God – both the written

---

[1] The sole of the foot, in Hebrew, is also referred to as the 'palm' of the foot.

Word and the incarnate Word (Yeshua). Likewise, our work (ב) should resemble the Word (ב) as we become more like Yeshua in our obedience to the Word of God. God's Word should always be reflected in our actions. This relationship is described by Yeshua when He said:

> "I am the vine, you are the branches. He who abides in Me and I in him, he bears much fruit, for apart from Me you can do nothing. If anyone does not abide in Me, he is thrown away as a branch and dries up, and they gather them, and cast them into the fire and they are burned. If you abide in Me, and My words abide in you, ask whatever you wish, and it will be done for you. My Father is glorified by this, that you bear much fruit, and so prove to be My disciples."[2]

A Word About Love

The fruit Yeshua desires is the fruit of the spirit – love, joy, peace, patience, kindness, goodness, faithfulness, gentleness and self-control.[3] Regrettably, there are those in the redeemed community who think they can produce this fruit apart from works. They think that if they can just produce enough warm feelings about God and others, they will somehow always fulfill His will for their lives. This is a grave error.

Love – the primary fruit of the spirit – is also given first place in God's commandments. When asked what the greatest commandment was, Yeshua answered, *"And you shall love the Lord your God with all your heart, and with all your soul, and with all your mind, and with all your strength."*[4] But, how can we love Him with all of our strength apart from action? Though love may be accompanied by strong emotions, love is *not* an emotion.

Most people think that the opposite of love is hate. This is incorrect. The opposite of hate is affection. Affection and hate are emotions, but love isn't. Love is much more than mere affection. Love is actively denying one's self for the sake of another. The opposite of love is selfishness. We show love for God by turning from our own selfish desires to fulfill His will. This is why the Master said, *"Whoever has My commands and obeys them, he is the one who loves Me."*[5]

---

[2] John 15:5-8
[3] Galatians 5:22
[4] Mark 12:30 (quoting Deuteronomy 6:5)
[5] John 14:21

When Yeshua answered the question concerning the greatest commandment, He added, *"The second [commandment] is this, 'You shall love your neighbor as yourself.' ..."*[6] This requires that we *do* unto others as we would have them *do* unto us. By God's definition love is either active or it is not love.[7]

The eight remaining fruits of the spirit (all of which are facets of love) also require action. We will begin to resemble our Lord – as כ resembles ב – when we begin to do His works. It is only by this that we give glory to the Father and prove ourselves disciples of Yeshua.[8]

Along these lines, the *Talmud* provides a clever way of measuring a person's character, all based on the letter *kaf* (כ). It states, "In three ways can a person's true character be perceived: with his *kos* (כוס); with his *kis* (כיס); and with his *kas* (כעס)."[9] What do these three words mean? They are a person's 'cup', 'wallet', and 'anger', respectively. In other words, the way a person handles his use of alcohol, his money, and his anger, reveals the true nature of that person's character. So, may each of us seriously examine our own *kos*, *kis*, and *kas*!

Eating the Fruit of Our Labor

John records the story of Yeshua's disciples presenting Him with food. But He declined their offer of food saying, *"I have food to eat that you do not know about."* When asked where this food came from He answered, *"My food is to do the will of Him who sent Me and to accomplish His work."*[10]

The reason so many believers today are unfulfilled in their spiritual lives is that they hop from fellowship to fellowship looking only to be fed rather than feeding upon the food of which Yeshua spoke. The food that sustained Him was to do the good works that God had commissioned Him to do. If we want to be fed spiritually, we must follow Messiah's example. The book of Psalms states, *"When you shall eat the fruit of your 'palms' [*כף *(kaph)], you will be happy and it will be well with you."*[11]

Our food must be to *do* the will of God who sent us to serve others. Sadly, this is the food which so many believers *"do not know about"*. This connection between *work* and *food* is confirmed by the fact that the Hebrew word for 'palm' (כף, *kaf*) also means

---

[6] Mark 12:31 (quoting Leviticus 19:18)
[7] John 14:23-24
[8] John 15:8
[9] *Talmud: Eruvin* 65b
[10] John 4:32-34
[11] Psalm 128:2

'spoon'.[12] Furthermore, the Torah states that a 'spoon' (כף, *kaf*) was used in the Temple to offer the daily incense on the golden altar. In the same way, the work of our *palms* should ascend before God as incense so as to bring Him pleasure in our service.

Returning to Yeshua's words *"My food is to do the will of Him who sent Me ..."*, it is interesting to note that the word מצות can be pronounced in two different ways. If מצות is pronounced *mitzvot*, it means 'commandments'. But, if it is pronounced *matzot*, it means 'unleavened bread'. This is certainly no coincidence!

The Letter of Possession and Similarity

When *kaf* (כ) is added to the front or the back of a word it changes the meaning of that word in one of two ways. Examining the influence that the letter *kaf* (כ) has on words will provide insight into how its truths can influence our own lives. When *kaf* (כ) is prefixed to a word, it means 'like' or 'as'. For example, when the word מלך (*melech*) 'king' has a כ added to the front, it becomes כמלך (*cha'melech*), 'like a king'. Similarly, if we attach כ to the front of כלב (*celev*) 'dog, it becomes ככלב (*ce'calev*) 'like a dog'.

On the other hand, when the letter *kaf* (כ) is added to the end of a Hebrew word it becomes possessive. For example, if *kaf* is added to the word חסד (*chesed*) 'kindness', it becomes חסדך (*chas'decha*) 'your kindness'.

What lessons may we derive from *kaf*'s effect upon words? Think of life as a word to which the כ of *good works* may be attached. If others can see the good works interwoven into your life, then you will be living a life *like* Messiah's who *"went about doing good"* by investing His life serving God by serving others.[13] Later, when you reach the *end* of your life, you will *possess* the rewards that God has prepared for you. The connection between *kaf* (כ) and 'possession' teaches that few things in life ever come into our possession without the work of our 'palms'.

Enlarging the Door

Yeshua said, *"Let your light shine before men in such a way that they may see your good works, and glorify your Father who is in heaven."*[14] When our good deeds are done humbly for God's glory and for our neighbor's good, we make the way to God more attractive and inviting to others. Note that *kaf*'s (כ) final form – ך – looks like an enlarged *dalet* (ד),

---

[12] This dual meaning is logical because a spoon is simply a mechanical substitute for the palm of the hand.
[13] Acts 10:38
[14] Matthew 5:16

which means 'door'. This illustrates that the man who is filled with the attributes of the *kaf* (כ) provides an enlarged door for those who would enter God's kingdom.

It can also be said that when the כ ('palm') faces out at the end of a word – away from itself in a gesture of open-handed generosity – it becomes a large door (ך) of invitation to the needy. May God grant that we perform our good works for His glory so that we – like the final *kaf* (ך) – may present an enlarged door of invitation to those who do not know Yeshua as their Messiah.

Yeshua's Greatest Accomplishment

Kaf is the root of the word '*kipah*' (כיפה), the head covering worn by observant Jewish men.[15] *Kaf* (כ) has the same shape as a *kipah*, or cap, and is also the root of the word *kippur* (כפור) as in *Yom Kippur* – the Day of Atonement (literally the "Day of Covering"). This is the sixth holy day on the biblical calendar and was the only time of the year in which the high priest would enter the Holy of Holies of the Temple. There he would sprinkle the blood of a bull and a goat before the Ark of the Covenant so as to *cover* Israel's sins from God's sight.[16] Atonement – covering our sins – is mistakenly thought to be Messiah's greatest accomplishment. In truth, He did not merely cover our sins. He accomplished infinitely more.

The writer of Hebrews explains *"For it is impossible for the blood of bulls and goats* [animals sacrificed on the Day of Atonement] *to take away sins."*[17] Only the blood of Messiah was potent enough to actually *remove* our sins, and that is exceedingly better than merely covering them over. As the writer of Hebrews put it: *"…we have been sanctified through the offering of the body of Yeshua Messiah once for all."*[18] Understandably then, one can examine the Apostolic Scriptures and note that nowhere does it refer to Messiah's sacrifice as an *atonement*.[19] The Scriptures consistently refer instead to His sacrifice as having the effect of *removing* our sins entirely. John the Immerser prophesied this at his first encounter with Yeshua when he said *"Behold, the Lamb of God who takes away the sin of the world!"*[20]

---

[15] From *kipah* we derive the English word 'cap'.
[16] See Chapter 1.
[17] Hebrews 10:4
[18] Hebrews 10:10
[19] Although the KJV mistranslates the word καταλλαγη (*katallage*) as 'atonement' in Romans 5:11, it should be translated 'reconciliation' as in verse 10 and in every other place καταλλαγη is used.
[20] John 1:29

Our salvation is based entirely upon God's grace, but our rewards are based upon our works. In a world of doctrinal extremes this balancing truth is rarely heard. Those with a legalistic mindset tend to emphasize good works at the expense of the sovereignty of God's grace, while others put great stock in God's grace but ignore the importance of works. One will quote, *"For by grace you have been saved, through faith, and that not of yourselves, it is the gift of God, not as a result of works."*[21] And another will reply, *"...faith without works is dead".*[22] Both statements are true. But living exclusively by one without the other creates imbalance and results in a lopsided faith. It is correctly said that we are not saved by faith *plus* works, but by faith *that* works.

Obviously, if one's faith in God is not strong enough to alter one's behavior, neither will it be strong enough to alter one's destiny. G.K. Chesterton wrote, *"There are people who pray for eternal life and don't know what to do with themselves on a rainy Sunday."*[23] In other words, what are we going to do with eternity if we do not know how to use the little time we have now? And what is the purpose for which God has so graciously saved us? It is that we should fulfill the destiny for which we were created – to perform *"good works in Messiah Yeshua"*.[24] May God grant that we grasp the magnitude of the salvation that is ours through Messiah Yeshua, the Savior who saves to the uttermost.

---

[21] Ephesians 2:8-9
[22] James 2:26
[23] As quoted by Rabbi Harold Kushner in <u>To Life! A Celebration of Jewish Being and Thinking</u> (Little-Brown, 1993), pg. 294.
[24] Ephesians 2:10

12

ל | *Lamed*

A Light to the World

---

*The spiritual life is an intelligent life,
one of knowledge and wisdom, not ignorance.*
R' ABRAHAM J. TWERSKI

Lights of the World

The letter *lamed* (ל) is unique in two ways: it is the tallest of the letters and it stands at the center of the alphabet. The shape of *lamed* (ל) has been compared to a watchtower or lighthouse established as a sentinel at the heart of the alphabet. In Torah scrolls the base of the ל is formed by a *kaf* (כ - the letter which symbolizes good deeds) atop which stands a *vav* (ו) in the shape of a flame, as if the good works inspired by the Holy Spirit were giving light and warmth to all those around.

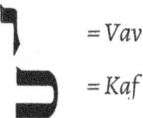
= Vav
= Kaf

Perhaps Yeshua was thinking of *lamed* (ל) when He said to His disciples:

> "You are the light of the world. A city set on a hill cannot be hidden, nor does anyone light a lamp and put it under a basket, but on the lampstand, and it gives light to

all who are in the house. Let your light shine before men in such a way that they may see your good works, and glorify your Father who is in heaven."[1]

As the flame-like protrusion stands atop the *kaf* (כ) in the formation of the *lamed*, so our good deeds should provide a platform for the display of God's light. Yeshua said, *"I am the light of the world"*,[2] but in the passage above He says that *we*, His followers, are the light of the world. In both cases the light referred to is the life of Yeshua – a life of godly good works done through the same spirit that worked through Yeshua and now dwells in us.

The arrangement of the ו (*vav*) supported by the כ (*kaf*, which means 'palm') also illustrates the verse, *"Therefore humble yourselves under the mighty hand of God, that He may exalt you at the proper time."*[3] Only the humble, who have been dealt with by God's hand, can produce works that are truly good. This is the essence of holy living – living a life like His. As the *vav* (ו) stands atop the *kaf* (כ), so the man who is filled with good works will be like a city on a hill whose light shines forth to illumine a dark world. This then gives us a glance at the kind of person represented by *lamed* (ל).

Knowing the Truth

The word *lamed* (למד) means to 'learn' and is the root which forms the words 'teach', 'study' and *Talmud* (תלמוד). We must *learn* to live a holy life that shines brightly in this dark world. To do so requires a disciplined dedication to the truth, which, according to scripture, is what earns a believer the title of *Christian*.

Luke tells us *"the disciples were first called Christians at Antioch."*[4] The term 'Christian' (or 'little Messiah') was not a title the disciples chose for themselves. They would never have been so presumptuous. It was the nonbelievers in Antioch who gave them this title. Though it was likely given in a derogatory vein, the disciples must have deemed it a great honor to be alleged of being so much like their Master.

The Bible tells us that the title Christian was given to 'disciples', which prompts the question, what is a disciple? The answer is found in John's gospel:

---

[1] Matthew 5:14-16
[2] John 8:12
[3] 1 Peter 5:6
[4] Acts 11:26

> So Yeshua was saying to those Jews who had believed Him, "If you continue in My word, then you are truly disciples of Mine, and you will know the truth, and the truth will make you free."[5]

We learn from this that a true disciple must be one who both believes upon Yeshua, and continues in His word. To "continue in His word" requires study of His word. Only then can we really know the truth and experience the freedom it brings. Many frustrated believers do not understand why they do not experience true freedom in their lives – freedom from habits, guilt, and unforgiveness, to mention a few. They do not experience freedom because they do not know the truth, and they do not know the truth because they do not study and obey the Torah. This principle lies at the core of the letter *lamed* (ל). If we endeavor to lead holy lives that provide light for a dark and dying world, we must be students of God's Word so that we will be free to live lives that are truly *Christian* in the biblical sense.

We must be careful not to limit our studies only to the Apostolic Scriptures as if only this part of the Bible has anything to teach us about Yeshua and the redeemed life. After His resurrection, Yeshua spoke to His disciples from the *Tanach* explaining His mission: *"Then beginning with Moses [i.e. the Torah] and with all the Prophets, He explained to them the things concerning Himself in all the Scriptures* [i.e. the Tanach]."[6] When our eyes are opened to see Yeshua in the Torah, we will also realize that the Torah is actually the *handbook* for the Christian life. In fact, the Torah is the handbook for being human.

We have learned that *beit* (ב) is the first letter of the Torah. However, the very last letter of the Torah is *lamed* (ל). When we combine the first and last letters of the Torah we derive the word לב (*lev*) 'heart' because the Torah is the revelation of God's heart.

Lamed's size and position at the center of the alphabet have also earned it the distinction of representing the King of Kings.[7] Interestingly, if we add *lamed* (ל) to its neighbors – *kaf* (כ) and *mem* (מ) – we derive the word מלך (*melech*) 'king'. Truly, Messiah the King is seated at the *heart* (לב) of both the Torah and the Hebrew alphabet and is the focus of the teachings contained in both. May God open our eyes to recognize the true heart of the Torah. If we look deeply into the Torah, we will see our Messiah on every page.

---

[5] John 8:31-32
[6] Luke 24:27
[7] Monk, p.138.

The Balanced Messianic Life

Again, *lamed* (ל) stands at the core of the Hebrew alphabet and means 'to learn'. In light of this, it is a regrettable phenomenon that a large segment of modern Christianity puts so much emphasis upon "spiritual" experiences at the expense of knowing God's Word. Both are important, but one without the other results in lopsided faith (if it could be called faith at all). Yeshua was aware of this imbalance when He rebuked the Pharisees saying: *"You are mistaken, not understanding the Scriptures nor the power of God."*[8]

To understand the proper balance of knowledge and experience we must learn the lesson of the salt crystal. Yeshua said ...

> *"You are the salt of the earth. But if the salt has become tasteless, how can it be made salty again? It is no longer good for anything, except to be thrown out and trampled under foot by men."*[9]

Anyone who has studied basic chemistry knows that salt is made of two elements – sodium and chlorine. From these two elements we derive the scientific name for salt – sodium chloride (NaCl)[10]. When these two elements are combined they make our food tastier and provide a mineral necessary for good health. But, in their individual states sodium and chlorine are poisons! Sodium is a crystal that is explosive when exposed to water. And chlorine is a gas that is fatal if inhaled. Separately, sodium and chloride are deadly. Combined, they are a life-sustaining substance.

An important lesson is to be learned from this: When we focus upon experience to the neglect of God's Word, we become like sodium – unstable, explosive, and poisonous. On the other hand, when we concentrate only upon study of scripture while neglecting the operation of God's spirit in our lives, we become like chlorine – a deadly gas. Or, to summarize it in another way:

> If you have knowledge without power, you will *dry up*.
> If you have power without knowledge, you will *blow up*.
> If you have knowledge *and* power, you will *grow up*.

---

[8] Matthew 22:29

[9] Matthew 5:13

[10] Though it is purely coincidental, if we convert the chemical abbreviation for salt – NaCl – into Hebrew letters – נאכל – they spell *ne'echal*, 'eaten'.

If we would be salt that does not *"become tasteless"*, then we must maintain a healthy balance of knowing the Scriptures and living them out. The alternative is poisonous. With God's help, we can maintain our saltiness by maintaining our balance and thereby grow to know Messiah through the lessons *lamed* (ל) illustrates.

The Age of Full Strength

Lamed (ל) has a numerical value of thirty. Several individuals in the Bible began to accomplish great things when they reached the age of thirty. Joseph was sold into slavery by his brothers when he was seventeen years old. He spent part of the next thirteen years serving Potiphar, and the rest of those years in prison. But, when he reached the age of 30 he was elevated to ruler of Egypt as Pharaoh's righthand man.[11]

Saul was thirty years old when he became king of Israel, and David was also thirty when he became king.[12] Additionally, Luke tells us that Yeshua was thirty years old when He began His public ministry.[13]

This is very curious, and certainly not coincidence. The question is why God orchestrated events so that each of these individuals was promoted to these special positions of service at 30 years of age? It may have to do with the Torah's guidelines concerning priests. Seven times in the Torah it is stated that the priests that serve in the Tabernacle must be at least thirty years of age.[14]

The *Mishnah* states, *"...at thirty years old [one attains] full strength..."*[15] In Hebrew, this phrase reads: בן שלשים לכח (*ben shilishim lakoach*), which literally translates to *"a son of thirty for strength"*. To this day, a Hebrew speaker refers to his age as a "son of" a certain number of years. Likewise, a female refers to herself as the "daughter of" a certain number of years.

So, does one automatically reach 'full strength' when one reaches the age of thirty? Possibly. But, I am interested here in spiritual strength – the spiritual strength achieved only if we reflect the lessons and truths embodied in the *lamed* (ל), whose numerical value is thirty.

---

[11] Genesis 41:46
[12] 1 Samuel 13:1; 2 Samuel 5:4
[13] Luke 3:23
[14] Numbers 4:3,23,30,35,39,43,47
[15] *Pirkei Avot* 5:25 (*Pirkei Avot* means 'Chapters of the Fathers' and is the one tractate of the *Talmud* that contains no commandments or rulings. It contains wisdom passed down from the Sages, including Gamaliel – Apostle Paul's teacher.)

Knowledge of YHVH

At the risk of being repetitive, I must draw your attention once again to the fact that *lamed* (ל) is constructed of a *vav* (ו) and a *kaf* (כ). If we add the numeric values of these two letters, we find that they equal 26 (כ = 20, ו = 6; 20 + 6 = 26), which is the numeric value of God's name *YHVH*, יהוה (י = 10, ה = 5, ו = 6, ה = 5; 10 + 5 + 6 + 5 = 26). This important connection between *Lamed* – the letter which stands at the center of the alphabet – and God's name emphasizes that the heart of what God wants us to learn through His alphabet is knowledge of Himself. We must approach the Bible not as if it were merely a portrait of God, but as a window through which we see the light of the Almighty Himself.

Note that *lamed* (ל) is the only letter whose top reaches above the line from which all of the other letters are suspended. It is as if this letter is permitted to poke its head above the clouds where all is clear and bright and see God in a way that is not granted to those who do not pursue Him by learning His Word and obeying it. If we add the numeric values of the letters which spell *lamed*'s full name – למד – we find that they equal seventy-four (ל = 30, מ = 40, ד = 4; 30 + 40 + 4 = 74). This is also the numeric value of the word בעב (*b'av*, 'in the thickness'),[16] a word which is found in the passage that says:

> Adonai said to Moses, "Behold, I will come to you in the thickness of the cloud, so that the people may hear when I speak with you and may also believe in your forever."[17]

To know God intimately, we must penetrate "the thickness" which surrounds Him. This is done only through study of His Word and prayer.

Blessing and Punishment

In our discussion of the letter *zayin* (ז) we learned how God has the authority to bless as well as to punish. This truth is reinforced by two unusual appearances of *lamed* (ל) in the Torah. The first one we shall consider is an oversize *lamed* (ל) found in the verse: "And Adonai uprooted them from their land in anger and in fury and in great wrath, and cast them into another land, as it is this day."[18]

---

[16] ב = 2, ע = 70, ב = 2; 2 + 70 + 2 = 74
[17] Exodus 19:9
[18] Deuteronomy 29:28

The phrase *"and cast them"* is one word in Hebrew: וישלכם (*vayash'licheim*). This word, with its oversize *lamed*, should be a constant reminder that the day of God's wrath is coming when He will exercise His authority as king to uproot and thrust people into a place to which they have no desire to go.

An even more unusual form of the letter *lamed* is found in the phrase: *"... Isaac had finished blessing Jacob..."*[19] The word "finished" is כלה (*kilah*). When this phrase is printed in Torah scrolls, the ל in *kilah* has an unusual looking crownlet attached to its top, as shown in the illustration below.

The Sages suggest that the crownlet atop this *lamed* (ל) is reaching over as if to bless the *hei* (ה).[20] The odd appearance of this letter, plus the word and phrase in which it is contained, suggest a scenario: a time is coming when this life will be 'finished' (כלה, *kilah*) and the King of Kings (ל) will bless those who have run their course in faith and obedience to His Word.

A Final Insight

The name of the Jewish people – ישראל (*Israel*) – begins with the smallest of the letters (י) and ends with the largest (ל). This is the story of Israel's spiritual history as well as our own. From small beginnings the Holy Spirit (י) works in our hearts, eventually leading us into the eternal presence of the King (ל). God is faithful, and if He has begun a good work in you – even if it is as small as a *yud* (י) – you can be *"... confident of this very thing, that He who began a good work in you will perfect it until the day of Messiah Yeshua."*[21]

---

[19] Genesis 27:30
[20] Munk, op.cit., pg. 141.
[21] Philippians 1:6

13

מ, ם | *Mem*

Living Waters

"Then the angel showed me the river of the water of life, as clear as crystal, flowing from the throne of God and of the Lamb down the middle of the great street of the city."
REVELATION 22:1-2

The Center of it All

In the previous chapter I stated that *lamed* (ל) is located in the middle of the alphabet. However, since the Hebrew alphabet contains an even number of letters, there is not one letter at the center, but two – *kaf* and *lamed* (כ and ל).

אבגדהוזחטיכלמנסעפצקרשת
△

However, there is another method to determine the center of the alphabet. Let me explain. *Mem* (מ) is the second of five letters having two forms. We have already encountered the first of these – *kaf* – whose two forms are כ and ך. When *mem* is found at the beginning or in the middle of a word it appears as מ. But, when *mem* ends a word it appears as ם. If we spell out the name *mem* (מם), we see that it contains two מ's – a normal and a final form.

If we include these five final forms with the 22 standard letters of the alphabet, we derive a total of 27 letters. If we place these 27 letters in a row (as shown below), we discover that מ (*mem*) occupies the center position.

אבגדהוזחטיכךל[מ]םנןסעפףצץקרשת

13 letters — 13 letters

This now provides us with a *third* center letter – כ (*kaf*), ל (*lamed*), and מ (*mem*). If we combine these three center letters we will discover who dwells at the center – מלך (*melech*) 'King'. How appropriate!

In its position at the heart of the Hebrew alphabet, *mem* (מ) divides it into two halves of thirteen letters each. Recall that 13 is the numerical value of 'love' (אהבה, *ahavah*) and 'one' (אחד, *echad*). Also, recall that 13 + 13 is the numerical value of God's name – YHVH (יהוה). These values surrounding *mem* (מ) make perfect sense when we realize that *mem* (מ) is the first letter of משיח (*Mashiach*) 'Messiah'.

Additionally, *mem* (מ) – like *lamed* (ל) – is constructed from the letters *kaf* (כ) and a *vav* (ו). But, whereas *lamed* has the *vav* (ו) standing atop the *kaf* (כ), *mem* (מ) has the *vav* standing to the left of the *kaf*.[1]

vav ו+כ kaf
⇩
מ
mem

The numeric values of these two letters add up to 26 – the number of God's name YHVH. Hence, these two letters at the center of the alphabet – ל and מ – share several things in common. But, whereas *lamed* (ל) stands tall like a lighthouse, *mem* (מ) flows like water. Let me explain.

The word *mem* (מם) is a shortened form of מים (*ma'im*) which means 'water'. In chemical terms water is designated as H_2O, which means that a molecule of water is comprised of two atoms of hydrogen (H_2) and one atom of oxygen (O). Water's chemical form can also be written H + O + H. Jewish scholars point out the obvious resemblance this pattern bears to the Hebrew spelling of water (מ + י + ם). As coincidental

---

[1] This combination of letters applies only to the normal form of *mem*, not the final form.

as this may seem, we must remember that the God who created the Hebrew language is the same God Who created water.

The Number of Transition

Mem (מ) has a numerical value of 40, and the Scriptures are replete with examples of the number 40. Here are a few:

- It rained for 40 days and 40 nights while Noah was in the ark.
- Isaac was 40 when he married Rebecca.
- Moses spent 40 years as a prince of Egypt.
- Moses spent 40 years as a shepherd in Midian.
- Moses was on Mt. Sinai for 40 days and 40 nights.
- The Israelites spent 40 years in the wilderness.
- Saul reigned over Israel for 40 years.
- David reigned over Israel for 40 years.
- Solomon reigned over Israel for 40 years.
- Yeshua was tested in the wilderness for 40 days.
- Yeshua appeared to His disciples over a period of 40 days after His resurrection.

Aside from their association with the number 40, what do all of these things have in common? They all represent a time of transition from one condition or state to another. In each case, after forty days (or years) things had completely changed. After 40 years in the wilderness, the Israelites were ready to enter Canaan. After 40 days in the wilderness, Yeshua was ready to begin His ministry. After leading the Israelites for 40 years, Moses was told to pass the leadership to Joshua.

Since *mem* (מ) has a numerical value of 40, it is appropriate that it should stand at the center of the alphabet as we transition from the first 13 letters to the final 13 letters. Likewise, *mem*'s name means 'water', which is also an element of transition. In Judaism, when a person completes one phase of life in order to begin another, he or she immerses themselves in a *mikveh* (מקוה) – a ritual immersion tank.[2]

Some instances would include:

- Prior to a wedding ceremony.

---

[2] In Christianity this is referred to as a baptismal tank or baptistry.

- Each month after a woman's menstrual cycle.
- Before a *Bat-* or *Bar-Mitzvah*.
- When converting to Judaism.
- When repenting of sin.
- When preparing to ascend to the Temple.
- Prior to *Yom Kippur* (The Day of Atonement).

In each example we see a transition from one phase of life to another. This helps us understand why Yeshua was immersed – He was ending His life as a carpenter (or stone mason) and beginning His life as rabbi, teacher and deliverer of Israel.

Thus, we can see the connection between the number 40 and ritual immersion – they both represent transition and change. How perfectly that these come together in the letter *mem* (מ), which has a numerical value of 40 and whose name means 'water'.

Water from the Rock

A curious play on words discovered by the Sages[3] is based upon an incident found in the book of Numbers:

Then Moses lifted up his hand and struck the rock twice with his rod, and water came forth abundantly, and the congregation and their beasts drank.[4]

The word for 'rock' used in this passage is סלע (*sela*).[5] Its three letters are *samech* (סמך), *lamed* (למד), and *ayin* (עין) respectively. The names of these three letters are spelled out in the diagram below.

Sela
↓

סמך	samech
למד	lamed
עין	ayin

---

[3] R'Chaim of Czernowitz (1760-1818), <u>Be'er Mayim Chaim</u>.
[4] Numbers 20:11
[5] This is obviously a different word from אבן (*evan*) 'stone' which we encountered in chapter 1. Also, this word is different from the word סלה (*selah*) that is found frequently in the Psalms.

Now that we have spelled out the names of the three letters which comprise *sela* 'rock', let's imagine the box containing these nine letters as the rock which Moses struck with his staff. Just as Moses struck the rock twice, we shall do the same. With the first blow the letters beginning each word are knocked off. Like this…

$$\begin{array}{c} ס\!\!\!/\ מ\ ך \\ ל\!\!\!/\ מ\ ד \\ ע\!\!\!/\ ו\ י \end{array}$$

With the second blow the last letters were knocked off. Once again, like this…

$$\begin{array}{c} ס\!\!\!/\ מ\ ך\!\!\!/ \\ ל\!\!\!/\ מ\ ד\!\!\!/ \\ ע\!\!\!/\ ו\!\!\!/\ י \end{array}$$

After these two blows, the only letters remaining are two מ's and a י which can be arranged to spell מים (*maim*) 'water'. And thus, like Moses, we acquire water from the rock.

As unusual as it may seem for a rock to give forth water, the Torah describes an even stranger event. In this event water stood up like a wall of rock. This occurred, of course, when God parted the Red Sea so that the Israelites could safely cross. The Torah says:

> "*At the blast of Your nostrils the waters were piled up. The flowing waters stood up like a heap. The deeps were congealed in the heart of the sea.*"[6]

In recognition of this miraculous event, tradition directs scribes to print this account in Torah scrolls in such a way that the lines of print resemble a wall. The illustration below shows a portion of this passage[7] in which the lines are arranged like courses of stone in a wall.

---

[6] Exodus 15:8
[7] Exodus 15:1-19 ("The Song by the Sea")

אַפִּיךָ נֶעֶרְמוּ מַיִם נִצְּבוּ כְמוֹ־נֵד
נֹזְלִים קָפְאוּ תְהֹמֹת בְּלֶב־יָם׃ אָמַר
אוֹיֵב אֶרְדֹּף אַשִּׂיג אֲחַלֵּק שָׁלָל תִּמְלָאֵמוֹ
נַפְשִׁי אָרִיק חַרְבִּי תּוֹרִישֵׁמוֹ יָדִי׃
נָשַׁפְתָּ בְרוּחֲךָ כִּסָּמוֹ יָם צָלֲלוּ כַּעוֹפֶרֶת בְּמַיִם
אַדִּירִים׃ מִי־כָמֹכָה בָּאֵלִם יְהוָה מִי
כָּמֹכָה נֶאְדָּר בַּקֹּדֶשׁ נוֹרָא תְהִלֹּת עֹשֵׂה
פֶלֶא׃ נָטִיתָ יְמִינְךָ תִּבְלָעֵמוֹ אָרֶץ׃ נָחִיתָ
בְחַסְדְּךָ עַם־זוּ גָּאָלְתָּ נֵהַלְתָּ בְעָזְּךָ אֶל־נְוֵה
קָדְשֶׁךָ׃ שָׁמְעוּ עַמִּים יִרְגָּזוּן חִיל
אָחַז יֹשְׁבֵי פְּלָשֶׁת׃ אָז נִבְהֲלוּ אַלּוּפֵי
אֱדוֹם אֵילֵי מוֹאָב יֹאחֲזֵמוֹ רָעַד נָמֹגוּ
כֹּל יֹשְׁבֵי כְנָעַן׃ תִּפֹּל עֲלֵיהֶם אֵימָתָה
וָפַחַד בִּגְדֹל זְרוֹעֲךָ יִדְּמוּ כָּאָבֶן עַד־
יַעֲבֹר עַמְּךָ יְהוָה עַד־יַעֲבֹר עַם־זוּ
קָנִיתָ׃ תְּבִאֵמוֹ וְתִטָּעֵמוֹ בְּהַר נַחֲלָתְךָ מָכוֹן
לְשִׁבְתְּךָ פָּעַלְתָּ יְהוָה מִקְּדָשׁ אֲדֹנָי כּוֹנְנוּ
יָדֶיךָ׃ יְהוָה יִמְלֹךְ לְעֹלָם וָעֶד׃ כִּי
בָא סוּס פַּרְעֹה בְּרִכְבּוֹ וּבְפָרָשָׁיו בַּיָּם וַיָּשֶׁב יְהוָה עֲלֵהֶם אֶת־מֵי

Revealed and Hidden Truth

Because of the tiny opening that appears at the bottom of the normal form of *mem* (מ), it is said to be "open". The final form (ם) however, is said to be "closed". These open and closed forms are described in Jewish lore as representing both the *open* teachings and the *hidden* wisdom of the Torah. The *Talmud* states: "מ *represents the revealed Torah, and* ם *represents the Torah's secrets."*[8] This is typical of God's ways to hide particular insights from our understanding until the appropriate time. Solomon stated, *"It is the glory of God to conceal a matter, but the glory of kings is to search out a matter."*[9] The Bible is replete with examples of God revealing His hidden wisdom. Let's consider some examples.

Daniel had a great appreciation for God's ability to reveal hidden truth, especially since it saved his life and that of his friends on at least one occasion.[10] Daniel proclaimed, *"It is He who reveals the profound and hidden things; He knows what is in darkness, and the light dwells with Him."*[11]

Matthew described Yeshua's teachings with a quote from Psalms when He wrote, *"I will open my mouth in parables, I will utter things hidden since the foundation of the world."*[12]

---

[8] Shabbat 104a. In Jewish lore the open (מ) and closed (ם) *mems* in the word *maim* ('water') are said to represent the waters below the firmament (which are open to us) and the waters above the firmament (which are closed to us). See The Alef-Beit, pg. 194.

[9] Proverbs 25:2

[10] Daniel 2

[11] Daniel 2:22

[12] Matthew 13:35 (quoting Psalm 78:2)

Paul often stated that God had chosen him to reveal secrets that had been hidden from the beginning of time. He wrote:

> ... but we speak God's wisdom in a mystery, the hidden wisdom which God predestined before the ages to our glory; the wisdom which none of the rulers of this age has understood, for if they had understood it they would not have crucified the Lord of glory.[13]

If the rulers during Yeshua's ministry had understood the hidden wisdom Paul later explained, they would not have crucified Yeshua. However, God has a purpose in all that He does. Paul's letter to the Ephesians gives us a glimpse as to why God chose to conceal His plans and thus allow Messiah to be crucified:

> To me, the very least of all saints, this grace was given, to proclaim to the Gentiles the unfathomable riches of Messiah, and to bring to light what is the administration of the mystery which for ages has been hidden in God who created all things.[14]

What is this mystery?

> ...the mystery which has been hidden from the past ages and generations, but has now been manifested to His saints, to whom God willed to make known what is the riches of the glory of this mystery among the Gentiles, which is Messiah in you, the hope of glory.[15]

This secret is the life-saving message of the gospel that is now being proclaimed to the entire world. The present gospel of God's grace is so very gracious that it is difficult to fathom. But, as with the wine at Cana, God has saved the best for last.[16] The good news that the Word of God proclaims to Jews and Gentiles alike goes far beyond what could ever have been imagined before Paul's day.

---

[13] 1 Corinthians 2:7-8
[14] Ephesians 3:8-9
[15] Colossians 1:26-27
[16] John 2:1-10

Though this subject is worthy of a book of its own (and several fine books have been written on this topic[17]), my purpose here is to emphasize that God can, and does, hide things from us so that they may be revealed at a later time, or that we may experience the joy that comes only from searching the Scriptures and uncovering them for ourselves. This is the meaning of the closed *mem* (ם).

The Shape of Things to Come

One thing that is hidden from us is the future. Though the Bible reveals a great deal concerning future events, there is much that we must wait to discover. A major end-time event illustrated by the letter *mem* (מ) is the establishment of the Messianic Age. The prophet Zechariah paints a graphic picture of the events that will occur in Jerusalem on that day.

Jerusalem sits atop a mountain range running north and south between the Mediterranean Sea (to the west) and the Dead Sea (to the east). Zechariah wrote:

> And in that day living waters [מים, maim] will flow out of Jerusalem, half of them toward the eastern sea and the other half toward the western sea; it will be in summer as well as in winter. And Adonai will be king over all the earth. In that day Adonai will be one, and His name one.[18]

Each time *mem*'s name is spelled out – מים – this future event is portrayed in miniature. To illustrate, let's consider the geography of Israel. A map of the Dead Sea reveals it to be pinched in two near its southern end. The shape of the Dead Sea has been changing over time, especially in recent decades. During several visits to the Dead Sea over the last twenty years, I have been amazed at how this connecting strip of water has continued to narrow, almost to the point of nonexistence. Older maps show a fairly wide strip of water connecting the upper and lower parts of the Dead Sea, while newer maps depict the northern and southern parts as separate bodies of water.

This is prophetically significant because Ezekiel indirectly foretold this geographic change.[19] In his description of the Messianic Age an angel guides Ezekiel

---

[17] The author recommends <u>The Problem of Evil and the Judgments of God</u>, by A.E. Knoch (Concordant Publishing Concern, 1976).

[18] Zechariah 14:8-9

[19] Ezekiel's prophecy parallels that of Zechariah, except he dedicates nearly an entire chapter to a detailed description of the river that will flow eastward from Jerusalem.

through the precincts of Jerusalem as it will appear when Messiah reigns as King. This is how he describes the stream that will flow from the temple mount:

> *Then he brought me back to the door of the house, and behold, water was flowing from under the threshold of the house toward the east, for the house faced east. And the water was flowing down from under, from the right side of the house, from south of the altar.*[20]

The next several verses describe how the stream grows into a river, ever increasing in depth and width and bordered on either side by many trees. Then we come to an astounding account of the effect this river has upon the Dead Sea:

> *Then he said to me, "These waters go out toward the eastern region and go down into the Arabah; then they go toward the sea, being made to flow into the sea, and the waters of the sea become fresh."*[21]

The word 'Arabah' comes from a Hebrew word meaning 'dry' or 'burnt up' and refers to the dry desert area at the foot of the Judean hills along the shores of the Dead Sea. When the river that flows from the Temple enters the Dead Sea the waters will become fresh. If you have ever tasted water from the Dead Sea, you can appreciate the grand scale of this miracle. Nothing lives in the Dead Sea because its water is nine times saltier than ocean water and is so acidic that drinking a single teaspoon can be fatal. For this deadly body of water to someday become fresh will be a miracle indeed.

Ezekiel continues:

> *"It will come about that every living creature which swarms in every place where the river goes, will live. And there will be very many fish, for these waters go there and the others become fresh; so everything will live where the river goes. And it will come about that fishermen will stand beside it; from Engedi to Eneglaim there will be a place for the spreading of nets. Their fish will be according to their kinds, like the fish of the Great Sea, very many."*[22]

---

[20] Ezekiel 47:1 ("The house" is a reference to the Temple.)
[21] Ezekiel 47:8 (emphasis mine)
[22] Ezekiel 47:9-10

160 | In His Own Words

Here, Ezekiel describes fishermen catching fish in a body of water that is presently referred to as the Dead Sea. But notice that the prophecy refers to them fishing only along a portion of the sea, from En Gedi to En Eglaim. What about the rest of the Dead Sea?

"But its swamps and marshes will not become fresh; they will be left for salt."[23]

How can only a portion of the Dead Sea become fresh water and the rest remain salty? Only by making one body of water into two as is now the case. But why not make the entire Dead Sea fresh? Why leave any of it salty? The southern portion of the Dead Sea, which will remain salty, is one of the world's richest natural resources. Its waters contain vast supplies of gold, uranium, potash, bromine and other valuable minerals and metals.

Returning to the word מים (*maim*, 'water'), note that the middle letter is a *yud* (י) – the first letter of the word ירושלם – 'Jerusalem'. As we read in the prophecies of Zechariah and Ezekiel, waters shall flow from Jerusalem to the east and the west. On both sides of the *yud* (י) is found a מ (*mem*) – the letter meaning 'water'. The *mem* to the left (west) is a final form made of a single enclosed shape. But the *mem* to the right (east) is in two parts (formed of a כ and a ו) and denotes the Dead Sea that is also in two parts.

What an extraordinary God we have that He could hide these beautiful insights concerning future events in the Hebrew alphabet. Only our God, who knows the end from the beginning, could accomplish such things.

As we close this section, I must mention that the ultimate event we look forward to is the coming of the New Heavens and the New Earth when the New Jerusalem shall appear. The square shape of the final *mem* (used only at the end of a word) is an appropriate symbol for the new city that will be revealed at the end of the ages. John describes it as a city "*... laid out as a square, and its length is as great as the width.*"[24]

A Hidden Life With God

The theme of this present series of letters is the walk of faith. We have seen how *chet* (ח) is our yoke whereby we stay close to our Master. *Tet* (ט) illustrates how we must

---

[23] Ezekiel 47:11
[24] Revelation 21:16

learn to die to self. *Kaf* (כ) illustrates the good works for which we were created. And *lamed* (ל) illustrates the knowledge of God we gain as we walk in His ways.

So, what does *mem* (מ) represent?

The Jewish Sages teach that just as *lamed* (ל), like a flame, always tries to climb higher and seek new levels of knowledge of God, *mem* (מ), like water, always seeks the lowest level of humility. In fact, when two sages disagreed on an issue the rule was to adopt the opinion of the meekest, not the most brilliant. Is humility the primary teaching of the letter *mem*? Possibly. But, I believe it goes further than this and would teach us that there is a secret hidden life we must cultivate with God – a *closed* life, if you will. It is, after all, those things which are done in secret (ם) for which we shall be rewarded openly (מ). The Master stated, *"But you, when you pray, go into your inner room, close your door and pray to your Father who is in secret, and your Father who sees what is done in secret will reward you."*[25]

When we stand before God to give an account of our lives may we hear Him say, *"Well done, good and faithful servant! You were faithful with a few things, I will put you in charge of many things. Enter into the joy of your Master!"*[26]

---

[25] Matthew 6:6
[26] Matthew 25:23

14

נ,ן | *Nun*

Humility, Fish, and the *Kahal*

> *"There is in this world nothing sacred but man,*
> *no sanctuary of God but the soul."*
> ANONYMOUS

Fishers of Men

On a recent trip to Rome I had the opportunity to tour the catacombs, a vast, complex underground network of burial chambers used by first-century believers. As I walked through seemingly endless stretches of tunnels, the guide pointed out many of the ancient Messianic symbols carved into the walls. The most frequent symbol, and one still prevalent among Christians, was of a fish. It was formed by two curved lines joined at one end as shown below:

Why was a fish such a popular symbol among early believers? One reason is that Yeshua compared men with fish when He told His disciples (several of whom were fishermen) that He would make them *"fishers of men"*.[1] The gospel was compared to a

---
[1] Matthew 4:19

fishing net which would draw people, like fish, from darkness into light.

Another reason the first-century *kahal* employed the fish symbol ...

⇨ **Reader:** Wait a minute! Stop the music! What is a *"kahal"*? Don't you mean "church"?

Okay, good question. let's pause here for a moment and talk about that word I just used – *kahal*. I use this word instead of 'church' for a very good reason. *Kahal* (קהל) is the word the *Tanach* itself uses for 'church'. I know what you must be thinking – "The *church* didn't begin until the New Testament." Though that is not true, I can't blame you for thinking that it is. After all, the cause of this confusion is more than 400 years old. Here is the story.

In 1604, King James of England commissioned a new English translation of the Bible. When he did this, he established fifteen rules to govern this ambitious project. Rule #3 reads as follows: *The old Ecclesiastical Words to be kept, viz. the Word* Church *not to be translated* Congregation *&c.*[2] In other words, King James insisted that the word *church* be employed throughout his translation rather than more accurate biblical terms. It is beyond the scope of this book to delve into the origins of the word *c-h-u-r-c-h*, but suffice to say that by 1604 this word did not describe the group of holy God-followers described throughout the Bible, but rather a formidable organization that wielded political power not only over the government of England and the rest of Europe, but also over the lives of the common people. This power even governed what they were allowed to believe. So powerful was this so-called "church" at the time, that it frequently executed those who did not toe its theological lines. This kind of governmental dominion was *not* what God had in mind for His holy people.

The Greek word translated 'church' is *ekklesia* (εκκλησια) – yes, the same basic word King James himself used in his Rule #3 – "Ecclesiastical". The word *ekklesia* means "a called-out people", or "a called together people". Hebrew has an exact equivalent of *ekklesia* which is (you guessed it) *kahal* (קהל). In fact, the Hebrew title for the book of *Ecclesiastes* (derived from εκκλησια) is *Kohelet* (קהלת) which is derived from *kahal* (קהל). The better we understand the Hebrew and Greek words that lie behind the word King James translated as 'church', the better we will understand the redeemed community that we have been mislabeling with this word.

First, we will realize that the *kahal* did not begin in the book of Acts, but rather

---

[2] Benson Bobrick, <u>Wide as the Waters: The Story of the English Bible and the Revolution It Inspired</u>, pg. 316.

back in Genesis where the word *kahal* (קָהָל) is first used.[3] In fact, the word *kahal* is used in the *Tanach* more frequently than the word *ekklesia* is used in the Greek Scriptures.[4]

Second, we will be able to understand Paul's teaching about how the Gentiles have been grafted into Israel. He did *not* say that the "church" has been grafted into Israel, but that the Gentiles have been grafted into the *kahal* of Israel. They – Israel – are the original "church" – not we Gentiles. And so, when the King James Bible was published in 1611, the word 'church' was used to translate *only* the Greek word *Ekklesia*, but words like 'multitude', 'company', 'assembly' and 'congregation' were used to translate the Hebrew word *kahal*.

There is much more to be said on this subject (and I am sorely tempted to say more here), but it deserves a book of its own. However, you will understand why I use the biblical term *kahal* when referring to what has been traditionally misunderstood as 'church'.

And so, continuing where we left off...

Another reason the first-century *kahal* employed the fish symbol is because the Greek word for fish ιχθυς (*ichthus*) forms an acrostic wherein the five Greek letters stand for *Yeshua Messiah, Son of God, Savior*.

Ι	Ιησούς	(*Yeseus*)	Yeshua
Χ	Χρίστος	(*Christos*)	Messiah
Θ	Θεού	(*theou*)	(of) God
Υ	Υιός	(*uios*)	Son
Σ	Σωτηρ	(*soter*)	Savior

Just as fish are connected with water, *mem* (מ, the letter which means 'water') is followed by *nun* (נ) – the letter whose name means 'fish'. As we study this letter, we shall see that its many seemingly unrelated characteristics fit neatly together to provide a message that is both instructive and timely. We begin our study of *nun* (נ) by looking at a unique passage to which we shall frequently refer in this chapter. Below, you can see how this passage – Numbers 10:35-36 – appears in a Torah scroll. Do you notice anything unusual?

---

[3] Genesis 28:3
[4] *Kahal* occurs 162 times. *Ekklesia* occurs 114 times.

> לָתוּר לָהֶם מְנוּחָה וַעֲנַן יְהוָה עֲלֵיהֶם יוֹמָם בְּנָסְעָם
> מִן הַמַּחֲנֶה ׆ וַיְהִי בִּנְסֹעַ
> הָאָרֹן וַיֹּאמֶר מֹשֶׁה קוּמָה יְהוָה וְיָפֻצוּ אֹיְבֶיךָ וְיָנֻסוּ
> מְשַׂנְאֶיךָ מִפָּנֶיךָ וּבְנֻחֹה יֹאמַר שׁוּבָה יְהוָה רִבְבוֹת
> אַלְפֵי יִשְׂרָאֵל ׆
> וַיְהִי הָעָם כְּמִתְאֹנְנִים רַע בְּאָזְנֵי יְהוָה וַיִּשְׁמַע יְהוָה

Look closely and you will see some lines which are bracketed by two *nuns* (נ). The passage in brackets is translated below:

> *Then it came about when the ark set out that Moses said, "Rise up, Adonai! And let Your enemies be scattered, and let those who hate You flee before You." When it came to rest, he said, "Return, Adonai, to the myriad thousands of Israel."*[5]

The Sages have given much attention to this passage in an attempt to answer the following questions:

- Why are these two verses set apart from the rest of the text?
- Why was the letter *nun* (נ) used to bracket them?
- Why are the two *nuns* sometimes written upside down and/or backwards?

Let's explore what the Sages have to say concerning this strange use of the letter *nun* (נ).

The Seven Books of Torah

The book of Numbers speaks primarily of the Israelites' journey through the wilderness, but the passage above speaks of the ark's journey. Since Moses recognized that Israel would always have enemies who would take every opportunity to attack, he began each leg of the journey with a plea that God would protect His people as they traveled to the land He had promised them. Whenever they paused in their journey, he would ask God to reside in their midst in such a way that the *"myriad thousands"* would experience His presence.

This passage has such a distinctive identity of its own that it is understandable

---

[5] Numbers 10:35-36

why it was set apart from the body of the surrounding text. In fact, the *Talmud* avers that this passage stands as an individual book of Torah![6] If the *Talmud* is correct, then the Torah actually contains seven books instead of five:

1. Genesis
2. Exodus
3. Leviticus
4. Numbers 1:1 to 10:34
5. Numbers 10:35-36
6. Numbers 10:37 to 36:13
7. Deuteronomy

This arrangement would then agree with the passage: *Wisdom has built her house. She has hewn out her seven pillars.*[7] – the seven pillars being the seven books of Torah upon which rests the house of wisdom. Though this is a clever concept, I think there is much better answer...

The Present Age

In several places among their writings the Sages alleged that these two verses are out of place. They are located between two stories neither of which appears to have any relationship to this passage. Preceding Numbers 10:35-36 is the account of Moses' invitation to his Gentile father-in-law Jethro to join the journeyings of Israel. And the passage following Numbers 10:35-36 is the account of God sending a consuming fire among the Israelites as punishment for their excessive complaining.

What the Talmudists did not realize is that the position of this unique passage provides a Torah picture of the current era in which we find ourselves – an era between Messiah's first coming and His return.[8] This is a period of time that began with God's invitation to the Gentiles (much as Moses' invitation to his Gentile father-in-law) to partake of the blessings that had originally been extended to Israel alone. And, this era will end when God purifies Israel in the crucible of end-time events (just as Numbers 10:35-36 is followed by a time of fiery judgment).

The current era forms a unique parenthesis in God's plan for Israel – a parenthesis that was utterly unforeseen by the Sages. It is a time in which God's presence

---

[6] *Shabbos* 115-116
[7] Proverbs 9:1
[8] In Christendom, this era is often called "the Church age".

abides in individual men and women, whether Jew or Gentile, by the Holy Spirit. The true *kahal* is not a religion, creed or denomination, but people who have individually given their allegiance to the God of Israel and His Messiah. Through this redeemed community, God has arisen so His spiritual enemies may *"be scattered"*, and we are commanded to stand against these enemies (Satan, sin and deception) clad in the spiritual armor that He has provided.

The block diagram below shows the parallels between Numbers 10:34-35 and this present age.

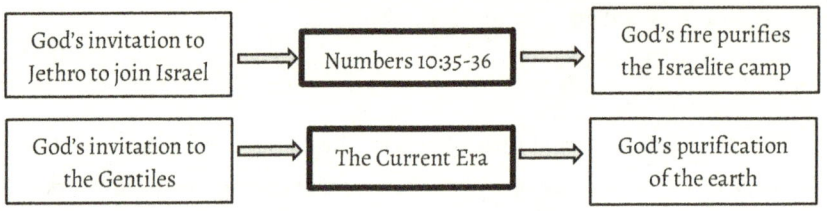

If this passage is a vignette of the current era, does it not make sense to bracket it with two 'fish' (*nuns*) – the universal symbol of the *kahal*?

If you are familiar with the Sabbath worship in a synagogue, you are aware that the highlight of the service is the removal, reading, and return of the Torah scroll to the *aron hakodesh* – the ark at the front of the synagogue where the Torah scroll is stored. This ancient tradition illustrates the central importance of God's Word to the Jewish people. At the moment the ark is opened to remove the scroll, Numbers 10:35 is chanted:

> *"Rise up, Adonai! And let Your enemies be scattered,*
> *and let those who hate You flee before You."*

The scroll is then lovingly carried up and down the aisles so that all present may honor it by touching it. The scroll is then unrolled, and the weekly portion is read aloud by individuals who are called up from the congregation. At the conclusion of the readings, the open Torah scroll is lifted up so that the words of the scroll are visible to all. While held aloft the following ancient blessing is chanted in Hebrew:

> *It is a tree of life to those who grasp it, and all its supporters are worthy. Its ways*
> *are ways of pleasantness and all its paths are peace. Turn us Lord to You and let us*

return. Renew our days as of old.[9]

After the scroll is rolled up, a second processional takes place amidst singing and chanting. When the scroll reaches the ark, Numbers 10:36 is quoted:

"Return, Adonai, to the countless thousands of Israel."

The ark is then closed.

This is how Numbers 10:35-36 is used both to introduce and conclude the reading of the Torah. During this present age God is using the community of believers to hold up His Word to the world as a Tree of Life. Believers today are living in this grand parenthesis wherein God is inviting both Jews and Gentiles to lift up the living Torah – Yeshua. Until the day that our precious Messiah returns, let us handle the Word of God humbly and with awe.

The Letter of Humility

Humility is a topic that is rarely addressed because anyone who is qualified to write on the subject is naturally reluctant to do so. My father enjoyed telling the story about a man whose church awarded him a medal for his outstanding humility ... and then had to take it away from him for wearing it to church. I write not as a candidate for the humility award, but as one who sees it as foundational to our understanding of the letter *nun* (נ).

Though humility should be deeply desired by all believers, its acquisition is usually accomplished only through pain and humiliation. We are commanded to humble ourselves, but we rarely achieve humility without considerable help.[10] God sometimes provokes humility by allowing us to experience the disastrous consequences of our own sin. Ironically, the Sages describe *nun* as the letter which not only represents humility,[11] but also a deep fall from purity to impurity – which is often just the kind of crisis that is necessary to produce humility. Most people in whom humility is evident can share experiences wherein they went through a spiritual downfall, wherein they learned to trust in God's love and grace instead of their own abilities and cleverness. For these, the prodigal son's story has become their own.

God said, *"But to this one I will look, to him who is humble and contrite of spirit, and who*

---

[9] Artscroll Siddur, pg. 445)
[10] James 4:10
[11] Talmud, *Berachot 4b*.

trembles at My word."[12]

For God's Word to be effective in our lives it must be received with humility. Whereas *mem* (מ) illustrates many truths concerning humility, *nun* (נ) illustrates truths about the humble person himself. This should not surprise us since 'fish' (נ) live in 'water' (מ) just as the humble man (נ) lives in humility (מ). Let us look at several ways in which the letter *nun* (נ) teaches us about living humbly.

The Missing *Nun*

Several of the Psalms are constructed as acrostics, such as Psalm 145. If you look at this psalm in Hebrew, you will observe that the first verse begins with א, the second with ב, the third with ג, and so on. But, when you reach the fourteenth verse of the psalm you will note that there seems to be a verse missing. Verse 14, which should begin with the letter *nun* (נ), skips instead to the next letter – *samech* (ס) which, as we shall learn in the next chapter, means 'support'. With this in mind, consider verse fourteen which begins with *samech*: *"Adonai supports all who fall and raises up all who are bowed down."*[13] The omission of a verse beginning with *nun* (נ) suggests that when we fall, God will erase the record of our sins and lift us up. The prophet Micah confirms this: *"He will again have compassion on us; He will tread our iniquities under foot. Yes, You will cast all their sins into the depths of the sea."*[14]

Returning to the inverted *nuns* of Numbers 10:34-35, one Rabbi suggests that these two upside-down letters represent the fact that Israel is in a state of נפילה (*n'philah*) 'downfall'. Note that this word also begins with נ. However, he also says that the נ's will be "reversed by God as soon as Israel returns again and adheres to the Holy Ark."[15] May God soon do so for Israel and for all who have fallen away from Him.

נ = 50

The letter *nun* (נ) has a numeric value of 50, a number that is closely related in meaning to the number 8 – whose themes are freedom and new beginnings. The reason these two numbers – 50 and 8 – are closely related is because they each begin new cycles. We have seen how 7 represents completion in time and 8 breaks free of the cycle in order to create a new beginning. Likewise, 49 (which is 7 x 7) also represents completions in time. The number 50 breaks out of the cycle to start a new beginning.

---

[12] Isaiah 66:2. See also 2 Chronicles 12:7; Daniel 10:12; James 1:21.
[13] Psalm 145:14
[14] Micah 7:19
[15] Munk, pg. 158

This is vividly demonstrated in the Torah, which commands that every fiftieth year slaves were to be freed, property returned to its original owners, and all debts canceled.[16]

Another example of freedom's connection to the number 50 is the story of the Exodus, which is mentioned exactly fifty times in the Torah. This story, describing deliverance from slavery to freedom, is the story of every Jew historically and of every believer spiritually.

The Sages have noted that in Torah scrolls, Numbers 10:34-35 is located exactly fifty paragraphs after the story of the giving of the Torah at Mount Sinai. But Jewish tradition has it that "when the final redemption will come, this passage will be returned to its proper place"[17] – exactly fifty paragraphs earlier.

Giving and Receiving

The Master said, *"Freely you received, freely give."*[18] The principle of giving and receiving is discussed frequently in Jewish writings. They teach that when one receives with genuine gratitude, one actually gives back to the giver at the same time. It is a feeling we all recognize when we make a gift to someone who receives it with joy and appreciation. We may have given them something physical, but they in turn have given us something spiritual. This is why one of the most effective ways we can experience happiness is to be generous toward others.

This principle applies also to our relationship with God. There is nothing we have that God needs. What do we have that we can give Him? Everything we have initially came from Him anyway. But, there is one thing we can give to God, and that is our gratitude. This is the one thing He cannot give Himself. It can only be given by us.

This principle of giving while at the same time receiving is taught be the Hebrew word for 'give' – נתן (*natan*). Note two things about this word. It begins and ends with *nun* (נ), the letter of humility. Also, it is spelled the same forward and backward. This illustrates that when we give, something is also given back.

Downfall, Humility, and Freedom

Nun (נ), the letter signifying humility, is a fitting letter with which to end this second series of Hebrew letters. One of the results of walking in faith is brokenness and humility, which allow the Holy Spirit to refine God's character within us. Freedom

---

[16] Leviticus 25:8-13
[17] Munk, op.cit, pg. 158
[18] Matthew 10:8

comes only through obedience to God and the only way to obey Him is to obey His Word. This requires humility. Not only does humility allow us to more fully appropriate God's Word, but God's Word also helps us to develop humility. Consider the following two passages:

> "He humbled you and let you be hungry, and fed you with manna which you did not know, nor did your fathers know, that He might make you understand that man does not live by bread alone, but man lives by everything that proceeds out of the mouth of Adonai."[19]

> "In the wilderness He fed you manna which your fathers did not know, that He might humble you and that He might test you, to do good for you in the end."[20]

Notice that in the first passage humility was required before God would give manna, while in the second, manna was given in order to produce humility. Manna is generally considered a picture of our spiritual food – God's Word.[21] Humility gives us access to God's manna, and God's manna in turn helps us develop true humility. This is also illustrated by the fact that *mem* (מ) and *nun* (נ) together spell מן – manna.

The Final *Nun*

Nun's final form graphically illustrates the connection between humility and God's Word. As you can see, the normal form of *nun* (נ) is bent over, which, according to the Sages, suggests humility.[22] On the other hand, the final form of *nun* (ן) stands straight and tall suggesting that the man who is humble in this life will stand tall at the judgment.[23] But, the final *nun* used in Torah scrolls looks quite different from that used in everyday print. In a Torah scroll it appears as an elongated *zayin* (ז), as shown below.

---

[19] Deuteronomy 8:3
[20] Deuteronomy 8:16
[21] John 6:58. *Manna* signifies the written Word as well as the incarnate Word, Yeshua.
[22] R' Schneur Zalman of Liadi, Likute: Torah 5:45ff. As cited in The Alef-Beit, op.cit.
[23] Compare Proverbs 18:12

As we learned in Chapter 7, *zayin* (whose name means 'weapon') represents the sword of the spirit which is the Word of God. In the same way, the humble man whose life is submitted to God will find himself as one in whom the Word of God is enlarged. His life will be one that is entirely transformed because his mind has been transformed by the indwelling Word.[24] Let us close this chapter with Paul's advice:

> *Do nothing from selfishness or empty conceit, but with humility of mind regard one another as more important than yourselves. Do not merely look out for your own personal interests, but also for the interests of others. Have this attitude in yourselves which was also in Messiah Yeshua, who, although He existed in the form of God, did not regard equality with God a thing to be grasped, but emptied Himself, taking the form of a bond-servant, and being made in the likeness of men. Being found in appearance as a man, He humbled Himself by becoming obedient to the point of death, even death on a cross.*[25]

Count Messiah's descending steps of humility:

> *Being in the form of God…*
> *Emptied Himself…*
> *Taking the form of a bond-servant…*
> *Being made in the likeness of men…*
> *He humbled Himself…*
> *Becoming obedient to death…*
> *Even death on a cross.*

Messiah descended in seven steps that ended in *"death on a cross"*. His humility was perfect and complete, giving Himself completely for our sakes. No being has ever traversed such a distance from glory to shame.

Though the majority of orthodox Judaism does not recognize Yeshua as the Messiah, they nevertheless recognize that Messiah will be a man of incredible humility. Consider the following:

> *The unique quality of Mashiach is that he will be humble. Though he will be the ultimate in greatness and will teach Torah to the Patriarchs and to Moshe Rabeinu,*

---

[24] Romans 12:2
[25] Philippians 2:3-8

peace be upon him, nonetheless he will be the ultimate in humility and self-nullification, teaching even simple folk.[26]

Returning to Paul's description of Messiah, observe in this passage (beginning with the bottom line) the seven stages of Messiah's glorification by the Father:

To the glory of God the Father.[27]
And every tongue confess that Yeshua the Messiah is Lord,..
And under the earth,...
And on earth...
At the name of Yeshua every knee will bow, of those...in heaven...
Bestowed on Him the name which is above every name, so that...
God highly exalted Him, and...

Truly, the seven steps of humiliation exemplify the bent shape of *nun*, while the seven steps of glorification exemplify the tall *zayin*-like shape of the final *nun*. Though Yeshua lived a life of humility culminating in a criminal's death on a cross, the story did not end there. His humiliation was followed by His glorification. And like the final *nun* which is found only at the end of a word, the Messiah's glorification will display to the universe His perfection as the Word of God made flesh. Truly this passage demonstrates the principle recorded by James, *"Humble yourselves in the presence of the Lord, and He will exalt you."*[28]

---

[26] Schneerson, Rabbi Yosef Yitzchak, HaYom Yom, pg. 75. (*"Moshe Rabeinu"* means "Moses our teacher".)
[27] Philippians 2:9-11
[28] James 4:10

Series Three

Promises and Warnings

15

ס | *Samech*

Supporting the Fallen

The Samech said: "O Lord, may it be Thy will to begin the creation with me, for Thou art called samech, the Upholder of all that fall". But God replied: "You are needed right where you are; you must continue to uphold all that fall."
Midrash Rabbah

A Letter of Support

With *samech* (ס) we begin our third series of letters, a series containing blessings, promises and warnings. *Samech's* name means to 'lean upon' or 'support'. It is fitting that *nun* (נ), symbolizing humility and downfall, should be followed by the letter which brings 'support'. As discussed in the previous chapter, the relationship of these two letters is illustrated by Psalm 145 in which the verses are ordered alphabetically as an acrostic. The fourteenth verse (which begins with *samech*) states:

> "Adonai upholds all who fall
> and raises up all who are bowed down."[1]

If we keep in mind how *nun* (נ) signifies downfall and humility, we could insert these letters as reminders like this:

> "Adonai upholds (ס) all who fall (נ)

---

[1] Psalm 145:14. The word 'uphold' in this verse is סומך (*someich*), which is from the root סמך (*samech*).

and raises up (ס) all who are bowed down (נ)."

Interestingly, the letters *nun* (נ) and *samech* (ס) together spell the word נס (*nes*) which means both 'miracle' and 'banner'. Sometimes when God comes to our rescue He does so in a miraculous way. After all, to *"uphold all who fall"* or to *"raise up all who are bowed down"* is one of the purposes of God's miracles. Likewise, this miracle of God's tender love and support in our lives is the 'banner' that displays to the world the kind of savior God truly is. As David wrote, *"You have given a banner (*נס*, nes) to those who fear You, that it may be displayed because of the truth."*[2]

We also see how *samech* (ס) symbolizes support when we consider that the foundation of Solomon's Temple was 60 cubits in length,[3] and *samech* (ס) has a numerical value of 60.

The Priestly Connection

The strength of *samech* (ס) is demonstrated in several ways which are closely related to the work and ministry of the Levitical priests. I say this because *samech*'s name – סמך – appears in the Torah in its root form most often in accounts describing the priests laying hands on the head of a sacrificial animal. The placing of a priest's hands on the sacrifice is phrased וסמך ידו (*v'smach yadoh*, "*...and he placed his hands...*"). Since *samech* (סמך) means to 'lean upon' or 'support', the word *v'smach* suggests that a priest did not merely lay his hands on the animal's head, but that he leaned his weight upon it – "*...and he supported [himself with] his hands...*".

Another connection between *samech* (ס) and the priestly office is found in the priestly blessing found in Numbers. This is often called the Aaronic blessing because it is the one by which God commanded Aaron to bless the people.

> *Adonai bless you, and keep you;*
> *Adonai make His face shine on you and be gracious to you;*
> *Adonai lift up His countenance on you, and give you peace.*[4]

This blessing is a standard fixture in synagogue liturgy. It is rare that one would attend a Sabbath service without hearing this blessing pronounced. The Sages see a number of connections between this blessing and the letter *samech*. But, to understand these connections we must look at this blessing as it appears in Hebrew.

---

[2] Psalm 60:4
[3] 2 Chronicles 3:3
[4] Numbers 6:24-26

יברכך יהוה וישמרך
יאר יהוה פניו אליך ויחנך
ישא יהוה פניו אליך וישם לך שלום

First, notice that the three lines of this blessing contain a total of 60 letters (15, 20, and 25 respectively) which equals the numerical value of ס. Next, note that the total number of words – fifteen – is the ordinal value of the letter ס (2 x 3 x 10 = 60; 2 + 3 + 10 = 15).

The Jewish Sages suggest that the sixty letters comprising the priestly blessing are what Solomon alluded to when he wrote:

> "Behold, it is the traveling couch of Solomon. Sixty mighty men around it, of the mighty men of Israel. All of them are wielders of the sword, expert in war. Each man has his sword at his side, guarding against the terrors of the night."[5]

We must understand that the priestly blessing's significance lies in the fact that it is the only blessing commanded by God for use by the priests. Therefore, its sixty letters are viewed as sixty warriors prepared to do battle in defense of God's people. Let us never underestimate the protective influence of God's blessing when it is declared in faith and obedience.

Surrounded with Protection

Samech's protective influence is also seen in the fact that it is the only one of the twenty-two regular letters that is a fully enclosed shape.[6] This is thought to picture God's surrounding perimeter of protection. Additionally, the first use of *samech* (ס) in the Bible is in the word הסבב (*hasovev*), meaning 'to surround' or 'encircle'.[7]

As *samech*'s (ס) name means 'to support' and its shape is one that surrounds, the promise of God in this letter is that He is omnipresent and thus able to surround, support, and protect us. The Bible is replete with God's promises to this effect:

> *For surely, Adonai, You bless the righteous;*
> *You surround them with Your favor as with a shield.*[8]

---

[5] Song of Songs 3:7-8
[6] The only other letter that forms a fully enclosed shape is the final form of *mem* (ם).
[7] Genesis 2:11
[8] Psalm 5:12

You are my hiding place; You preserve me from trouble;
  You surround me with songs of deliverance.[9]

As the mountains surround Jerusalem,
  So Adonai surrounds His people from this time forth and forever.[10]

Do not fear, for I am with you;
  Do not anxiously look about you, for I am your God.
I will strengthen you, surely I will help you.
  Surely I will uphold you with My righteous right hand.[11]

Samech's Warning

Samech holds a warning for us (as well as a promise) by virtue of its entirely enclosed shape. Because we are surrounded and protected by God, it is unnecessary for us to surround and protect our existence with self. We must guard against becoming 'closed in' and cut off from God by self-interest. If samech (סמך) is spelled backwards, it renders the word כמס (*kamas*) meaning 'concealed' or 'stored away'. If we lack faith in God's surrounding protection, we become prone to fears and insecurities which cause us to conceal ourselves from Him and from others.

Several Hebrew words indicating things that are closed off or hidden begin with *samech* (ס). Some examples are:

סתר	*satar*	'hiddenness'
סוד	*sod*	'secret'
סגר	*sagar*	'to close'

Let us take care to learn the lesson of the *samech* so that we will not suffer the consequences of being cut off from God's life-giving fellowship and protection.

The Conclusion

A cursory reading of Ecclesiastes can be a somewhat depressing experience, but I think this was Solomon's intention. After all, the constant refrain of Ecclesiastes is

---

[9] Psalm 32:7
[10] Psalm 125:2
[11] Isaiah 41:10

"under the sun", referring to the futility of mere physical existence in the physical world. However, when we come to the end of the book, Solomon provides an uplifting bit of advice that points us away from the physical and toward the spiritual. Here is the passage:

> *The conclusion, when all has been heard, is: fear God and keep His commandments, because this applies to every person.*[12]

An oversize *samech* is found here in the word סוֹף (*sof*) which means 'end' or 'conclusion'. It is as if Solomon is drawing a circle around what really matters in this life – fearing God and keeping His commandments. We know from Proverbs that fearing God is the beginning of wisdom, and keeping His commandments is the source of blessings.[13] By these two things, we can free ourselves from the limitations of only what exists "under the sun" and begin to walk with God in the realm of the spiritual.

If we will heed the lessons of *samech*, then we will not be guilty of smothering the light God has given us. Let us open ourselves instead to the Lord's gracious gift of Himself and to the service He would have us render to others. Then the blessing of our High Priest – Yeshua – will become a reality in our lives.

> *Adonai bless you, and keep you;*
> > *Adonai make His face shine on you and be gracious to you;*
> > *Adonai lift up His countenance on you, and give you peace.*

---

[12] Ecclesiastes 12:13
[13] Proverbs 9:10 / Deuteronomy 11:26-27 / Psalm 112:1

16

ע | *Ayin*

The Window of the Soul

"Only he who can see the invisible can do the impossible."
FRANK GAINES

The name of the letter *ayin* (ע) means 'eye' and is formed in such a way that the two strokes at the top of the letter resemble two eyes. In pre-Temple times this letter was circular in shape – O – which likewise resembles an eye. The Bible has much to say about the eye, and many of these lessons are illustrated by the letter *ayin* (ע). However, we shall begin our study of *ayin* (ע) by exploring its strong connections to three other letters of the alphabet. As we explore them, we shall discover both the promises and warnings represented by this letter.

Connection #1: The Word and the Spirit

Ayin (ע) is constructed from two Hebrew letters which we have already studied – *zayin* (ז) on the left attached to an enlarged *yud* (י) on the right.[1] It appears in Torah scrolls as shown below:

You may recall from our previous studies that *zayin* (ז – the 'weapon') represents the

---

[1] This is according to the *Mishnah Berurah*, the definitive halachic guide for Ashkenazic Jewry which includes a description of the proper formation of the letters for *tefillin* (phylacteries). Mishnah Berurah, vol. 1(B), pgs. 255-309 (Philipp Feldheim Inc., 1992).

Word of God, while *yud* (י – the only letter that 'hovers' above the line) represents the spirit of God. By combining these two letters to form *ayin*, God is illustrating that if we will walk according to His Word (ו) and His spirit (י), then we will have eyes (ע) to truly see Him. Therefore...

> If my spirit is filled with His spirit (represented by the י)...
> And my mind is filled with His Word (represented by ו)...
> Then my vision (represented by ע) will be filled with Him.

This principle is seen in what Yeshua said concerning true worship. He said that those who worship God must do so *"in spirit (י) and truth (ו) for such people the Father seeks (ע) to be His worshippers."*[2] These two balancing principles – the Word and the spirit – not only effect our own eyes but God's eyes as well. Here we are told that the eyes of God are upon those who walk in the spirit and the Word. The Bible instructs us to *"...walk by faith, not by sight."*[3] Faith, however, must be grounded in something reliable and, in the case of the believer, must be placed in God's Word (ו) so that we may receive the guidance of the Holy Spirit (י).

These truths are also borne out by the fact that in Aramaic the word *ayin* (עין) means 'sheep', and according to Jewish belief the "eye of the sheep is continuously looking towards its shepherd while the eye of the shepherd is continually watching over his sheep."[4]

True sight results from knowledge of the Word and sensitivity to the spirit. This is borne out by the gematria of the two letters which comprise *ayin*. *Zayin* (ז) has a numeric value of seven, and *yud* (י) ten. If multiplied, these two numbers equal 70, which is also the numeric value of the letter *ayin* (ע).[5]

Connection #2: The Power of Silence

Ayin (ע) also bears a strong connection to the letter *aleph* (א) – the first letter of the alphabet. *Aleph*, the 'Lord and Master' of the alphabet, is similar to *ayin* in that they are both silent letters. An important lesson is to be learned from this. We know that *aleph* represents YHVH – the one true God – but why did He also designate *ayin* as a

---

[2] John 4:23
[3] 2 Corinthians 5:7
[4] The Alef-Beit, pg. 224. (Aramaic is a Semitic language closely related to Hebrew and was the common tongue in first-century Israel. Aramaic is also written using Hebrew letters.)
[5] (ז = 7, י = 10; 7 x 10 = 70 = ע)

second silent letter? The answer can be found in the Psalm that says: *"Cease and know that I am God."*[6] The letter representing God and the letter representing sight are both silent because it is only in stillness, silence and "ceasing" that we may truly know Him.

Because the world is a noisy place (just as our enemy wants it) we must learn to retreat into necessary silence (even if it means retreating to a closet) so that we may experience stillness with God. Only in silent intimacy do we grow to know Him as He is. This is also illustrated by the fact that the word עין (*ayin*) means 'a spring' of water. When we commune with God in silence we are able to drink deeply from the source of living water and our thirst for meaning will be satisfied.[7]

Connection #3: An Effective Witness

Another letter that is also constructed from a *yud* (י) and a *zayin* (ז) is the letter *gimel* (ג), which pictures the Holy Spirit as messenger to those in need. Looking closely at *gimel* as it appears in Torah scrolls, you will see how it is comprised of a *zayin* (ז) leaning on a *yud* (י).

In Connection #1 we learned that we must be filled with both God's spirit and God's Word. In Connection #2 we learned that we truly come to know God as we practice being silent before Him. Both of these truths will equip us to fulfill the role illustrated by *gimel* (ג), namely, to take the good news of Yeshua to those in need. What is the lesson *gimel* (ג) seeks to teach? As you may recall from chapter 3, *gimel* (ג) pictures a man walking westward from the 'house' (*beit*, ב) toward the 'door' (*dalet*, ד) of the needy person. We resemble *gimel* in its mission to bring the good news of Yeshua only to the degree that we know God's Word (ז) and walk in His Spirit (י). If we are filled with Bible knowledge but not with God's spirit, we shall be like a *gimel* without a 'foot' (י) – we will know the way of salvation but lack the ability to effectively impart it to others. On the other hand, if we are filled with the Holy Spirit but do not know the Scriptures, we may have zeal but without knowledge resulting in the spread of confusion. We will then resemble the foot of the gimel without the *zayin* (ז) – just a *yud* (י) wallowing in the dirt.

---

[6] Psalm 46:10
[7] John 7:37

The lessons taught by the letter *ayin* are reflected in Paul's prayer for the believers in Ephesus:

> *I pray that the eyes (ע) of your heart may be enlightened, so that you will know (ו) what is the hope of His calling, what are the riches of the glory of His inheritance in the saints, and what is the surpassing greatness of His power (י) toward us who believe...*[8]

If we will walk in His spirit, meditate upon His Word and commune with Him in quietness, then Paul's prayer will find fulfillment in our lives.

Our Spiritual Clothing

According to Jewish legend, Adam and Eve were not entirely naked while in the Garden of Eden – they glowed with God's *shekinah* glory as light radiated from their bodies. Though this is may only be a legend, it is nevertheless a beautiful one. If true, it explains Paul's words when he wrote that God sent His Son "... *in the likeness of sinful flesh.*"[9] Why not simply state that Yeshua came "in flesh"? Why add the word "sinful"? Possibly, Paul is alluding to this legend. For had Yeshua come in the likeness of "sinless" flesh, He might have walked about glowing with the light of God's glory. Talk about distracting! As Isaiah prophesied concerning the Messiah's appearance: "... *He has no stately form or majesty that we should look upon Him, nor appearance that we should be attracted to Him.*"[10]

But, Yeshua did, in fact, manifest a magnificent and glorious appearance on one occasion – when He was transfigured in the presence of Peter, James and John. Matthew records it this way:

> *And He was transfigured before them, and His face shone like the sun, and His garments became as white as light.*[11]

Based upon the legend of Adam and Eve's translucence before their fall, Jewish tradition teaches that we shall once again have bodies that will glow with God's divine presence. They celebrate this belief on Saturday evenings at the end of *Shabbat* with

---

[8] Ephesians 1:18-19
[9] Romans 8:3
[10] Isaiah 53:2
[11] Matthew 17:2

a beautiful ceremony wherein they bid farewell to the Sabbath until its arrival again the following Friday night.[12] At one point in the ceremony the participants look at the reflection of light on their fingernails. Why the fingernails? They are the only part of the body that is translucent and are viewed as a promise that just as Adam and Eve once had bodies that were luminous, one day we too will have such spiritual bodies.

But, when Adam and Eve sinned, the lights went out and they saw only their own skin and realized that they were truly naked. Hence, we, their children, also have bodies of opaque skin. I mention this because if we take the word for 'light' – אור (*or*), and substitute ע for א, we derive the word עור (*or*) 'skin'. Note that both words have the same pronunciation – *or*. Won't it be wonderful when someday this earthly *or* (עור) 'skin') is replaced with *or* (אור 'light')!

Warnings

Ayin also contains several warnings for us, especially against walking according to mere human sight. During the days of the Judges, God's primary criticism of His people was that every man did *"what was right in his own eyes"*.[13] And in the Sermon on the Mount, Yeshua refers to the 'eye' twelve times as He warned against its misuse. Let us examine some of His remarks and consider how they are illustrated by the Hebrew alphabet.

> *"If your right eye makes you stumble, tear it out and throw from you. It is better for you to lose one of the parts of your body, than for your whole body to be thrown into Gehenna."*[14]

If our conduct is dictated only by what we see, then we have little hope of seeing God's Kingdom. In Ecclesiastes, Solomon used the phrase *"under the sun"* twenty-nine times and emphasized each time that the things which we can see and pursue in this physical realm (*"under the sun"*) are all 'vanity' (הבל, *hevel*) or 'breath'. Solomon also used this word – 'vanity'/'breath' – twenty-nine times in Ecclesiastes. "Under the sun" twenty-nine times, and "vanity" (or "breath") twenty-nine times – what was Solomon trying to teach us by this?

The phrase "under the sun" (תחת השמש, *tachat hashemesh*) is a reference to the limitations of this physical world. The word "vanity"/"breath" (הבל, *hevel*) is a

---

[12] This ceremony is called *Havdalah*, meaning 'separation'.
[13] Judges 17:6 / 21:25
[14] Matthew 5:29

reference to the brevity of time. A world limited by this space and time is not a world that can truly satisfy the soul breathed into us by the immeasurable and eternal Creator.

הבל = "breath' or 'vanity' (29x) = brevity of TIME
תחת השמש = "under the sun" (29x) = limitations of SPACE

We must look beyond the limitations of this world and the brevity of this earthly life to find true satisfaction for our souls. This lesson is demonstrated by substituting an *aleph* (א) in place of its silent twin, *ayin* (ע), in the spelling of the word עין (*ayin*, 'eye'). This substitution renders the word אין (*ein*) which means 'nothingness', 'falsehood', or 'emptiness'. This illustrates that without God (א) in our lives, what the physical eye sees is really nothing.

עין = 'eye'
אין = 'nothing'

Paul wrote, *"While we look not at the things which are seen, but at the things which are not seen. For the things which are seen are temporal, but the things which are not seen are eternal."*[15]

A Good Eye

Yeshua taught:

> *"The eye is the lamp of the body. So then if your eye is good, your whole body will be full of light. But if you eye is evil, your whole boy will be full of darkness. If then the light that is in you is darkness, how great is the darkness! No one can serve two masters, for either he will hate the one and love the other, or he will be devoted to one and despise the other. You cannot serve God and wealth."*[16]

---

[15] 2 Corinthians 4:18
[16] Matthew 6:22-24

The terms Yeshua used in this passage – "good eye" and "evil eye" – are common Hebrew idioms. In Jewish tradition an *ayin tovah* ("good eye") equals generosity, and an *ayin ra'ah* ("evil eye") equals greed. A greedy man whose eyes are closed to others is full of darkness since he is turned in upon himself. Paul warns us not to be self-absorbed, but counsels, *"…do not merely look out for your own interests, but also for the interests of others."*[17] The generous person looks to the needs of others and thus is full of light, radiating goodness wherever he goes.

In light of the above, it is interesting to note that in Hebrew the words for 'rich man' (עָשִׁיר, *ashiyr*) and 'poor man' (עָנִי, *ani*) both begin with *ayin* (ע). Perhaps God is trying to teach us that our prosperity (or lack of it) may depend upon the way we use our eyes. Let us never use our eyes to feed our greed, nor pray to God to satisfy it.

The person who only looks upon the outward appearance of people and things is profoundly blind to the greater reality. He sees only the surface, and not the depths. We noted earlier that the word אוֹר (*or*) 'light' is a homophone for עוֹר (*or*) 'skin'. Interestingly, if we change the pronunciation of the word for 'skin' (עוֹר) to *iveir*, it no longer means 'skin'. It means 'blind'. As I said, people who look only at the outward appearance – the 'skin' – of people and things, are profoundly 'blind' to the greater reality.

A further study of *ayin* (ע) reveals a powerful and dangerous source of deception which lies behind the eyes. Let us first explore the truths in the following passage:

> *"Why do you look at the speck that is in your brother's eye, but do not notice the log that is in your own eye? Or how can you say to your brother, 'Let me take the speck out of your eye,' and behold, the log is in your own eye? You hypocrite, first take the log out of your own eye, and then you will see clearly to take the speck out of your brother's eye."*[18]

In this passage Yeshua alludes to several ungodly character traits: criticism, self-righteousness, hypocrisy, jealousy, pride, and spiritual blindness. How can a person with a log in his eye even begin to see a speck in someone else's? How can we hope to correct an error in others that is so blatant in ourselves? Self-deception is the most powerful deception of all. It makes a person blind to his own faults while at the same time making him painfully aware of the same faults in others.

This brings us once again to the need for studying and obeying the Word of God

---

[17] Philippians 2:4
[18] Matthew 7:3-5

so that we will be as those who not only walk in the light but are also filled with light. If we do not walk in the light of God's Word, we will be like the person described by James:

> *But prove yourselves doers of the Word, and not merely hearers who delude themselves. For if anyone is a hearer of the Word and not a doer, he is like a man who looks at his natural face in a mirror. For once he has looked at himself and gone away, he has immediately forgotten what kind of person he was.*[19]

This person probably would not remember seeing the plank in his own eye even after the mirror had faithfully reflected its presence. Satan intends to blind us with falsehoods so that we cannot see the truth. Paul warns of this when he writes: *"...the god of this age has blinded the minds of the unbelieving so that they might not see the light of the gospel of the glory of Messiah, who is the image of God."*[20]

Let us be careful in how we use our eyes. We must take custody of them so that we will not repeat the sin of Eve who "*... saw that the tree was good for food, and that it was a delight to the eyes...*".[21] Eve did not perceive the forbidden fruit as good for food until after she began to entertain Satan's lie. But, once Eve yielded up the control of her eyes, she also yielded control of her actions.

The Sages claim that the power of Satan lies behind the eye. This statement is based on what happens when the first two letters of עין are shifted one letter to the left in the alphabet. When we shift the letter ע one letter over to ס, and we shift י one letter over to ט, we derive סטן (*satan*) – a homophone of *Satan* (שטן). Truly, the deceptive power of Satan (סטן) does literally lie behind the eye (עין).

...פעסנמלכיטח...
...פעסנמלכיטח...

It was for the purpose of directing their eyes to the truth that God commanded Israel to wear *tzitzit* ('tassels') on the corners of their garments. These were to be constant reminders before their eyes to remember His commandments.

---

[19] James 1:22-24
[20] 2 Corinthians 4:4
[21] Genesis 3:6

"It will be tzitzit (ציצת) for you to look at and remember all the commandments of Adonai, so as to do them and not follow after your own heart and your own eyes, after which you played the harlot."[22]

Whether or not you wear *tzitzit* on the corners of your garments, there is nevertheless something upon which you are directed to fix your eyes, as stated by the author of Hebrews: *Fixing our eyes on Yeshua, the author and perfecter of faith, who for the joy set before Him endured the cross, despising the shame, and has sat down at the right hand of the throne of God.*[23]

---

[22] Numbers 15:39
[23] Hebrews 12:2

17

פ, ף | *Peh*

The Power of Speech

"Adonai, open my lips, that my mouth may declare Your praise."
PSALM 51:15

The Power of Speech

Following *ayin* (ע) the 'eye', is *peh* (פ) the 'mouth'. This sequence illustrates the principle that only after one sees and understands should one open one's mouth and speak.

The order of the letters in this series – *samech* (ס), *ayin* (ע), and *peh* (פ) teach an important priority:

> ס = *Support* – strength and containment of one's thoughts and ideas
> ע = *Eyes* – examination of one's thoughts and ideas
> פ = *Mouth* – resulting speech and action

This pattern agrees with the verse which commands the wearing of *tefillin* (phylacteries):

> *"Moreover, it will serve you as a sign on your arm [ס] and as a reminder between your eyes [ע], so that Adonai's Torah may be in your mouth [פ]; for with a strong*

hand Adonai brought you out of Egypt."[1]

Peh has two forms: the closed (פ) and the open (ף). The closed form is used at the beginning and in the middle of words, while only at the end of a word is an open form used. The obvious lesson here again is: learn to keep silent (פ) before you open your mouth (ף).

Peh (פ) is constructed from a *kaf* (כ) which symbolizes a 'cup' (כוס, *kos*) or 'container' (כלי, *kli*). But, notice what is in this container – a *yud* (י) symbolizing the Holy Spirit and spirituality. The *yud* (י) in the *peh* (פ) illustrates that the mouth should 'contain' only words of godliness. Our speech should be controlled by God's spirit. When the mouth becomes a vessel (כ) ruled by the spirit (י), then His Word (ב) will be found there, which, in the case of *peh*, is literally true. Look inside the *peh* (פ) below and you will see what I mean.

Peh → בפ ← Beit

Notice the silhouette of a *beit* (ב) inside the פ. In Torah scrolls, every closed *peh* is formed this way. This is a constant reminder of God's command to Joshua:

> *"This Book of the Torah (ב) shall not depart from your mouth (פ), but you shall meditate on it day and night, so that you may be careful to do according to all that is written in it. For then you will make your way prosperous, and then you will have success."*[2]

Recall that the first letter of the Torah is an oversize *beit* (ב). In light of the fact that the outline of a ב exists inside the פ, it has been suggested that surrounding the very first letter of the Torah must be an even larger, though invisible, פ.[3] And to whom would this invisible 'mouth' (פ) belong? It would, of course, belong to God who gave His Word to the world. As Paul stated, all scripture is "God-breathed".[4] In other words, our invisible God, represented by the invisible פ, breathed forth the words of

---

[1] Exodus 13:9
[2] Joshua 1:8
[3] Alef-Beit, pg. 256.
[4] 2 Timothy 3:16

Torah, whose first letter is an enlarged ב (*beit*).

The Torah says that God spoke *"mouth to mouth"* with Moses.[5] The Torah (ב) that God spoke from His mouth (פ) went into Moses' mouth (פ) enabling him to speak God's Word (ב) to the Israelites.

But, when God called him to go to Egypt and speak to Pharaoh, Moses complained of his inability to speak, saying he was *"heavy of mouth"*.[6] God, however, did not remove his speech impediment, but instead promised that He would be with him in the midst of his weakness. God said to Moses, *"I will be with your mouth."*[7] Now think about *that* for a moment. The great "I AM" said, "I (אנכי, *anochi*) *will be with your mouth."* When one considers that the numeric value of *peh* (פ) is 80, and the numeric value of "I" (אנכי, *anochi*) is 81,[8] one can grasp the significance of God's words to Moses, *"I will be with your mouth"*, because "I" equals פ +1 (80+1). In other words, the One (1) Who was with Moses' mouth (פ) was the great "I" of "I AM" – YHVH.

Interestingly, Moses was 80 years old when he began to converse with God *"mouth to mouth"*. Likewise, we know that Yeshua was about 30 years old when He began His public ministry, and 30 is the total numerical value of the two letters which together comprise the shape of פ (כ and י).

Warnings

Perhaps it is unnecessary to warn of the dangers which accompany the misuse of the mouth since the Scriptures repeatedly warn of the consequences of an unruly tongue, such as:

> *And the tongue is a fire, the very world of iniquity. The tongue is set among our members as that which defiles the entire body, and sets on fire the course of our life, and is set on fire by Gehenna.*[9]

But the Hebrew provides some delightfully interesting insights which may benefit us.

Pharaoh, the evil tyrant from whom God delivered the Israelites, is a prime example of one who misused his mouth during several attempts to destroy the Jewish

---

[5] Numbers 12:8. Most versions mistranslate this as "face to face".
[6] Exodus 4:10
[7] Exodus 4:12
[8] א =1, נ =50, כ =20, י =10; 1 + 50 + 20 + 10 = 81.
[9] James 3:6

people. By his powers of speech he had the Jewish people enslaved, commanded that their children be cast into the Nile, made false promises to Moses, boasted against God, and initiated military operations against the Israelites as they neared the Red Sea. A study of Pharaoh's life reveals a man of evil actions and of evil speech.

The name 'Pharaoh' is spelled פרעה. The first and last letters of his name spell פה (*peh*) 'mouth', and the two letters inside Pharaoh's 'mouth' spell רע (*rah*) 'evil'. Thus we see that Pharaoh's mouth was constantly filled with evil.

As Pharaoh began to fear the Jewish people under his rule, he said, *"Come, let us deal wisely with them, lest they multiply..."*[10] In Hebrew, the phrase *"lest they multiply"* is פן ירבה (*pen yirbeh*. Note that this phrase begins with the letter פ.) Two verses later, the Torah says, *"...the more they afflicted them, the more they multiplied..."*[11] In Hebrew, the phrase *"the more they multiplied"* is כן ירבה (*chen yirbeh*). Notice that this phrase is identical to the previous one except that it begins with *kaf* (כ) instead of *peh* (פ). The Sages state that פ's 'tooth' had been pulled thus rendering it כ.

פן ירבה = "lest they multiply"
כן ירבה = "the more they multiplied"

It is an irrefutable scriptural principle that when the wicked attack the righteous, it is the wicked who are ultimately broken and the righteous who are ultimately benefited. As the Psalmist wrote: *"You have shattered the teeth of the wicked."*[12]

Moving ahead a few more verses, we read that Pharaoh embittered the Israelites' lives *"with crushing harshness"*.[13] In Hebrew the phrase *"with crushing harshness"* is בפרך (*b'pharech*). The Sages derive an insight from this by pronouncing the letter פ (*peh*) – which, as we know, means 'mouth' – so that the word reads ב-פ-רך (*b'peh rach*) which means *"by a soft mouth"* or *"with soft speech"*. This provides insight into how Pharaoh's tactics in Egypt were similar to Satan's in Eden.

The only weapon Satan has is his mouth filled with poisonous lies. Yeshua said that Satan *"is a liar and the father of lies"*.[14] Only through deception can Satan rob us of our freedom, and it is only through God's truth that freedom can be regained.

---

[10] Exodus 1:10
[11] Exodus 1:12
[12] Psalm 3:7
[13] Exodus 1:14
[14] John 8:44

So Yeshua was saying to those Jews who had believed Him, "If you continue in My word, then you are truly disciples of Mine, and you will know the truth, and the truth will make you free."[15]

Let us immerse our minds in the Word of Truth so that the enemy cannot rob us *b'peh rach* – "with soft speech". Let us also put on God's full armor so that when the enemy attempts to snap his jaws upon us he will shatter his teeth.

The drama that occurred in the Garden of Eden is actually pictured in the arrangement of the Hebrew alphabet itself. The Torah tells us that God placed two trees in the midst of the Eden – the Tree of Life, and the Tree of the Knowledge of Good and Evil. Think of these two trees as you study the Hebrew word for 'tree' (*eitz*):

עץ

We were introduced to the letter on the right in the previous chapter. It is *ayin* (ע), which means 'eye'. We learn more about the letter on the left in the next chapter. It is *tzaddi* (צ),[16] which means 'righteous'. These two letters, which somewhat resemble trees, spell the word 'tree' (*eitz*). Considering their respective meanings, we can imagine the tree on the right (which is facing left) as the Tree of Knowledge. It's name reminds us that Satan appealed to the eyes in this temptation of Adam and Eve. And, we can imagine the letter on the left (which is facing right) as the Tree of Life, since its roots are deeper, and its name means 'righteous'.

Now, let's place these two letters in their proper places in the alphabet:

. . . . ע פ צ . . . .

Do you recognize the letter between the two 'trees'? It is, of course פ (*peh*) 'mouth'. But, unlike the mouths of Adam and Eve, this mouth is ready to feed from the tree whose name means 'righteous' – the Tree of Life.

If only we can learn the lesson that is so graphically illustrated here. Let us turn our backs to the things that tempt us with our eyes, and pursue those things that are righteous and life giving. Let us also remember the words of John at the end of

---

[15] John 8:31-32
[16] Tzaddi is one of the five letters that have two forms: צ and ץ.

Revelation: *Blessed are those who wash their robes, so that they may have the right to the Tree of Life…*[17]

A Word Appropriately Spoken

Solomon wrote:

> *Like apples of gold in settings of silver is a word that is spoken appropriately.*[18]

How can our words be like golden apples? And, what are the *"settings of silver"* to which Solomon refers?

In Hebrew, 'gold' (זהב, *zahav*) ends with ב, and the word for 'silver' (כסף, *ceseph*) ends with פ. Can you see how *gold* (ב) belongs in settings of *silver* (פ)? If you recall how *beit* (ב) is silhouetted inside the letter *peh* (פ), then you will be able to understand Solomon's allegory.

When the words of wisdom from God's Torah (ב) reside in mouths (פ) that are surrendered to His Lordship, then the resulting words will be *"fitly spoken"* like apples of gold in settings of silver.

> *Adonai, who may abide in Your tent? Who may dwell in Your holy hill?*
> *He who walks with integrity, and works righteousness,*
> *And speaks truth in his heart, and does not slander with his tongue …*[19]

---

[17] Revelation 22:14
[18] Proverbs 25:11
[19] Psalm 15:1-3

18

צ,ץ | *Tzaddi*

The Righteousness of the Saints

"The wicked man flees though no one pursues,
but the righteous are as bold as a lion."

PROVERBS 28:1

The Principle of the Menorah

If you have read this book in chapter sequence, you will have noticed that each series of seven letters is introduced by a page showing the letters atop a stylized menorah. This was not done merely for aesthetic purposes. Rather, it was done because the pattern of the menorah is found throughout the scriptures. Before considering the letter *tzaddi* (צ), which stands at the center of our third and last series of letters, it is necessary to introduce the remarkable principle of the menorah.

The golden menorah described in Exodus 25:31-40 was a lamp fueled from a reservoir of oil in its base. The central branch supported three branches on either side, each culminating in a decorative cup supporting a flame. The purpose of the menorah was to provide light in the Holy Place of the Tabernacle and, later, in the Temple. The menorah is such a prevalent image of Judaism that it has become Israel's national symbol.

The predominant place given to this symbol is not by accident. God has ordained the menorah as His pattern for presenting the light of truth throughout the

Scriptures. For example, David wrote that God's Word is *"... a lamp to my feet and a light for my path."*[1] If we analyze the structure of this verse in Hebrew, its menorah pattern is revealed.

נר לרגלי דברך ואור לנתיבתי

A lamp | to my feet | (is) Your Word | and a light | to my path.

Note that this verse is comprised of only five words in Hebrew (as opposed to around 14 words in English). The middle word is דברך (*d'varecha*) *"Your word"* – which is fitting for the central branch of this menorah. The first two words are נר לרגלי (*ner l'rag'li*) *"to my feet"*, and the last two words are ואור לנתיבתי (*v'or lin'tivati*) *"and a light to my path"*. Thus, if we were to match the flow of the words to the Hebrew, the verse would read, *"A lamp to my feet is your Word, and a light to my path."*

Although the menorah described in Exodus had seven branches, a menorah may actually have any number of branches.[2] But regardless of the number of branches in a menorah, the center branch is considered to be the most important because it supports those on either side. I mention this because the Bible in general, and the Torah in particular, are constructed according to a menorah pattern. For instance, the five books of the Torah may be compared to a Menorah as shown below.

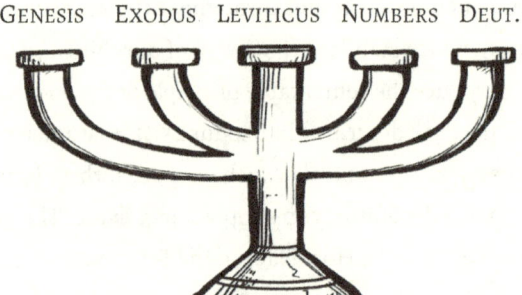

GENESIS   EXODUS   LEVITICUS   NUMBERS   DEUT.

---

[1] Psalm 119:105 The Word 'lamp' in this verse is *neer* (נר), from which we derive the word *menorah* (מנרה).
[2] The menorah used for celebrating Hanukkah, for instance, has nine branches.

In the illustration we see Leviticus standing in the center with Genesis and Exodus radiating out to one side, and Numbers and Deuteronomy radiating out to the other. As we shall see, this arrangement is not the product of human ingenuity, but is a design supported by the Hebrew scriptures in a most amazing way. Now, follow closely as we see an astounding menorah pattern revealed by this arrangement.

The illustration below contains the opening verses of Genesis. If we begin with the last letter of בראשית (*barasheit*, "In the beginning"), which is *tuv* (ת), and begin counting, we find the word *Torah* (תורה) spelled out at 50-letter intervals. You can check this yourself in the illustration. The four letters that spell תורה (*Torah*) are circled.

בראשית ברא אלהים את השמים ואת הארץ
והארץ היתה תהו ובהו וחשך על פני תהום ורוח
אלהים מרחפת על פני המים ויאמר אלהים יהי
אור ויהי אור וירא אלהים את האור כי טוב
ויבדל אלהים בין האור ובין החשך ויקרא
אלהים לאור יום ולחשך קרא לילה ויהי ערב
ויהי בקר יום אחד

The same equidistant lettering phenomenon occurs in Exodus. Beginning with the first *tuv* (ת) in Exodus, we once again find the four letters of תורה (*Torah*) spelled out at intervals of 50 letters. The following passage from Exodus 1:1-7 has the four letters of תורה (*Torah*) circled.

> וְאֵלֶּה שְׁמוֹת בְּנֵי יִשְׂרָאֵל הַבָּאִים מִצְרָיְמָה אֵת
> יַעֲקֹב אִישׁ וּבֵיתוֹ בָּאוּ רְאוּבֵן שִׁמְעוֹן לֵוִי וִיהוּדָה
> יִשָּׂשכָר זְבוּלֻן וּבִנְיָמִן דָּן וְנַפְתָּלִי גָּד וְאָשֵׁר וַיְהִי
> כָּל נֶפֶשׁ יֹצְאֵי יֶרֶךְ יַעֲקֹב שִׁבְעִים נָפֶשׁ וְיוֹסֵף הָיָה
> בְמִצְרָיִם וַיָּמָת יוֹסֵף וְכָל אֶחָיו וְכֹל הַדּוֹר הַהוּא
> וּבְנֵי יִשְׂרָאֵל פָּרוּ וַיִּשְׁרְצוּ וַיִּרְבּוּ וַיַּעַצְמוּ בִּמְאֹד
> מְאֹד וַתִּמָּלֵא הָאָרֶץ אֹתָם

We shall skip over Leviticus (the center branch of our menorah) for a moment and move on to Numbers – the fourth book of the Torah. If we examine the opening paragraph, we once again find the word *Torah* spelled out in 50-letter intervals, but with a difference. Instead of *Torah* being spelled תורה, it is spelled backward – הרות. Here is the passage (Numbers 1:1-4) with every 50th letter circled beginning with the ה (*hei*) at the end of the word משה (*Moshe*, 'Moses'):[3]

> וַיְדַבֵּר יְהוָה אֶל מֹשֶׁה בְּמִדְבַּר סִינַי בְּאֹהֶל מוֹעֵד
> בְּאֶחָד לַחֹדֶשׁ הַשֵּׁנִי בַּשָּׁנָה הַשֵּׁנִית לְצֵאתָם מֵאֶרֶץ
> מִצְרַיִם לֵאמֹר שְׂאוּ אֶת רֹאשׁ כָּל עֲדַת בְּנֵי יִשְׂרָאֵל
> לְמִשְׁפְּחֹתָם לְבֵית אֲבֹתָם בְּמִסְפַּר שֵׁמוֹת כָּל זָכָר
> לְגֻלְגְּלֹתָם מִבֶּן עֶשְׂרִים שָׁנָה וָמַעְלָה כָּל יֹצֵא צָבָא
> בְּיִשְׂרָאֵל תִּפְקְדוּ אֹתָם לְצִבְאֹתָם אַתָּה וְאַהֲרֹן וְאִתְּכֶם
> יִהְיוּ אִישׁ אִישׁ לַמַּטֶּה אִישׁ רֹאשׁ לְבֵית אֲבֹתָיו

Proceeding to the last book of the Torah – Deuteronomy – we find an arrangement similar to that in Numbers. Once again, the word *Torah* is spelled backward (הרות), but this time at internals of 49 letters instead of 50. Here is the passage (Deuteronomy 1:5-8) beginning with the ה (*hei*) at the beginning of the word (התורה, *ha-torah*) "the Torah":

---

[3] It is assumed that the reason God chose to start the count from the *hei* (ה) of Moses' name rather than one of the *hei*'s that appear previously in the passage is that the Torah was given *through* Moses.

צ - Tzaddi | 203

> בְּאֶרֶץ מוֹאָב הוֹאִיל מֹשֶׁה בֵּאֵר אֶת הַתּוֹרָה הַזֹּאת
> לֵאמֹר יְהוָה אֱלֹהֵינוּ דִּבֶּר אֵלֵינוּ בְּחֹרֵב לֵאמֹר רַב
> לָכֶם שֶׁבֶת בָּהָר הַזֶּה פְּנוּ וּסְעוּ לָכֶם וּבֹאוּ הַר
> הָאֱמֹרִי וְאֶל כָּל שְׁכֵנָיו בָּעֲרָבָה בָהָר וּבַשְּׁפֵלָה
> וּבַנֶּגֶב וּבְחוֹף הַיָּם אֶרֶץ הַכְּנַעֲנִי וְהַלְּבָנוֹן עַד הַנָּהָר
> הַגָּדֹל נְהַר פְּרָת רְאֵה נָתַתִּי לִפְנֵיכֶם אֶת הָאָרֶץ בֹּאוּ
> וּרְשׁוּ אֶת הָאָרֶץ אֲשֶׁר נִשְׁבַּע יְהוָה לַאֲבֹתֵיכֶם

Thus far we have seen the principle of the menorah demonstrated in the arrangement of these four books of the Torah: Genesis and Exodus comprise the two branches on one side of the Menorah, while Numbers and Deuteronomy comprise the two branches on the opposite side. In the first two branches the word *Torah* is spelled forward, but in the opposite two branches it is spelled backward. This arrangement suggests that *Torah* is 'radiating' outward in both directions from the center branch – Leviticus.

Let's take a look now at the central branch of our menorah – Leviticus. Its first line is pictured below:

> וַיִּקְרָא אֶל מֹשֶׁה וַיְדַבֵּר יְהוָה אֵלָיו מֵאֹהֶל מוֹעֵד

Instead of the word תורה (*Torah*) spelled out in 50- or 49-letter intervals, we find God's name – יהוה (*YHVH*) – spelled out in eight-letter intervals. The picture is now complete. From *YHVH* radiates the books of the Torah.

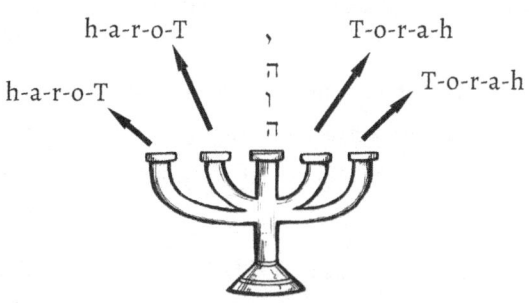

Why is the name of *YHVH* in Leviticus spelled at intervals of eight letters? As we have learned, the number eight is the number of life, and the name of the 8th letter of the alphabet – *chet* (ח) – is traditionally a symbol for life.

It is beyond the scope of this chapter to explore all of the possible reasons why an interval of fifty was employed for spelling the word 'Torah' in three of the branches. But one reason for the 50-letter intervals may be because the Torah was given to Moses on the 50th day after the exodus from Egypt. In the biblical calendar this day is called *Shavuot*. In Christianity it is known as *Pentecost*. On the other hand, the number 49 (used for the intervals in Deuteronomy) is equal to 7 x 7, and seven is used frequently in the Bible to signify completion and wholeness. Thus, Deuteronomy brings the Torah to completion.

Before we return to the letter *tzaddi* (צ) and discuss its relationship to the menorah, it is necessary to look at one more example of the principle of the menorah in Scripture. This one is contained in the opening sentence of the Bible as shown below.

בראשית ברא אלהים (את) השמים ואת הארץ

Here we see that the first sentence of the Bible – *"In the beginning, God created the heavens and the earth"* – contains seven words in Hebrew. Although it is tempting to discuss other features of the menorah pattern created by these seven words, we will direct our attention only to the word which stands at the very center of this sentence – את (*et*). Note that it is spelled using the first and last letters of the alphabet.[4] In Revelation, Yeshua is called the *Alpha* (A) and *Omega* (Ω). These are the first and last letters of the Greek alphabet – the language in which the Apostolic Scriptures were written. Therefore, *alpha* and *omega* (A Ω) in Greek correspond to *aleph* and *tuv* (את) in Hebrew.[5] Do you grasp the significance of this? Here, in the very first verse of the Bible stands Yeshua the *Alpha* and *Omega* (A Ω) – or *Aleph* and *Tuv* (את) – as the focal point of creation.

John may have had this in mind when he wrote of Yeshua: *"All things came into being through Him, and apart from Him nothing came into being that has come into being. In Him was life, and the life was the Light of men."*[6] Could the picture be more perfect? In

---

[4] *Et* (את) is an untranslatable Hebrew word which always points to the direct object of a sentence.
[5] Revelation 22:13
[6] John 1:3-4

this menorah we see creation radiating from Yeshua (את) – the *"Light of men"* and the Light of the world.

I have introduced the principle of the menorah because the Hebrew alphabet itself is constructed according to this divine pattern. As previously discussed, the alphabet consists of three series of seven letters each, plus the last letter, *tuv* – ת (which stands alone for reasons we shall discuss later). Each series of letters is arranged according to the principle of the menorah with the center letter of each series embodying the heart of that series' message. Let's briefly review the first two series of letters and consider the supporting central branch of each one.

Our first series of letters introduced the story of the gospel. The letter at the center from which the other six letters radiate is *dalet* (ד) the 'door', and Yeshua is the door through whom man comes to God. This is the heart of the message contained in the first series of letters.

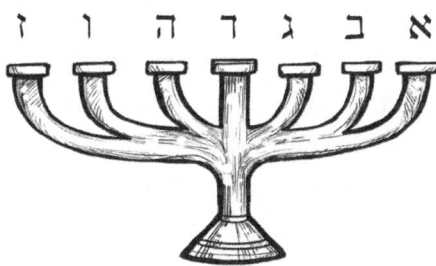

Our second series of letters speaks of the believer's life of service. At the center of this series we find the letter *kaf* (כ), which means 'palm' of the hand. As discussed in chapter 11, the palm is the Hebrew symbol for all work and service. From this letter radiate the six letters comprising the message dealing with maturity, good works, and service to God and to others.

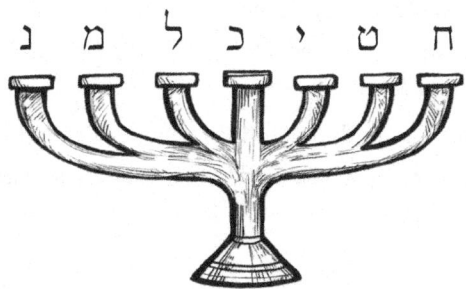

Our third, and final series, is comprised of the letters filled with promises and encouragement as well as warnings, has *tzaddi* (צ) at its center. From *tzaddi* radiate both the promises awaiting the individual who hungers and thirsts after righteousness, as well as the warnings which accompany unrighteous living.

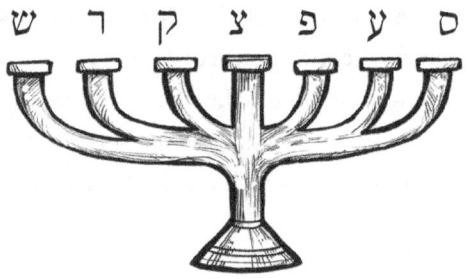

Tzaddi (צ) is an exceedingly important letter because its name – צדי (*tzaddi*) – is the root of the word צדיק (*tzaddik*), which means 'righteous man'. It is fitting that *tzaddi* (צ) should follow *ayin* (ע) rather than precede it since *"...the eyes of the Lord are toward the righteous"*.[7] And one can easily see that the *ayin* (ע) is facing the left toward *tzaddi* (צ).

Seeking Righteousness

Though *tzaddi* (צ) is the root of the word meaning 'righteous', *tzaddi* itself comes from the root צוד (*tzod*) meaning 'to hunt'. Understandably, righteousness is something that everyone should seek after. Yeshua encouraged this when He said, *"Blessed are those who hunger and thirst for righteousness, for they shall be satisfied."*[8] Seeking worldly pleasures and reward should not be the practice of a true believer because, although pleasure and earthly reward are not inherently evil, the pursuit of them leads to ruin and destruction.[9] Yeshua promised, *"But seek first His kingdom and His righteousness, and all these things will be added to you."*[10]

Along with having his needs met, the righteous individual will also receive divine protection. Solomon wrote, *"When the whirlwind passes, the wicked is no more, but the*

---

[7] 1 Peter 3:12
[8] Matthew 5:6
[9] 1 Timothy 6:9
[10] Matthew 6:33

righteous has an everlasting foundation."[11] If we will seek God's kingdom and righteousness above all, we will be like the righteous man who remains standing after the storm has passed. This protection extends even beyond this life to the day in which we will stand before God at the Judgment. However, this is not the case with the unrighteous person. David wrote *"Therefore the wicked will not stand in the judgment, nor sinners in the assembly of the righteous."*[12]

These truths are graphically illustrated by the two forms of *tzaddi*. The normal form of this letter suggests a man kneeling with his hands uplifted to heaven: צ. But, when *tzaddi* appears at the end of a word it suggests a man standing tall with upraised arms: ץ. The Sages teach that *tzaddi* (צ) represents the humility of the righteous person in this world, and its final form – ץ – represents their great reward in the World to Come.

A Tale of Two Trees

A fascinating occurrence of the final *tzaddi* (ץ) is found in the story of the Garden of Eden. The Torah tells us that in the center of the garden God planted two trees – the Tree of Life, and the Tree of the Knowledge of Good and Evil. Eating from the first was permitted, but eating from the second was forbidden. The former would give life, but the latter would result in sin and death. Though we touched on this in the previous chapter, here we will discover another insight into the Hebrew word for 'tree' (*eitz*):

$$עץ$$

Note that the letter on the right is an *ayin* (ע) looking toward the left. And the letter on the left is a *tzaddi* (ץ) looking toward the right. Throughout the Scriptures the terms 'left' and 'right' have special significance. 'Left' always represents the physical, and 'right' always represents the spiritual.[13] Don't these two letters – ע and ץ – standing side by side look like two trees? The one on the right – ע – means 'eye' and is peering toward the left, or the 'physical'. But, the one on the left – ץ – means 'righteous'. It has deeper roots and is peering toward the right, or the 'spiritual'.

We are continually confronted with the same choice that was presented to Adam

---

[11] Proverbs 10:25
[12] Psalm 1:5
[13] For examples see Proverbs 3:16; Ecclesiastes 10:2; Matthew 6:3, 25:33.

and Eve. As they were confronted with a choice of two trees – one leading to life and one to death – so we must constantly make decisions with the same outcomes. Solomon wrote, *"There is a way which seems right to a man, but its end is the way of death."*[14] We must be cautious not to follow what is pleasant to the eye, but what is right in God's sight. Our way is the wrong way. But His way always leads to righteousness and life.

Living by Faith

This righteous letter – *tzaddi* (צ) – is formed from a *nun* (נ) with a *yud* (י) resting on its back.[15] We have learned from previous chapters that *nun* (נ) symbolizes humility and *yud* (י) symbolizes the spirit of God. The connection here is clear: a righteous man (צ) is one who is humble (נ) and upon whom the Holy Spirit (י) rests.

God desires for His people to be righteous. As we grow in righteousness we also grow in godliness, for the righteous man displays godly character in all that he says and does. The relationship between righteousness and godliness is suggested by the fact that *tzaddi* (צ) resembles the letter *aleph* (א) – the letter which represents the one true God more than any of the other Hebrew letters. Recognizing the similarity between these two letters, one noted rabbi wrote, *"The form of the tzaddi in general is the 'female' counterpart of the form of the aleph."*[16] This profound insight takes on new meaning for the believer in light of the fact that the *kahal* – those who have been made righteous (צ) through Messiah – are the bride of Messiah (א). The quote continues, *"The tzaddi (צ) represents the complete stature of the souls of Israel, while the aleph (א) the Master of the Universe [i.e. God] chooses the tzaddi (צ) to be His eternal mate."*

In three instances the Apostolic Scriptures quote the verse from Habakkuk which states, *"the righteous man will live by his faith."*[17] But what is faith? If faith is nothing more than wishful thinking, we will live our lives with our fingers crossed hoping that what we believe may actually be true. If faith is just a religion made up of rules and regulations, then we will live a life of sheer legalism. So, how can we truly *"live by faith"* if our definition of faith is flawed?

The pattern God provides us for the life of faith is found in the story of Abraham. The Torah states that he *"believed in Adonai [i.e. had faith in Him], and He credited it to him as righteousness"*.[18] But when it says, *"Abram believed in Adonai"*, what did that belief

---

[14] Proverbs 14:12
[15] Mishnah Berurah, Vol. 1B, pg. 299.
[16] Yitzchak Ginsburgh, The Alef-Beit, pg. 270.
[17] Habakkuk 2:4
[18] Genesis 15:6 (CJB)

look like? What form did Abram's faith take?

Faith is not a feeling or a set of beliefs. Everyone has those to one degree or another. But, a close examination of Abraham's life reveals that genuine faith is loving obedience to God. This kind of faith does not spring up overnight. Abraham walked with God for years before He credited Abraham's faith as righteousness. In other words, God does not ask us for a "leap of faith" but a walk of obedience. Faith is not works. But faith is the spiritual impetus that brings forth works. After all, faith without works is dead.[19]

Each time God speaks to us and we obey Him in faith, God regards it a righteous act. The hallmark of the righteous man is faithfulness – faithfulness to God's Word and to God's voice.[20] It is our godly obedience which weaves for us a garment of righteousness. God describes His bride as being clothed in fine linen. And what is this linen? It is the "righteous acts of the holy ones".[21] There is a righteousness that comes purely from grace, but there is also a righteousness that is the outworking of God's spirit through us as we cooperate with Him.

Outside of faithful obedience to God and His Word we have no righteousness of our own. Paul discovered that true righteousness comes only from pursuing Messiah in obedience, and stated his goal:

> …so that I may gain Messiah, and may be found in Him, not having a righteousness of my own derived from the Torah, but that which is through faith in Messiah, the righteousness which comes from God on the basis of faith.[22]

The root word for 'faith' is אמן (amen) – the word with which we traditionally end prayers. Amen (אמן) has a numeric value of 91.[23] This same word is also equal to צ+א.

Let us be careful to live righteously and humbly so that all the promises represented by our final series of letters may radiate from us in such a way that we can be a *menorah* in a dark world. This should be our desire. It is what Yeshua desires for us. In this way we can fully satisfy His will when He said:

> *"You are the light of the world. A city on a hill cannot be hidden. Nor does anyone*

---

[19] James 2:17, 26
[20] Exodus 15:26; 19:5-6
[21] Revelation 19:7-8
[22] Philippians 3:8-9 (CJB)
[23] א = 1, מ = 40, נ = 50; 1 + 40 + 50 = 91

light a lamp and put it under a basket, but on the lampstand, and it gives light to all who are in the house. Let your light shine before men in such a way that they may see your good works, and glorify your Father who is in heaven."[24]

---

[24] Matthew 5:14-16

19

ק | *Kof*

Holy Unto the Lord

---

*"It is a great deal better to live a holy life than to talk about it.
Lighthouses do not ring bells and fire cannon to call
attention to their shining – they just shine."*
Dwight L. Moody

A Letter of Holiness

During the days of the Temple, if one found a container marked with the letter *kof* (ק) it was assumed that its contents were consecrated. This letter was used to label sacred objects because *kof* (ק) traditionally symbolizes קדושה (*kadushah*) 'holiness'. Isaiah tells us that the angels in heaven praise God saying, *"Kadosh, kadosh, kadosh is Adonai of hosts, the whole earth is filled with His glory."*[1] Of all the letters of the alphabet, in the Jewish mind this one most specifically symbolizes holiness.

Our God is holy, and He desires holiness on behalf of His people saying, *"You shall be holy, for I – Adonai your God – am holy."*[2] But, what is holiness? And how does it differ from righteousness?[3]

Many believers have the mistaken notion that holiness and righteousness are

---

[1] Isaiah 6:3
[2] Leviticus 19:2
[3] Represented by the letter *tzaddi* (צ).

equivalent, or that holiness is merely the result of righteous living, neither of which is the truth. Righteousness must be established on the foundation of holiness. Hence, when God makes a person holy, righteous acts are to be the result. Indeed, confusion concerning righteousness and holiness arises because we misunderstand what holiness is.

In its strictest sense the word *kadosh* was a secular word having neither good nor bad connotations. To be holy – *kadosh* – essentially means to be set apart for a special purpose, regardless of whether that purpose is godly or wicked. However, most of the occurrences of this word in the *Tanach* are in regard to godly purposes.

Other terms commonly used to translate *kadosh* are 'sanctified' or 'consecrated'. Though these are considered 'religious' terms today, during Bible times they had no such religious connotations. It was over a long period of time these words eventually came to be used strictly in a religious sense. Again, the word *kadosh* – represented by the letter *kof* (ק) – simply means to set apart something or someone for a particular use or purpose. For example, when a Jewish woman becomes engaged to be married she enters a period of *kedoshin* – separation from others for the sake of her future husband. Similarly, in the book of Exodus God commanded Moses to sanctify [i.e. make *kadosh*] the altar in the Tabernacle, meaning that it was to be used only for God's purposes.[4] The Bible also speaks of people, animals, and other objects made *kadosh*.

Two Aspects of Holiness

Holiness, according to scripture, possesses two aspects which we must clearly understand. First, holiness is a state which is the result of relationship or position and not performance. Accordingly, we are made holy by our relationship with Yeshua the Holy One. Paul stated that Yeshua has become to us *"righteousness and sanctification, and redemption."*[5] The fact that we have been 'sanctified' (or, 'made holy') should not come as a surprise to us. After all, did we not come into a new relationship with God when we dedicated [i.e. 'set aside'] our lives to Him? Furthermore, the act of ritual immersion is a picture of this new relationship wherein we turned away from our past way of living and set ourselves apart – *kadosh* – to God.

That holiness is not the product of personal righteousness is best illustrated in the account of Aaron the High Priest. God instructed Moses that Aaron and the

---

[4] Exodus 40:10
[5] 1 Corinthians 1:30

priests were to be attired in *"garments of holiness"* so as *"to minister to Me"*.[6] Aaron was holy not because of personal righteousness, but because God simply chose him to be set apart to serve Him in the Tabernacle. In keeping with this, Aaron was to wear a golden head-plate inscribed with the words קדש ליהוה (*Kadosh la-YHVH*) – *"Holy unto Adonai"*.[7] Despite Aaron's role in the worship of the golden calf, Aaron went on to wear the holy garments and golden head-plate in his service to God. There is much more to be said on this subject, but we must move on to the second aspect of holiness.

Although holiness is a result of our relationship with God, there is another aspect of holiness that requires our constant maintenance. This is the part we play. In addition to the holiness described thus far, our behavior can either enhance or damage our position of holiness. The Bible's constant appeal to us is to live righteously because we have been made holy. Peter puts it best when he writes to believers:

"…who are chosen according to the foreknowledge of God the Father, by the sanctifying work of the spirit, to obey Yeshua the Messiah…"[8]

However, Paul wrote to the Romans:

"…For just as you presented your members as servants to impurity and to Torah-lessness, resulting in further Torah-lessness, so now present your members as servants to righteousness, resulting in sanctification."[9]

In essence, Peter is saying that we have been made holy in order that we may live righteously, and Paul is saying that we are to live righteously so that we may grow in holiness. Consequently, we see the aspect of being made holy as well as the aspect of developing holiness. The more one yields one's mind, time, strength and talents in service to God, the more one sets oneself apart entirely to Him in holiness.

Our pursuit of righteousness confirms the position of holiness in which God has established us. Paul put it this way:

"Not that I have already obtained it or have already become perfect, but I press on

---

[6] Exodus 28:4
[7] Exodus 28:36
[8] 1 Peter 1:1-2. The numeric value of *yud* (י, the letter which represents the Holy Spirit) is 10. The numeric value of *kof* (ק) is 100, or 10 x 10. The Holy Spirit's (י) goal is to lead us to greater holiness (ק).
[9] Romans 6:19

so that I may lay hold of that for which also I was laid hold of by Messiah Yeshua."[10]

There is a holiness whereby Yeshua takes hold of us, and there is the exercise of holiness whereby we take hold of Him. The first brings salvation, and the second brings fruitfulness. Again, God is holy and therefore commands us to be holy by separating ourselves from the standards and appetites of this world and pledging our loyalty to Him.

A Lesson from the Exodus

The aspects of holiness and righteousness are best illustrated by God's redemption of the Israelites from Egypt. When He took them out of Egypt through the body and blood of the Passover lamb, they became a holy people – set apart to God. They had a lot to learn about righteousness, but that would come later.

After a tentative journey to Mount Sinai, God gave them His Torah so that they would know how a holy and free people should live. *"... what great nation is there that has statutes and judgments as righteous as this whole Torah which I am setting before you today?"*[11] God gave His righteous laws to Israel so that they could become a righteous people.

However, forty days after Moses ascended Sinai to receive God's instruction, the people at the foot of the mountain fashioned a golden calf and engaged in the appalling sin of idol worship. But, there was one group that did not participate – the tribe of the Levites. As a reward for their righteousness, they were elevated to a level of *greater* holiness by being set apart as the priestly tribe.

In other words, all the Israelites were established as *holy* when they were separated from Egypt. But, they were not yet *righteous*. At the incident of the golden calf, the Levites responded with righteousness and were elevated to a higher degree of *holiness* by being set apart to serve as Israel's priests. I can think of no better illustration of the beautiful dance between holiness and righteousness than this. May each of us continue to grow in both of these aspects of our redemption so that we may become ever more effective servants to God.

The Marriage of Holiness and Righteousness

As holiness and righteousness are inseparable in the life of the godly person, likewise *kof* (ק) is an integral part of the word צדיק (*tzaddik*, 'righteousness one'). Note that this word begins with *tzaddi* (צ – the letter of 'righteousness') and ends with *kof* (ק – the letter of 'holiness').

---

[10] Philippians 3:12
[11] Deuteronomy 4:8

Righteousness must be wedded to holiness. When we try to be righteous apart from being holy, our righteous acts are tainted and insufficient. But when combined with holiness, righteous acts are genuinely righteous. In fact, the letters in the middle of צדיק (tzaddik, 'righteousness one') spell די (diy) 'sufficient'.[12] By the same token, when we claim holiness but do not live righteously, such 'holiness' is fruitless, lukewarm, and nauseating in God's sight.

Kof (ק) is comprised of two letters – a kaf (כ) and a ... well, there is a dispute as to what the other letter is. According to authorities, the kaf (כ) is suspended over a vav (ו). If this is correct, then the two letters that comprise kof have a total numeric value of 26 – the number of God's name YHVH.[13] Since kaf (כ) symbolizes the 'palm' of the hand, this arrangement depicts God's hand suspended over a man (depicted by the vav – ו). Could there be a more apt picture of holiness than this? One who has forsaken worldliness so as to unite with God has truly come under God's protective hand.

However, there is a second possible letter combination. In many Torah scrolls the kof (ק) is constructed as a kaf (כ) suspended over a zayin (ז) – the letter that symbolizes the sword of the spirit – God's Word. This version of kof is shown below.

Again, kaf means 'palm of the hand', thus creating a picture of a hand grasping a sword by its hilt. This provides us with another powerful image. A holy individual – ק – is an instrument of the Word (ז) in God's hand (כ). May we all be found to be such.

In Aramaic, the name of the letter kof is pronounced kufa (קופא), which means "eye of a needle". Yeshua said, *"For it is easier for a camel to go through the eye of a needle than for a rich man to enter the kingdom of God."*[14] In speaking of the eye of the needle, could Yeshua (who spoke and taught in Aramaic) have been referring to the letter kufa (ק)? Could He have been saying that it is easier for a camel to pass through a ק than for a rich man to enter the Kingdom of God? That a camel of 'holiness' has a better chance of entering God's kingdom than a man of riches? Who knows? But, it is

---

[12] The word diy (די) will be familiar to those who sing *"Dayeinu"* ("It Would Have Been Enough") at the Passover Seder.

[13] Kaf (כ) = 20 and vav (ו) = 6; 20 + 6 = 26.

[14] Luke 18:25

something to ponder.[15]

Warnings

In light of all that *kof* teaches concerning holiness, it may come as a surprise to discover that *kof*'s name – קוֹף – actually means 'monkey'! Huh? What does a monkey have to do with holiness?

One Jewish theologian answers that question this way:

> *When a man does not elevate himself beyond the ordinary, when a man does not act in a way to create sacredness, when a man does not endow his situation with holiness, man is no more than an ape.*[16]

Jewish theology speaks frequently of man's 'animal nature' and how holiness is easily mimicked, or 'aped'. Apart from indwelling godliness we can become even worse than animals, and the Sages frequently remind us that we must clothe our souls in holiness and righteousness lest our animal natures dominate us.

Paul conveyed a similar thought when he said:

> *"...that, in reference to your former manner of life, you lay aside the old self, which is being corrupted in accordance with the lusts of deceit, and that you be renewed in the spirit of your mind, and put on the new self, which in the likeness of God has been created in righteousness and holiness of the truth."*[17]

Notice that *kof* is the only letter (apart from some final forms) that extends below the line. In addition to representing 'holiness' (*kadushah*), ק also represents the depths to which we can sink if we follow our animal natures.

Kof's Two Faces

Aside from *hei* (ה), *kof* is the only letter that is created from two separate unattached strokes of the pen. The *Mishnah Berurah* makes it clear that these two strokes are

---

[15] It is worth noting that the Aramaic word for 'camel' (גמלא, *gamla*) also means 'rope' (depending upon the context). Therefore, Yeshua may have actually said, *"It is easier for a rope to go through the eye of a needle than for a rich man to enter the Kingdom of Heaven."* In either case, the point of the analogy is clear.
[16] Robert M. Haralick, The Inner Meaning of the Hebrew Letters, pg. 269.
[17] Ephesians 4:22-24

never, under any circumstances, to come into contact with one another.[18] But, the Torah contains two exceptions to this rule. Twice in the Torah *kof* (ק) is written with the vertical and horizontal strokes connected. The first instance of this variant ק is found in Exodus:

> Now when Moses saw that the people were out of control – for Aaron had let them get out of control to become a laughingstock among their enemies…[19]

In this tragic account of Israel's swift descent into sin and idolatry we see all vestiges of holiness erode to the point that the people became a *"laughingstock among their enemies"*. The variant ק is contained in the word בקמיהם (*b'kameihem*), which means *"to their enemies"*. Whenever our holiness deteriorates into carnality, we become a laughingstock to our enemies and thus subject God's name to ridicule and mockery. This passage illustrates *kof* the 'monkey' – man's animal nature. When the people indulged their animal passions they left God in order to worship an animal. They became like monkeys worshipping a golden calf. Though some scientists wrongly declare that we evolved from apes, we do know this much is true: when we forget God and follow our animal passions we *devolve* into monkeys.

The only other passage containing a variant ק (in which the vertical and horizontal strokes touch) is found in the book of Numbers:

> Now on the day that Moses had finished setting up the Tabernacle, he anointed it and consecrated it with all its furnishings and the altar and all its utensils, he anointed them and consecrated them also. Then the leaders of Israel, the heads of their fathers' households, made an offering. (They were the leaders of the tribes. They were the ones who were over the numbered men [הפקדים]).[20]

This verse opens a lengthy chapter (89 verses) describing the gifts each tribe brought before the Lord. The phrase *"the numbered men"* is one word in Hebrew: הפקדים (*ha'pakudim*). A better translation of *ha'pakudim* is *"those who were mustered"* or *"gathered"*.

Note the dramatic contrast between these two passages containing the variant

---

[18] Op.cit., Vol.1B, pg. 301.
[19] Exodus 32:25
[20] Numbers 7:1-2

ק's. In the first, the Israelites *"were running wild"* in idolatrous, orgiastic worship of the golden calf. This illustrates *kof* as the letter whose name means 'monkey'. But in the second, the Israelites with dignity and love presented God with the very best they had to offer. This passage illustrates *kof* as the letter of *kadosh* – 'holiness'. These two variant *kofs* present us with a choice that every individual must make: either to yield our will to our animal passions, or yield our life to the lofty service of God. May we respond to God's call by serving and worshipping Him in the beauty of holiness.

Training Our Monkey

Let us return for a moment to our discussion concerning righteousness and holiness. Recall that *tzaddi* (צ) symbolizes righteousness, and *kof* (ק) symbolizes holiness. Now, consider the word below:

$$\leftarrow צחק \rightarrow$$
$$\uparrow$$

Note that on the right (and facing toward the right) is the letter *tzaddi* (צ), and on the left (and facing left) is the letter *kof* (ק).[21] At the heart of this word is the letter *chet* (ח) which symbolizes life. Thus, this word portrays a life (ח) that is balanced between righteousness and holiness and between the physical and spiritual (left and right). When our life is in such perfect balance, what then is the result? Laughter. And that is exactly what this word צחק (*tzichak*) means – 'to laugh'. You may recognize this as the root of Isaac's name *Yitzchak* (יצחק) which means 'laughter'. Could there be a more perfect representation of a life of joy and laughter?

Conclusion

When we demonstrate through acts of righteousness the holiness which is ours through Yeshua's sacrifice, we are well-pleasing in God's sight.[22] The marriage of holiness and righteousness provides light for our walk as well as light to a dark world. As Yeshua stated, *"You are the light of the world. A city set on a hill cannot be hidden."*[23]

The two letters which represent holiness and righteousness – ק and צ – when

---

[21] Recall that right and left always represent the spiritual and the physical respectively.
[22] Hebrews 10:14
[23] Matthew 5:14

joined, spell the word קץ (*ketz*), which means 'end' or 'destruction'. This word is used in the verse which states, *"Man puts an end to the darkness..."*[24] Truly, when we walk in holiness (ק) and righteousness (צ) then darkness in our lives comes to an end.

The book of Hebrews invites us to separate ourselves to God and to identify with His Son, Yeshua.

> *Therefore Yeshua also, that He might sanctify the people through His own blood, suffered outside the gate. So, let us go out to Him outside the camp, bearing His reproach. For here we do not have a lasting city, but we are seeking the city which is to come.*[25]

Yeshua was not executed in the Temple precincts, but outside Jerusalem at Golgotha, the *"place of the skull"*. To commit ourselves to a God who cannot be seen may appear ridiculous and wasteful in the eyes of the world, but bearing the disgrace that Yeshua bore is the price of holiness. This is the response God welcomes when He says, *"Therefore, come out from their midst and be separate"*, says the Lord. *"And do not touch what is unclean, and I will receive you."*[26] Note, however, that He does not say, *"...come out from their midst and be isolated..."*. How then could we bear light to those who exist in darkness?

Let us look at one final invitation that God extends to us to enter into this holy relationship as depicted by *kof* (ק):

> *Therefore, I urge you, brothers, by the mercies of God, to present your bodies a living and holy sacrifice, acceptable to God, which is your spiritual service of worship. And do not be conformed to this world, but be transformed by the renewing of your mind, so that you may prove what the will of God is, that which is good and acceptable and perfect.*[27]

Note the phrase, *"... present your bodies a living and holy sacrifice ..."*. This is how the animal nature is dealt with – by yielding our body as living sacrifice to God. Only in this way will God's will – His Torah – be demonstrated in our lives.

This principle is beautifully illustrated in the Levitical sacrifices. The skins of the

---

[24] Job 28:3
[25] Hebrews 13:12-14
[26] 2 Corinthians 6:17
[27] Romans 12:1-2

animals were never burned on the altar.[28] What was inside the skin ascended to God upon the smoke of the altar, but the skins themselves became the property of the priests to be used as parchment for the writing of Torah scrolls. Do you see the application? As we yield ourselves to God as living sacrifices, everything within us is given up to God, but the outer container – our flesh – remains behind. In this way, our bodies, including our speech and actions, serve as *"living epistles"* written by God for the world to read.[29]

My prayer is that God may mark us, as were the holy vessels in the Temple, with the letter ק so as to designate us *kadosh* unto the Lord, and that we will be living Torah scrolls for His glory.

---

[28] Leviticus 7:8
[29] 2 Corinthians 3:3

20

ר | *Resh*

Human Reasoning vs. Obedience

"Nothing in a person's life is closer to the spirit than his mind."
WATCHMAN NEE

We are prone to follow our own inclinations whenever our will conflicts with God's will. We may readily admit that Adonai is our God, yet fail to consult His will in important decisions. Instead, we limit God to the boundaries of our own reason as if our intellect was equal to His.

Watchman Nee, one of the great Christian witnesses of the twentieth century, wrote "We act as if there were two persons in the universe who are omniscient: God and myself."[1] Nee contends that our greatest hindrance to obeying God is our own human reasoning. Though God invites us, *"Come now, and let us reason together"*,[2] we tend to live our lives according to our own powers of reason and neglect the blessed life that results from obedience to His will. These are the lessons of the letter *resh* (ר).

The shape of *resh* (ר) is traditionally believed to depict the back of the head. Even its name – ריש (*resh*) – is equated with ראש (*rosh*) 'head'. However, *resh* (ר) has several definitions: 'head', 'chief', 'master', 'prince', 'leader', 'commander', and 'poverty'.[3] Though the last definition may seem dissimilar to the others, it reminds us that if we

---

[1] Watchman Nee, <u>Spiritual Authority</u>, pg. 102.
[2] Isaiah 1:18
[3] Two examples where *resh* is translated 'poverty' may be found in Proverbs 13:18 and 28:19.

allow ourselves to be ruled by the head – making it our master and leader – then we will suffer spiritual poverty.

The False Center

Though *resh* (ר) appears near the end of the alphabet, mathematically it stands at the very center. By this I mean that *resh* (ר), with a numerical value of 200, stands mathematically halfway between א (*aleph*) which equals 1, and ת (*tuv*) which equals 400. *Resh* (ר) does not dwell at the actual center of the alphabet, only at its mathematical/logical center. *Resh* is located very near the end of the alphabet between the letter *kof* (ק) and *shin* (ש) which together spell שקר (*sheker*) 'falsehood'. We will be prone to deception if our lives will revolve around a false center – human reasoning. The tendency to enthrone human logic at the core of our being is very common today. But, attempting to live our lives in this way will lead to emptiness and frustration.

Do not misconstrue what I am saying – in no way should we denigrate God's gift of reasoning. (I have used reason to prepare this book and you must use reason to comprehend it.) However, we must appreciate that our powers of reason are limited. Reason should be used to augment our faith in God and His Word, not substitute for it.

Note how *resh* (ר) is similar in appearance to the letter *beit* (ב),[4] and recall that *beit* (ב) represents the Word of God – the 'house' wherein resides God's truth. The difference between ב and ר is that *beit* (ב) rests on a firm foundation, teaching us that our knowledge and reasoning must be established on the solid foundation of God's Word. *Resh* (ר), on the other hand, has no foundation and could be easily toppled. This illustrates that if we proudly lean on our own understanding (instead of on God's Word) we will certainly fall.[5] Solomon (the wisest man in history) makes this clear:

> *Trust in Adonai with all your heart and do not lean on your own understanding. In all your ways acknowledge Him, and He will make your paths straight.*[6]

Notice that Solomon does not say that we should never use our understanding. He says only that we should not lean upon it. Our human reasoning is like a paper wall. If we lean on it, we are certain to fall. The purpose of our God-given power of

---

[4] This similarity also extends to their numeric values: ב = 2; ר = 200.
[5] Proverbs 16:18
[6] Proverbs 3:5-6

reason is to enable us to appreciate what He *has done*, rather than try to determine what He is going to do. This is why *resh* (ר) appears near the end of the alphabet. Reasoning makes a wonderful caboose, but it is an inept locomotive. Just as ר follows צ and ק, so logic (ר) must follow 'righteousness' (צ) and 'holiness' (ק), because logic is incapable by itself of leading us to righteousness and holiness.

The Impersonator

You may have noted the similarity between *resh* (ר) and *dalet* (ד). Recall that *dalet* (ד) means 'door' and stands at the center of the series of letters dealing with the Gospel. Just as it is easy to confuse *resh* with *dalet*, it is also easy to misconstrue reason for a door by which we can come to God.

Likewise, we are prone to confuse knowledge with wisdom, and substitute correct opinion for faith. Consider what the community in Laodicea thought of its spiritual state, and compare it to what God says of their true condition.

> *"Because you say, 'I am rich, and have become wealthy, and have need of nothing,' and you do not know that you are wretched and miserable and poor and blind and naked."*[7]

The gap that existed between the Laodiceans' true condition and their perceptions of their condition could not have been greater. Like the Laodiceans, we are fallen creatures and our reasoning powers are faulty at best. The further we drift from truth the more blind to truth we become, though our human reasoning attempts to convince us that we are fine.

God describes the gulf that exists between our thoughts and His by saying:

> *For as the heavens are higher than the earth, so are My ways higher than your ways and My thoughts than your thoughts.*[8]

This is illustrated by the fact that the very first word in the Bible to begin with *resh* (ר) is *rakiya* (רקיע), which means 'gap' or 'division'. It is used to describe the gulf between the heavens and the earth.[9]

Resh (ר) also resembles the letter י (*yud*), which symbolizes the Holy Spirit. One

---

[7] Revelation 3:17
[8] Isaiah 55:9
[9] Genesis 1:6

rabbi commented on this similarity this way, "When the *yud* (י)...makes himself big and proud, he becomes the *resh* (ר)."[10] What he is saying is that pride can change a spiritual life (י) into a life lived merely according to human reasoning (ר). Reliance on human reasoning is a direct result of pride and is fueled by vain accumulation of knowledge. Therefore, we must be careful in our quest for knowledge because *"knowledge makes arrogant..."*[11] and pride can cause us to confuse our knowledge and reasoning powers (ר) with spirituality (י).

This is not to say that knowledge obtained by study is insignificant or evil. God forbid. The Bible commands us to study so as to prevent future shame.[12] Only let us be careful to walk in humility, making knowledge our servant and not our 'master' (*resh*, ריש).

As we can see, *resh* (ר) bears a resemblance to a number of other letters, and scribes are warned to take great care when forming a *resh* lest it be mistaken for one of these. One rabbi writes:

> The *resh* ר must be drawn with great care. If the corner at the back of its head is not clearly rounded, it will look like a dalet ד. If its roof is too short, it will look like a *vav* ו, and if its tail is too long, it will look like a final *kaf* ך.[13]

Likewise, human reasoning, education, logic, knowledge (each good in its own right) are easily mistaken for something they are not.

Human Reasoning or Faith?

The tendency to substitute human reasoning for faith can progress to deadly extremes if one begins to deify the human mind. This is a common error today as people progressively become *"lovers of self"* with the result that they are *"always learning and never able to come to the knowledge of the truth"*.[14] In modern times the deification of the intellect has become an idolatrous religion. Judaism's foremost declaration – the *Shema* – contains a warning of this danger.

---

[10] Lawrence Kushner, <u>The Book of Letters</u>, pg. 71.
[11] 1 Corinthians 8:1
[12] 2 Timothy 2:15
[13] Kushner, op. cit.
[14] 2 Timothy 3:1,2,7

שְׁמַע יִשְׂרָאֵל יְהוָה אֱלֹהֵינוּ יְהוָה אֶחָֽד

This fundamental statement of Judaism is translated: *"Hear, O Israel, Adonai is our God, Adonai is One."*[15] You will notice that the final letter of the prayer is an enlarged *dalet* (ד) contained in the word אחד (*echad*) 'one'. The Sages have explained that this irregularity occurs so that the *dalet* (ד) will not be mistaken for a *resh* (ר), thus rendering *echad* (אחד) as *achar* (אחר) 'another'. Substituting ר for ד would render the prayer: *"Hear, O Israel, Adonai our God is [just] another Lord."* Let us also take care that we not make an idol of human reasoning (ר) to the point that we obey it as if it were 'another' god.

אחד = 'one'

אחר = 'another'

Salvation Through Faith, Not Human Reasoning

A common error found among believers is to confuse knowledge with maturity, action, wisdom, or even salvation. As important as knowledge is – including knowledge of the Scriptures – it cannot by itself solve our problems. No one knows the Bible better than Satan himself, yet thus far it has done nothing to improve his character. It has been said that if you educate a devil, all you get is a clever devil.

What God requires of us seldom accords with our human reasoning, yet every miracle recorded in scripture required obedience to something which, at the time, seemed foolish. In fact, the greatest miracle in history is something that seems foolish to the logic of human reasoning. Paul wrote: *"For the message of the cross is foolishness to those who are perishing…"*[16] To think that I must entrust my life to a Jewish carpenter who lived 2,000 years ago – believing that He lived a sinless life, was crucified, and then rose from the dead – goes entirely beyond the realm of logic and human reasoning. However, what at first appears as foolishness is, in fact, divine wisdom.

Once again, Paul writes:

> *For indeed Jews ask for signs and Greeks search for wisdom. But we preach Messiah crucified, to Jews a stumbling block and to Gentiles foolishness.*[17]

---

[15] Deuteronomy 6:4
[16] 1 Corinthians 1:18
[17] 1 Corinthians 1:22-23

This agrees with Yeshua's statement that if we want to enter the Kingdom of Heaven, we must become like little children – relying upon faith rather than logic.[18]

Since human reasoning was the vehicle through which sin entered the world, God has ordained faith as the vehicle by which sin is defeated. God planted two unique trees in the Garden of Eden – the Tree of Life and the Tree of the Knowledge of Good and Evil. Following human logic, Adam and Eve ate of the latter in blatant disobedience to God's command.[19] The result? We (Adam and Eve's children) are disposed to make decisions the same way. We choose every path according to anticipated benefit ("good") or dreaded unpleasantness ("evil") to ourselves. Hence, God chose to introduce salvation by channels which lie outside of human logic. Paul explains it this way:

> *For since in the wisdom of God the world through its wisdom did not know God, God was well-pleased through the foolishness of the message proclaimed to save those who believe.*[20]

When we partake of God's grace through faith, it is like eating from the Tree of Life. It awakens the spirit within us to grasp the brilliance of God's plan of the cross. Only then does His perfect reasoning begin to make sense to us, as Paul confirmed:

> *We have received, not the spirit of the world, but the spirit that is from God, so that we may know the things freely given to us by God.*[21]

Peace, Rest and Joy

When our hearts and minds are made alive by God's spirit, we enter into a supernatural peace and rest. This can be illustrated by taking the letters of the word ראש (*rosh*) 'head' and promote each letter to the next consecutive letter (ר becomes ש; א becomes ב; and ש becomes ת), we derive the word שבת (*Shabbat*) 'Sabbath'. May God give us grace to move beyond a merely logical existence (ראש) to one of peace and Sabbath rest (שבת).

---

[18] Matthew 18:22
[19] Genesis 3:6
[20] 1 Corinthians 1:21
[21] 1 Corinthians 2:12

Another byproduct of spiritual wisdom is joy. This is illustrated by taking the word ראש (*rosh*) 'head' and 'demoting' the ר from the front of the word to the rear, which renders the word אשר (*asher*) 'happy'. In the same way, when we demote human reasoning from master to servant, we will experience true joy and happiness (אשר) in our walk of faith.

$$ראש = \text{'head'}$$
$$אשר = \text{'happy'}$$

God does not want us to be mentally feeble, for the development of the mind is not contrary to faith nor spirituality. On the contrary, we are to love God *"with all our mind"*,[22] which precludes worshipping God in ignorance. God does not want us to be ignorant of His will or of His ways. He wants to make our minds fresh and new, able to grasp His perfect will for us. But, we must first learn holiness by submitting our minds to God's lordship as Paul instructs:

> *And do not be conformed to this world, but be transformed by the renewing of your mind, so that you may prove what the will of God is, that which is good and acceptable and perfect.*[23]

It is in this way that God will fortify our minds so that we can master alien thoughts instead of letting them master us. Once again, Paul writes:

> *We are destroying speculations and every lofty thing raised up against the knowledge of God, and we are taking every thought captive to the obedience of Messiah.*[24]

Conclusion

In short, *resh* (ר) teaches that the mind is a wonderful servant but an unreliable master. If we make the mind a well-trained servant, it will bring us spiritual riches. But, if we make human reasoning our master, we will come to spiritual poverty. Let me provide one last illustration to drive home this point.

---

[22] Luke 10:27
[23] Romans 12:2
[24] 2 Corinthians 10:5

Consider the following passage:

> *Thus says Adonai: "Cursed (ערור, arur) is the man who trusts in man and makes flesh his strength, whose heart turns away from Adonai. He is like a shrub (ערער, arar) in the desert, and shall not see when good comes. He shall dwell in the parched places of the wilderness, where no one dwells. Blessed is the man who trusts in Adonai, whose trust is Adonai. He is like a transplanted tree by water, that sends out its roots by the stream, and does not fear when heat comes, for its leaves remain green, and is not anxious in the year of drought, for it does not cease to bear fruit."*[25]

This passage contrasts a wild desert shrub (ערער, arar) with a fruit tree transplanted by a river. The *arar* bush is a beautiful shrub-like plant found in the desert. But, its luscious-looking fruit are actually inedible and filled with dry, powdery fibers. Its name – *arar* (ערער) – is almost identical to the word for 'cursed' – *arur* (ערור). And who is this 'cursed' person whom God compares to the *arar* shrub? He is *"the man who trusts in man and makes flesh his strength, whose heart turns away from Adonai."*

Note the spelling of ערער – an *ayin* (ע, which means 'eye') followed by *resh* (ר, which means 'head'). Then the sequence is repeated: eye – head – eye – head. Could any spelling more perfectly depict the person who lives according to his own eyes and reasoning?

If a man does not trust in God, he unthinkingly trusts in himself instead. He is cursed like the *arar*. He may be deceptively attractive, but has nothing of substance to offer the spiritually thirsty.

May God bless us like the tree transplanted by the river that we may bear fruit in season, and not be *arur* ('cursed') like the *arar*. May He also grant us sharp minds trained to discern truth from error so that we may serve Him as workmen who need not be ashamed.

---

[25] Jeremiah 17:5-8

21

ש | *Shin*

Peace and Protection

"With God in charge of our defenses, there will be peace within."
T.T. Faichney

Perfect Shalom

Shin (ש), the last in our third series of letters, completes many themes and insights contained in the preceding twenty letters. One rabbi has written that *shin* (ש) represents the "totality of an overall process, one that is שלם [shaleem]."[1] Shaleem (שלם) means 'whole', 'full', 'complete' and we shall see how these concepts are reflected in *shin* (ש), the initial letter of *shaleem*.

From *shaleem* we derive the word *shalom* (שלום) 'peace'. The phrase "perfect peace" in Hebrew is שלום שלם (*shalom shaleem*).[2] The word for 'peace' is derived from a root that means 'full' and 'complete' because peace is much more than the mere absence of conflict. Peace is the culmination of a process – a finished work. The word *shalom* 'peace' is also the traditional Hebrew word for both greeting and farewell – another example of how *shin* (ש) represents the "totality of an overall process". As we shall discover, peace and completion are inseparable because one is the result of the other.

To help us understand the lessons of the letter *shin* (ש) we will examine two

---

[1] Robert M. Haralick, op.cit., pg. 295.
[2] This phrase is not found in the *Tanach*. Although the KJV uses the phrase *"perfect peace"* in Isaiah 26:3, this is not a literal translation. There the phrase is *shalom shalom*, "double peace".

particularly sacred articles in Jewish life – the *mezuzah* and the *tefillin*. Though these objects may be unfamiliar to Gentile readers, they are daily fixtures in the life of the observant Jew. These two objects require our special consideration because each displays a prominent letter – ש.

The Mezuzah

A *mezuzah* is a rectangular container which is attached to the right-hand doorpost of a home. It has a large *shin* (ש) displayed on its front like the one in the illustration below.

Sealed within the *mezuzah* is a small hand-printed parchment scroll prepared according to the same carefully prescribed procedures observed in the preparation of a *Sefer Torah*.[3] (See below.)

This scroll contains a passage beginning with *shin* (ש) in the word שמע (*shema*) 'Hear!'. Following is the first paragraph of the passage in English:

---

[3] See note on pg. xii.

Hear, O Israel! Adonai is our God, Adonai is One! You shall love Adonai your God with all your heart and with all your soul and with all your might. These words, which I am commanding you today, shall be on your heart. You shall teach them diligently to your sons and you shall talk of them when you sit in your house and when you walk by the way and when you lie down and when you rise up. You shall bind them as a sign on your hand and they shall be as frontals on your forehead. You shall write them on the doorposts of your house and on your gates.[4]

The literal meaning of *mezuzah* (מזוזה) is 'doorpost' – the same word that is used in the passage above. The instructions to write God's commandments on the door frames of the home have been taken quite literally, resulting in the appearance of a *mezuzah* on the doorposts of Jewish, as well as many Christian homes.

Printed on the back of the *mezuzah* scroll are the letters ש-ד-י. These letters are the initials for שׁוֹמֵר דַלְתוֹת יִשְׂרָאֵל (*shomer doltot Yisrael*) "Guardian of the doors of Israel". The three letters ש-ד-י also spell one of God's names – *Shaddai*. (See below.)

שדי, *Shaddai* →

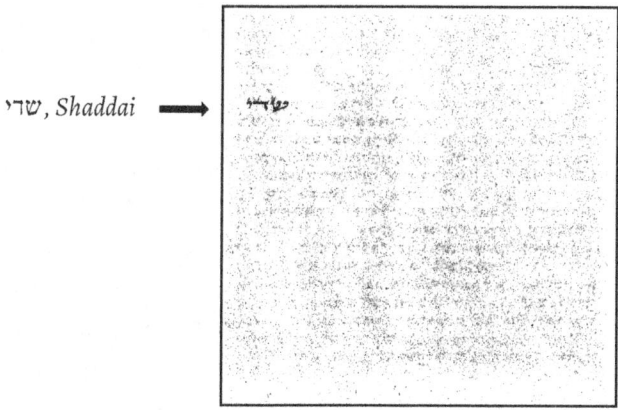

From the above we can see that the *shin* (ש) displayed prominently on the outside of the *mezuzah* can stand for three things:

שומר	Shomer	Guardian
שדי	Shaddai	Shaddai
שמע	Shema	Hear!

---

[4] Deuteronomy 6:4-9

Though the *mezuzah* illustrates many truths, we will consider only these three aspects here.

Guardian of Peace

The presence of the *mezuzah* serves as a constant visual reminder of the exodus from Egypt when the blood of the Passover lamb was placed on the lintel and doorposts of each Jewish home. On that memorable night the angel of death passed through the land of Egypt and slew the firstborn of man and beast. God commanded each Israelite family to remove a lamb from the flock and place its blood on the exterior door frame of the home because...

> *The blood will be a sign for you on the houses where you live. And when I see the blood I will pass over you, and no plague will befall you to destroy you when I strike the land of Egypt.*[5]

The Passover lamb is one of the Bible's primary representations of Yeshua. Consider some of the parallels between the Passover lamb and Yeshua – the *"Lamb of God"*.

The lamb was a male	- Ex. 12:5
The lamb was examined for four days	- Ex. 12:3,6
The lamb was without blemish	- Ex. 12:5; Luke 23:22
The lamb was killed while in the prime of life	- Ex. 12:5-6
The lamb was slain publicly	- Ex. 12:6; Luke 23:33-38
The lamb was slain in the evening	- Ex. 12:6; Luke 23:44-46
None of the lamb's bones were broken	- Ex. 12:46, John 19:33,36
The lamb's blood brought life	- Ex. 12:13, 23; John 6:53-57
The lamb's body brought deliverance	- Ex. 12:11, 31-37; Heb. 10:10

God commanded Israel to observe this momentous day throughout its generations on the 14th day of *Nissan*, the same day on which Yeshua was crucified nearly 1,500 years later as the *"Lamb of God Who takes away the sins of the world"*.[6] For hundreds of years the annual Passover feast was celebrated to commemorate Israel's

---

[5] Exodus 12:13
[6] John 1:29

deliverance from slavery. But when Yeshua came, He added another dimension to the Passover observance. He said, *"Do this [Passover Seder] in remembrance of Me."*[7] As the blood of the Passover lamb provided physical redemption for the Israelites, the blood of Yeshua provides spiritual redemption for all men.

The Israelites had no other recourse but to entrust their lives entirely to God's protection. Consequently, they experienced life and peace instead of death and mourning. As the blood of the lamb was placed on the doorposts to protect the Israelites, so the *mezuzah* containing the Word of God is attached to the doorpost as a reminder that we are protected by the "Guardian of the doors of Israel". God's Word is a guardian to the individual whose life is committed to living by it. The *mezuzah* is not a good luck charm, but a reminder of the protection God promises to those who obey Him, and thus serves as a sign that peace (*shalom*) reigns within the home. It is a sign to all who cross the threshold that they are entering a small corner of God's Kingdom – a home where God's commandments are followed. After all, God reigns wherever His commandments are obeyed.

It has been observed that Israel is the world's *mezuzah* – the doorway through which the Messiah entered the world. This idea of Israel as a *mezuzah* is supported by Jerusalem's topographic similarity to a ש. It is well-known that the three narrow valleys that run north and south through Jerusalem all connect at the southern point of Mount Zion thus forming topographically the shape of the letter *shin* (ש).[8]

The Bible commands us to pray for the peace of Jerusalem (ירושלם) whose name means "city of peace".[9] As improbable as peace in Jerusalem may seem today, peace will come when the Prince of Peace returns to rule as Israel's true and lawful King. The very name 'Jerusalem' is a promise that someday this city will truly become a "city of peace".

Aside from the physical *mezuzah* on the doorpost of the home, we should also mount a spiritual *mezuzah* on the doorpost of our hearts. This is not an imaginary stretch since it is the heart that Yeshua referred to when He said that He knocks at the door.[10] If we have invited Him into our lives, then let us affix a *mezuzah* of shalom to the doorposts of our hearts so that the world may know that the Prince of Peace

---

[7] Luke 22:19
[8] The Kidron Valley runs along the eastern edge of Jerusalem. The Hinnom Valley runs along the western edge and bends toward the Kidron at its southernmost point. The Valley of the Cheesemakers no longer exists, but it used to run north and south through the center of Jerusalem to join the Hinnom Valley in the south.
[9] Psalm 122:6
[10] Revelation 3:20

reigns within.

Paul promised that through prayer God's 'peace' (shalom) would 'guard' (shamir) our hearts:

> *Be anxious for nothing, but in everything by prayer and supplication with thanksgiving let your requests be made known to God. And the peace of God, which surpasses all comprehension, will guard your hearts and your minds in Messiah Yeshua.*[11]

Shaddai – the All-Sufficient God

The large decorative *shin* (שׁ) displayed on the *mezuzah* also stands for שׁדי (Shaddai). This name is derived from the Hebrew word שׁד (shad) – a woman's 'breast'. *Shaddai* could therefore be translated "the breasted one", meaning the provider and sustainer of life. Though it may seem uncomfortable to think of God as "the breasted one", it is nevertheless a name He gave to teach us that He cares for His people like a mother for her children.[12] The שׁ on the *mezuzah* is a constant reminder that we may always rely upon God to supply all of our needs. The *mezuzah* also reminds us of Yeshua's words: *"But seek first His kingdom and His righteousness, and all these things will be given to you as well."*[13]

As commanded in the *mezuzah* scroll, may you learn to *"Love Adonai your God with all your heart and with all your soul and with all your strength."* These three – heart, soul, and strength – correspond to the three vertical strokes of the *shin* (שׁ).

שׁמע – Shema – "Hear!"

A fascinating insight into the association of *shin* (שׁ) with the *mezuzah* is gained by carefully examining the procedure by which a Hebrew servant showed eternal devotion and love for his master. The master-servant relationship described in the Torah was quite different from the master-slave relationship practiced in early America and elsewhere in the world. The biblical laws governing slavery were so humane that at the end of his period of indenturement (no one was ever forcibly kept in slavery for

---

[11] Philippians 4:6-7

[12] In no way do I align with the present theological trend which attempts to paint God in a female role. The Bible consistently refers to God in masculine terms. But, by the same token, femininity itself is an extension of God's character since God himself created femininity.

[13] Matthew 6:33

life)[14] the slave sometimes chose to remain a servant to his master for the remainder of his life. In such cases, the Torah prescribes the following ritual by which a person remained attached to his master.

> If you buy a Hebrew servant, he is to serve you for six years. But on the seventh he shall go out as a free man without payment. If he comes alone, he shall go out alone. If he is the husband of a wife, then his wife shall go out with him. If his master gives him a wife, and she bears him sons or daughters, the wife and her children shall belong to her master, and he shall go out alone. But if the servant plainly says, 'I love my master, my wife and my children. I will not go out as a free man.' Then his master shall bring him to God, then he shall bring him to the door or the doorpost. And his master shall pierce his ear with an awl. And he shall serve him permanently.[15]

What a curious way for a servant to demonstrate his devotion to his master! Aside from leaving a blood stain on his master's doorpost, this process also left a permanent hole in the servant's ear. As strange as this demonstration of devotion may seem to us, it was, nevertheless, God's ordained method by which a servant was to express his determination to serve his master for the rest of his life.

David refers to this ritual in Psalm 40. This psalm describes his rescue by God from dreadful trouble and despair. But, his deliverance generated such joy and gratitude that he determined to serve God forever. David expressed his devotion thus:

> Sacrifice and meal offering You have not desired.
> My ears You have pierced;
> Burnt offering and sin offering You have not required.
>
> Then I said, "Behold, I come.
> In the scroll of the book it is written of me.
> I Delight to do Your will, O my God.
> Your Torah is within my heart."[16]

---

[14] In all fairness, there is some dispute about this when it comes to Gentile slaves. But, it is beyond the scope of this book to go into a theological discussion here.
[15] Exodus 21:2-6
[16] Psalm 40:6-8

David's desire to follow God forever is expressed by this allusion to the passage in Exodus 21.

The author of Hebrews employs this same passage as a depiction of Messiah. Examine how the writer of Hebrews quotes the same psalm:

> *Therefore, when He comes into the world, He says, "Sacrifice and offering you have not desired, but a body You have prepared for Me. In whole burnt offerings and sacrifices for sin You have taken no pleasure. The I said, 'Behold, I have come (in the scroll of the book it is written of Me) to do Your will, O God.'"*[17]

Though the writer is obviously quoting the passage in Psalms, it appears he has made a flagrant error. Notice that the phrase in Psalm 40 – *"but my ears you have pierced"* – is replaced with – *"but a body you prepared for me"*. How can one reconcile this quote with the passage in Psalms from which it was obviously taken?

What we see here is actually a common teaching technique employed by the Jewish rabbis. Frequently, a Torah teacher will quote a familiar passage while inserting or substituting words. This is not done with the intention to mislead the student (since Hebrew students are thoroughly familiar with the *Tanach*, especially the Torah and Psalms), but as a simple and quick method of revealing a deeper meaning called a *midrash*.[18]

In this *midrash* the writer is using the servant whose ear was nailed to the door as a picture of Messiah who was nailed to the cross – a demonstration both of His devotion to His Father and of His love for the Bride, the *kahal*. This is why the phrase *"My ears you have pierced"* is changed to *"a body you prepared for Me."* Through the centuries, every time a servant offered his ear to be nailed to the doorpost of his master's house, he was keeping alive a picture of the Messiah who would someday come to offer His body to be pierced on a cross.

Note again the parallels between the servant in Exodus and the Messiah in Hebrews: The servant loves his master and is dedicated to him. Likewise, the Messiah loves His Father and is dedicated to His service (*"I have come to do your will, O God"*). The servant loves the bride whom his master has given him, and Messiah loves His bride whom His Father has given Him. For the servant to secure his relationship with his bride his blood had to be shed. Similarly, for Messiah to secure His bride His blood was also shed.

---

[17] Hebrews 10:5-7
[18] From the word דרש *d'rash*, 'to search out'.

Whereas the servant's ear was nailed to the wooden doorpost, Messiah's body was nailed to the cross. Both the servant's act of dedication and Messiah's crucifixion were performed publicly. And just as the servant's scar became a sign of love and devotion, Messiah also bears the marks of the crucifixion. And just as the servant's ear was nailed to the doorpost (where a *mezuzah* is fastened), so Yeshua was crucified in Jerusalem – the '*mezuzah*' of the world.

Interestingly, the 'awl' used in Psalm 40 for piercing the servant's ear is מרצע (*mar'tzeiah*), which has a numerical value of 400.[19] Why is this important? This is the same numerical value of the letter ת (*tuv*), whose name means 'cross'. This reinforces the connection between the analogy between the piercing of the servant's ear and the crucifixion of Yeshua's body.

To Hear is to Obey

But, why was it the ear that had to be nailed to the doorpost? The ear is the organ of hearing and, significantly, the first word contained in the *mezuzah* scroll is "Hear!". God invites us – even commands us – to put our ear to the place where the Lamb's blood was applied and hear what our Savior has accomplished for us. If God has our ear, He has our obedience. This is demonstrated by the fact that the word for 'discipline' (*mishma'at*, משמעת) has *shema* as its root.

Paul wrote, "... *faith comes from hearing, and hearing by the word of Messiah.*"[20] May God grant us grace to keep our ear to the Word that we, like the devoted servant, may be found obedient to God our Master. Then we shall someday hear, "*Well done, good and faithful servant! You have been faithful with a few things. I will put you in charge of many things. Come and share your Master's happiness!*"[21]

In Chapter 4 we examined the letter *dalet* (ד), whose name means 'door'. Amazingly, if we combine *dalet* (ד) and *shin* (ש, which stands for שמע, *shema*, "Hear!"), we derive שד (*shad*) which, as we have seen, is the root for *Shaddai* (שדי) – "the all sufficient One" – which is printed on the back of the *mezuzah* scroll.

The *mezuzah* – a simple and beautiful object – is marvelously full of symbolism and truth. Whenever we behold the ש displayed on the mezuzah it reminds us of three important lessons: God is our Guardian (שמר, *shomer*) and our All-Sufficient One (שדי, *Shaddai*), whose Word we must be diligent to hear (שמע, *shema*) and obey. As you fasten a *mezuzah* to the doorpost of your home, let it remind you to be a

---

[19] מ = 40; ר = 200; צ = 90; ע = 70; 40 + 200 + 90 + 70 = 400.
[20] Romans 10:17
[21] Matthew 25:21

devoted servant who offers his ear to be nailed to his master's doorpost, for the *mezuzah* represents the place where the lamb's blood was applied, the servant's ear was pierced, and where the Word of God is recorded.

The Letter of Flame

The second object in which the *shin* (ש) figures prominently is the head *tefillin* – a cube-shaped leather box worn by orthodox men on the forehead during prayer.[22] Two tefillin are worn – one on the head and one on the arm – but it is the head *tefillin* that we will be discussing shortly.

Each *tefillin* contains four passages of scripture. The hand *tefillin* contains these four passages on a single piece of parchment while the head *tefillin* has four small compartments containing the same four passages on individual scrolls. As with *mezuzah* scrolls, *tefillin* scrolls are prepared to the same exacting standards as a *Sefer Torah*. Following are the four passages contained in each of the *tefillin*.

1st Passage:

> Then Adonai spoke to Moses, saying, "Sanctify to Me every firstborn, the first offspring of every womb among the sons of Israel, both of man and beast; it belongs to Me."[3] Moses said to the people, "Remember this day in which you went out from Egypt, from the house of slavery; for by a powerful hand Adonai brought you out from this place. And nothing leavened shall be eaten. On this day in the month of Aviv, you are about to go forth. It shall be when Adonai brings you to the land of the Canaanite, the Hittite, the Amorite, the Hivite and the Jebusite, which He swore to your fathers to give you, a land flowing with milk and honey, that you shall observe this rite in this month. For seven days you shall eat unleavened bread, and on the seventh day there shall be a feast to Adonai. Unleavened bread shall be eaten throughout the seven days; and nothing leavened shall be seen among you, nor shall any leaven be seen among you in all your borders. You shall tell your son on that day, saying, 'It is because of what Adonai did for me when I came out of Egypt.' And it shall serve as a sign to you on your hand, and as a reminder on your forehead, that the Torah of Adonai may be in your mouth; for with a powerful hand Adonai brought you out of Egypt. Therefore, you shall keep this ordinance at its appointed

---

[22] The word *tefillin* comes from the Hebrew word for 'prayer'. The English word for *tefillin* is 'phylacteries'.

time from year to year."[23]

2nd Passage

"Now when Adonai brings you to the land of the Canaanite, as He swore to you and to your fathers, and gives it to you, you shall devote to Adonai the first offspring of every womb, and the first offspring of every beast that you own; the males belong to Adonai. But every first offspring of a donkey you shall redeem with a lamb, but if you do not redeem it, then you shall break its neck; and every firstborn of man among your sons you shall redeem. And it shall be when your son asks you in time to come, saying, 'What is this?' then you shall say to him, 'With a powerful hand Adonai brought us out of Egypt, from the house of slavery. It came about, when Pharaoh was stubborn about letting us go, that Adonai killed every firstborn in the land of Egypt, both the firstborn of man and the firstborn of beast. Therefore, I sacrifice to Adonai the males, the first offspring of every womb, but every firstborn of my sons I redeem.' So it shall serve as a sign on your hand and as phylacteries on your forehead, for with a powerful hand Adonai brought us out of Egypt."[24]

3rd Passage

"Hear, O Israel! Adonai is our God, Adonai is one! You shall love Adonai your God with all your heart and with all your soul and with all your might. These words, which I am commanding you today, shall be on your heart. You shall teach them diligently to your sons and shall talk of them when you sit in your house and when you walk by the way and when you lie down and when you rise up. You shall bind them as a sign on your hand and they shall be as frontals on your forehead. You shall write them on the doorposts of your house and on your gates."[25]

4th Passage

"It shall come about, if you listen obediently to my commandments which I am commanding you today, to love Adonai your God and to serve Him with all your heart and all your soul, that He will give the rain for your land in its season, the early and

---

[23] Exodus 13:1-10
[24] Exodus 13:11-16
[25] Deuteronomy 6:4-9 (This is also the passage that is contained in the *mezuzah*.)

late rain, that you may gather in your grain and your new wine and your oil. He will give grass in your fields for your cattle, and you will eat and be satisfied. Beware that your hearts are not deceived, and that you do not turn away and serve other gods and worship them. Or the anger of Adonai will be kindled against you, and He will shut up the heavens so that there will be no rain and the ground will not yield its fruit; and you will perish quickly from the good land which Adonai is giving you. You shall therefore impress these words of mine on your heart and on your soul; and you shall bind them as a sign on your hand, and they shall be as frontals on your forehead. You shall teach them to your sons, talking of them when you sit in your house and when you walk along the road and when you lie down and when you rise up. You shall write them on the doorposts of your house and on your gates, so that your days and the days of your sons may be multiplied on the land which Adonai swore to your fathers to give them, as long as the heavens remain above the earth."[26]

These four passages contain the directive to bind God's commandments on the arm and forehead, which has been traditionally fulfilled by the donning of *tefillin*. The detailed construction of *tefillin* and the way they are wrapped and tied is the result of many centuries of tradition. In fact, we can be confidant that Yeshua wore *tefillin* as part of His daily practice.[27]

The narrow leather strap used to bind the head *tefillin* in place must be tied with a slip knot formed in the shape of the letter *dalet* (ד). Similarly, the hand *tefillin* must be bound to the arm, but with a knot formed in the shape of a *yud* (י). Externally, the hand and head tefillin are identical except that the head tefillin has a large *shin* (ש) embossed on either side. This letter, plus those formed by the two knots, spell שדי (*Shaddai*), the same word found on the back of the *mezuzah* scroll.

Upon examination of the head *tefillin*, one will notice that the two *shins* which appear on either side are not identical. The *shin* (ש) which appears on the right side is constructed normally with three vertical stokes, but the *shin* which appears on the left side is constructed with four vertical strokes as shown below.

---

[26] Deuteronomy 11:13-21

[27] Had Yeshua failed to observe the commandment to don *tefillin*, this would most certainly have been brought up at His trial. But, His accusers could not find anything to fault Him with. (Matthew 26:59-60)

One of the theories behind this four-pronged *shin* is that the wearer can tell the left side from the right. Another theory is that it is to remind the wearer of the four passages of Torah contained within the head *tefillin*. Although these may be valid reasons for this distinctive *shin*, there is a deeper lesson hidden in this ancient custom – one revealed by the Apostolic Scriptures. Before we see what light they shed on this subject we must explore further into the Jewish lore of the letter *shin* (ש).

Many have noted *shin's* (ש) similarity in appearance to a flame. This resemblance is not by chance. Although the word *shin* means 'tooth', Jewish mystical tradition teaches that the spiritual essence of *shin* is fire.[28] These two divergent images are really not so diverse. After all, fire and teeth do the same thing – consume.

Shin (ש) has another significant connection to fire in that when it is preceded by the letter *aleph* (א) the word שא (*aish*) 'fire' is created. Likewise, when *aleph* (א) is preceded by *shin* (ש) the word אש (*sah*) is created, which means 'go up' or 'ascend' as a flame. Additionally, the greatest fire of all, the 'sun' – שמש (*shemesh*) – begins and ends with *shin*.

The numerical value of *shin* also has Biblical connections to fire and flame. *Shin* (ש) equals 300, and Gideon attacked the Midianites with only 300 men armed with flaming torches in one hand and swords in the other.[29] Also, Samson burned the fields of his enemies by releasing 300 foxes with torches tied to their tails.[30]

Having seen the connection between fire and the ש on the head *tefillin*, let us read the description of *Shavuot* (Pentecost) as recorded in the book of Acts.

> When the day of Shavuot came, they were all together in one place. And suddenly there came from heaven a noise like a violent rushing wind, and it filled the whole house where they were sitting. And there appeared to them separate tongues of fire and they rested on each one of them. And they were all filled with the Holy Spirit and began to speak with other tongues, as the spirit was giving them utterance..[31]

---

[28] Ginsberg, pgs. 310-313. Haralick, pgs. 304-305. See also Sefer Yetzirah 3:9.
[29] Judges 7:16-22
[30] Judges 15:4-5
[31] Acts 2:1-4

Shavuot is a biblical holy day that commemorates the giving of the Torah on Mt. Sinai.[32] At that event God descended upon the mountain in flame, smoke, and thunder to meet with His faithful servant Moses. On the same day nearly 1500 years later the Holy Spirit descended upon faithful men and women with *"tongues of fire"*. At the first *Shavuot* God wrote His Torah on stone tablets, but at the latter *Shavuot* He wrote His Torah on human hearts.[33]

Shin (ש) – the letter of flame – appears on the head *tefillin* as a picture of God's spirit resting upon the heads of His faithful servants as it did at the giving of the Torah on Mount Sinai. This picture is brought into sharper focus by several words connected with this event, each beginning with *shin* (ש).

שבועות	Shavuot	'Pentecost'[34]
שבע	shiva	'seven'
שבתות	shabatot	'weeks'
שאון	shaon	'wind'
שמים	Shamaim	'Heaven'

The question remains, however, concerning the unusual *shin* on the left side of the head *tefillin* and why it is formed with four vertical strokes rather than with the customary three. The answer is found in Luke's account of *Shavuot* mentioned above.

> *And there appeared to them separated tongues of fire and they rested on each one of them.*

Notice the word 'separated' which in the King James Version is 'cloven' and comes from a Greek word which means 'divided'. (The Darby Translation renders the verse: *And there appeared to them parted tongues, as of fire, and it sat upon each one of them.*) For the *shin* on the head *tefillin* – with its unusual four strokes – to be consistent with the Acts account describing tongues of flame resting on the head, it too must be 'cloven', or 'parted'.

There is another reason why the letter *shin* (ש) is a fitting letter to represent the flame of the Holy Spirit resting upon the head of the believer. When God places His

---

[32] In Christianity the day is known as *Pentecost*.
[33] Hebrews 10:16 (quoting Jeremiah 31:33)
[34] Called the "Feast of Weeks" because it comes seven weeks after Passover.

spirit upon us and within us, He is placing the essence of His being within the essence of ours. What is the essence of God's being? The Torah gives us a hint.

When Moses inquired as to God's name, He told Moses it was:

אהיה אשר אהיה
Ehyeh   Asher   Ehyeh[35]

Note that at the heart of this holy name burns the letter of fire – the fire of God's holiness. May that same fire burn brightly within our spirits. May He descend upon us with power as He did upon Mount Sinai at the first *Shavuot* and as He did again upon the believers in Jerusalem – the City of *Shalom*, the city upon which the *shin* (ש) is eternally recorded.

These insights are reinforced by the blessing that is made when the head *tefillin* with its two *shins* (ש) is donned in the morning. The blessing is as follows:

> *From Your wisdom, O supreme God, may You imbue me; from Your understanding give me understanding; with Your kindness do greatly with me; with Your power cut down my foes and rebels. [May] You pour goodly oil upon the seven arms of the menorah, to cause Your good to flow to Your creatures. May You open Your hand and satisfy the desire of every living thing.*[36]

Though this ancient and beautiful blessing invites commentary, I want to draw you attention only to the phrase, "May You pour goodly oil upon the seven arms of the menorah…" When I make this blessing as I don *tefillin*, I imagine the two *shins* with their seven arms as tongues of fire which I am placing on my head, and I picture my heavenly Father pouring his oil down so that I might burn brightly for Him. In this way, each morning is a mini-Pentecost.

Two Aspects of Fire

Christianity has traditionally looked upon fire as having mostly to do with Hell, pain, suffering and destruction. However, this is not the stance of scripture. Every mention of fire in the Bible is ascribed to God's essence, holiness and purity. Consider for a moment just a few of the appearances of fire in the Word:

---

[35] *"I AM THAT I AM"* – Exodus 3:14
[36] The Expanded Artscroll Siddur (2010), pg. 9.

- God spoke to Moses from the burning bush.
- God's presence appeared on Mt. Sinai in fire.
- Elijah ascended into heaven in a chariot of fire.
- God led the Israelites through the wilderness with a pillar of fire.
- God surrounds Himself with angels called *seraphim* (literally 'burning ones').
- Flames of fire rested on the Apostles' heads on *Shavuot*,
- ... and the list goes on.

Messiah stated that "the eye is the lamp of the body".[37] With this in mind, what are we to make of John's description of Yeshua's angel on the Isle of Patmos? *"His head and His hair were white like white wool, like snow; and His eyes were like a flame of fire."*[38] If indeed the eyes are the lamp by which the soul looks out upon the world, then Yeshua's soul has fire as its essence. This aligns with the statement in the Torah: *"Our God is a consuming fire."*[39] No wonder John the Immerser tells us that Yeshua *"will immerse with the Holy Spirit and fire."*[40]

Since fire is so closely ascribed to God's essence, let's consider for a moment fire's dual nature: light and heat. These two aspects of fire are reflected in the Hebrew words and letters. The Hebrew word for 'fire' is אש (*aish*). It's two letters, א (*aleph*) and ש (*shin*), are the initials of its two aspects – light (אור, *or*) and heat (שרף, *saraph*).[41]

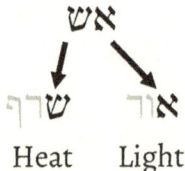

Heat   Light

These two aspects of fire are graphically depicted in the account of the blood covenant God established with Abraham. As we have learned in chapter 5, when a blood covenant was made, an animal was cut in half and the two men making the covenant would walk between the two halves, thus depicting that they were walking

---

[37] Matthew 6:22
[38] Revelation 1:14
[39] Deuteronomy 4:24, and quoted in Hebrews 12:29.
[40] Matthew 3:11
[41] *Saraph* is one of about ten Hebrew words translated 'heat' in the *Tanach*.

in 'one blood'.

However, when God made a blood covenant with Abraham, events took an unusual turn. Here is the account:

> Now when the sun was going down, a deep sleep fell upon Abram; and behold, terror and great darkness fell upon him ... It came about when the sun had set, that it was very dark, and behold, there appeared a smoking oven and a flaming torch which passed between these pieces.[42]

The first unusual thing about this covenant (other than the extraordinary fact that it was God Himself covenanting with a mere man) is that God caused Abraham to go into a deep sleep.[43] God knew that Abraham and his descendants would not be able to keep the stipulations of the covenant perfectly. Therefore, God took upon Himself the full responsibility for the covenant's fulfillment – including any punishments Abraham and his descendants might incur.

The second unusual aspect of this covenant is how God manifested His presence – a smoking oven and a flaming torch. However, when we consider the two aspects of fire, these two items make perfect sense. Though an oven and a torch are both vessels for fire, they have differing purposes. The purpose for an oven is to manifest fire's aspect of heat. The purpose of the torch is to manifest fire's aspect of light. Could God have more perfectly depicted His essence as a *"consuming fire"*?

"For Adonai your God is a consuming fire"

At the end of his life, Moses addressed the Israelites on the east bank of the Jordan and warned them to keep God's covenant, *"For Adonai your God is a consuming fire, a jealous God."*[44] In this statement we find both of the primary names of God: יהוה (YHVH) and אלהים (*Elohim*). According to Jewish theology, God's name יהוה represents His attribute of mercy, and אלהים (*Elohim*) represents God's attribute of strict justice. When both of these names are used together (as they are here) then both attributes are in view.

In keeping with our discussion of the letter *shin* (ש) and fire, we discover a fascinating insight when we consider the numerical values of the name אלהים (*Elohim*)

---

[42] Genesis 15:12, 17
[43] The Hebrew word used here is *tardeimah* (תרדמה). The only other place this word occurs in the Torah is Genesis 2:21 where God caused a "deep sleep" to fall upon Adam.
[44] Deuteronomy 4:24

when we spell out the names of its letters and calculate their values. Below, you will find the five letters of אלהים arranged vertically with the full name of each letter and numerical value of the letter's name beside it.

א	אלף	= 111
ל	למד	= 74
ה	הי	= 15
י	יוד	= 20
ם	מם	= 80
		300

And what is the significance of the number 300? It is the numerical value of the letter of fire – ש (*shin*).[45]

The New Jerusalem

In Chapter 23 we shall discuss how God elects to rest His *shekinah* in places that are cube-shaped. Among the examples we shall encounter in that chapter are the Holy of Holies and the New Jerusalem. Both of these are in the shape of a perfect cube and are places where God's spirit did – or will – dwell.

Tefillin are also shaped as a cube. Of course, this is not to say that the Holy Spirit dwells in leather boxes worn on the head and arm. These are merely physical symbols of spiritual truths. The head and hand *tefillin* are tactile reminders of the need to submit our thoughts and energies to the authority of God's will. The head *tefillin* reminds us that we are to love God with all of our mind. The hand *tefillin* (worn on the upper arm near the heart) reminds us to love God with all of our heart and strength.

Once again, consider the New Jerusalem described in the book of Revelation. There we are told that the city is surrounded by a wall and twelve gates, four on each side, and the city has no need of the sun because *"the glory of God gives it light, and the Lamb is its lamp."*[46] The light of the New Jerusalem is also evoked by the head *tefillin* with *shins* embossed on its two sides. Just as the head *tefillin* is sandwiched between two *shins* (ש), the word שמש (*shemesh*) 'sun' has a *mem* (מ) sandwiched between two *shins*. But, what is the meaning of this *mem* (מ)?

The New Jerusalem is described as having no need of the sun because God's glory

---

[45] For a fascinating discussion of fire and water, see Appendix B.
[46] Revelation 21:12-13,23

is its light and the Lamb is its lamp. The Lamb is Messiah – משיח (*Mashiach*). By placing the word *Mashiach* between the two ש's of the head *tefillin*, we derive the arrangement shown below. The word שמש (*shemesh*) 'sun' appears across the top, and משיח (*Mashiach*) 'Messiah' descends vertically.

$$\begin{array}{ccc} \text{ש} & \text{מ} & \text{ש} \\ & \text{ש} & \\ & \text{י} & \\ & \text{ח} & \end{array}$$

Although the compartments within the *tefillin* are sealed to prevent casual viewing of the contents, someday God will remove the veil from His holy living Word and Messiah – the Light of the World – will be revealed in such a way that all men will see Him, and…

> …*every knee will bow, of those who are in heaven and on earth and under the earth, and that every tongue will confess that Yeshua HaMashiach is Lord, to the glory of God the Father.*[47]

---

[47] Philippians 2:10-11

The Cross of Yeshua

22

ת | *Tuv*

The Power of the Cross

"If anyone would come after me, he must deny himself and take up his cross daily and follow me."

LUKE 9:23

The Principle of the Cross

The apostle Peter stated that Paul's writings contained some things that were difficult to understand.[1] One example is Paul's statement that he "boasts" in the cross of Messiah:

> *But may it never be that I would boast, except in the cross of our Lord Yeshua Ha-Mashiach, through which the world has been crucified to me, and I to the world.*[2]

How was it possible for Paul to *"boast"* in such a gruesome instrument of torture as the cross – the very implement upon which the Messiah was murdered? Crosses worn in the form of jewelry and displayed as decorations in homes and church buildings have become so familiar to us that the cross has lost its ability to strike terror in

---

[1] 2 Peter 3:16
[2] Galatians 6:14

our hearts. The cross has become something tame and comfortable – a decorative symbol.

But, this was not the case for someone living under harsh Roman rule in the first century. During that time the cross was an object of revulsion. No one who had witnessed a crucifixion ever forgot it. The horror of a live crucifixion is impossible for us to imagine, yet Paul wrote that he *boasted* in the cross of Messiah. To Paul the crucifixion and resurrection of Messiah were the most important events in human history and the focal points of all God's dealings with man.

The apostle John also made a strange comment concerning the cross. Though he was an eye-witness to Messiah's crucifixion, he referred to Yeshua as *"…the Lamb slaughtered before the world was founded"*.[3] What did John mean by this? Yeshua was crucified only about 2,000 years ago – during John's lifetime.

These statements reveal that John and Paul both viewed the cross as an eternal principle as well as an historical event. To them the cross was the principle upon which the universe was created, and upon which the world was redeemed. This is the principle of the cross: to lay down one's own life – one's rights – for the sake of another. This means saying *no* to self and saying *yes* to another.

God desires that this principle that was demonstrated by Messiah be demonstrated in us as well. Paul wrote:

> *Have this attitude in yourselves which was also in Messiah Yeshua, who, although He existed in the form of God, did not regard equality with God a thing to be grasped, but emptied Himself, taking the form of a bond-servant, and being made in the likeness of men. Being found in appearance as a man, He humbled Himself by becoming obedient to the point of death, even death on a cross.*[4]

Similarly, Yeshua said:

> "If anyone wishes to come after Me, he must deny himself, and take up his cross daily and follow Me."[5]

---

[3] Revelation 13:8 (CJB)
[4] Philippians 2:5-8
[5] Luke 9:23

The Goal of the Alphabet

Tuv's (ת) identity is of a different order than the other twenty-one letters and is the culmination of all the lessons they embody. *Tuv* (ת) is seen not only as completing the alphabet, but also as returning to the *aleph* (א). In Jewish tradition the Hebrew letters form a circle, or crown, with ת completing the circuit back to א.[6] In fact, the Sages describe the foot of the *tuv* (ת) as pointing toward the *aleph* (א). Thus, this chapter leads us back (or should I say 'forward'?) to *aleph* (א), the letter which represents the Father. This beautifully illustrates how every person must come to the Father through the cross – ת – of Messiah. If we begin with *tuv* (ת) and add the next two letters of the alphabet (א and ב, which together spell אב, *av*, 'Father') we derive the word תאב (*ta'av*) 'to desire' or 'long for'. Observe how this word is used in Psalm 119:

> I <u>crave</u> [תאב] your <u>salvation</u> [ישוע, Yeshua] Adonai, and your Torah is my delight.[7]

All of the letters of the alphabet point to ת, and ת points to אב (*av*) the Father. This illustrates what Yeshua meant when He said: *"I am the way and the truth and the life. No one comes to the Father but through Me."*[8]

ת a Cross?

Most people, when they learn that *tuv* (ת) represents a cross, usually respond with: Why would the language of Judaism, a religion which rejects Christianity, incorporate Christianity's most sacred symbol within its alphabet?

This question is easily answered if we remember that God, not man, designed the letters of the Hebrew alphabet. Consequently, if God chose *tuv* (ת) to represent a cross centuries before crucifixion was invented, then this is all the more proof that God is indeed the divine author of the *Aleph-Beit*.[9] If, as John wrote, Yeshua was crucified from *"before the world was founded"*, then God easily foresaw the need for including a cross in the *aleph-beit*.

---

[6] A Talmudic story describes the 22 letters of the *Aleph-Beit* as decorations encircling God's crown.
[7] Psalm 119:174 from <u>The Artscroll Tehillim</u>, (Mesorah Publications, Brooklyn, NY, 1995).
[8] John 14:6
[9] The word *tuv* (תו) is generally translated as 'sign' or 'mark', but in at least one Jewish grammar text, ת is explicitly referred to as a 'cross'. (<u>The Hebrew Teacher</u>, Hyman E. Goldin, Hebrew Publishing Company, New York, 1923.)

The question arises: if *tuv* (ת) represents a cross, why doesn't it look like one? Despite evidence suggesting otherwise, traditional Christian art portrays Yeshua as crucified upon a T-shaped structure. Though this design may have been used occasionally in crucifixions, it was not the norm. In a Roman style crucifixion, the executioner was not concerned with the aesthetics of the exercise. The form of the structure was dictated by convenience, not tradition. A crucifixion was equally as effective whether the victim was nailed to a tree, a wall, a post, or a T-shaped structure. It made no difference to the executioner if a victim was hung with his arms straight out to the side or over his head, or if his feet were placed together or wide apart in a spread-eagle position.[10]

In a place of frequent public executions, a more permanent arrangement would have been contrived for the convenience of the executioners. Thus, a typical crucifixion at Golgotha probably went as follows. The victim carried only the horizontal crossbeam (called the *patibulum*) on his shoulders to the place of execution. Upon arrival, his hands were nailed to the *patibulum* which was then hauled into position, raising its victim with it. The *patibulum* was then hung on hooks that were permanently fastened to vertical posts. This arrangement looked nearly identical to the letter *tuv* (ת).[11] The feet were then nailed either to another horizontal crosspiece near the ground, or to the vertical posts on either side, thus securing the victim in a spread-eagle position.

In light of the fact that the victim would have to be spread-eagled with his hands up and out and his feet spread wide apart, it is interesting to note that this is the shape of the pre-Temple (or *Paleo-Hebrew*) form of the letter *tuv* (ת), which is shaped like X. We have not discussed the pre-Temple form of the *aleph-beit* (which deserves a book of its own[12]), but in the case of the *tuv* (ת) we cannot afford to miss the amazing insight opened to us by the primitive form of this letter. The early form of *tuv* (ת) – X – is an illustration of Yeshua in the posture of crucifixion.

---

[10] For a fascinating theory on the origins of the "T"-shaped cross, see The Two Babylons by Alexander Hislop, Loizeaux Brothers, 1959.

[11] The films *Jesus of Nazareth* and *A.D.* portray just this kind of arrangement.

[12] The author recommends Hebrew Word Pictures, by Dr. Frank T. Seekins (Hebrew World Inc., 2012).

The Sin Offering

The principle of the cross is illustrated in some powerful ways by the Hebrew letters. Paul tells us that *"He made Him who had no sin to be sin on our behalf..."*[13] The Hebrew word for sin is חטא (*cheit*). If we fasten חטא ('sin') to the 'cross' (ת), we derive the word חטאת (*cha'tat*) which means 'sin offering'.

A poignant description of Yeshua's sacrifice as our sin offering is offered by the prophet Isaiah. This account was written almost 700 years before Yeshua's birth, yet it dramatically captures the sorrow of His death.

> *But He was pierced for our transgressions, He was crushed for our iniquities;*
> *the chastening for our well-being fell upon Him, and by His wounds we are healed.*
>
> *All of us like sheep have gone astray, each of us has turned to his own way,*
> *but Adonai has caused the iniquity of us all to fall on Him.*
>
> *He was oppressed and He was afflicted, yet He did not open His mouth. Like a lamb that is led to slaughter, and as a sheep that is silent before its shearers, so He did not open His mouth.*
>
> *By oppression and judgment He was taken away. And as for His generations, who considered that He was cut off out of the land of the living for the transgression of my people, to whom the stroke was due?*
>
> *His grave was assigned with wicked men, yet He was with a rich man in His death, because He had done no violence, nor was there any deceit in His mouth.*
>
> *Yet it was Adonai's will to crush Him, putting Him to grief. If He would render Himself as a guilt offering, He will see His offspring, He will prolong His days, and the good pleasure of Adonai will prosper in His hand.*[14]

The great Scottish author George MacDonald wrote, "The Son of God suffered unto death, not that men might not suffer, but that their sufferings might be like

---

[13] 2 Corinthians 5:21
[14] Isaiah 53:5-10

his." MacDonald understood that the graphic portrayal of Messiah's death in Gospels was provided to us so that we could learn a lesson about ourselves as well as our Savior. Though not a particularly popular subject, the subject of death is a very biblical one. Since no one gets out of this world alive, we may as well pay attention to what the Word teaches us about death, and how even it can be turned to our benefit. This is the principle of the cross, and we shall discuss how our death to self should reflect Messiah's death for us.

The Nature of Man

Nowhere do the Scriptures refer to a "sin nature" in man,[15] but they do refer to an inclination within the human heart toward evil. After God destroyed the world by a flood He stated, "...*the intent* [יצר, *yetzer*] *of man's heart is evil* [רע, *rah*] *from his youth...*"[16] Thus Judaism refers to this "evil inclination" as the *yetzer harah* [יצר הרע].[17] It is this *yetzer harah* that draws us away from a righteous life and stirs rebellion against our *yetzer hatov* (יצר הטוב) "good inclination". We can think of the *yetzer harah* as the force that lies behind sin and constantly nudges us toward it. Paul refers to the *yetzer harah* as the "old man" or "old self".[18] However, in Yeshua's crucifixion we see God's method for dealing with the *yetzer* – the power of sin.

When you perceive the devastation wrought upon Yeshua's body, you should also perceive what God has done to your own *yetzer harah*. Paul wrote:

> *For if we have become united with Him in the likeness of His death, certainly we shall also be in the likeness of His resurrection, knowing this, that our old self was crucified with Him, in order that our body of sin might be done away with, so that we would no longer be slaves to sin.*[19]

What Paul is saying is that through Yeshua's crucifixion the hands of your *yetzer harah* were nailed down so that you no longer have to do the things you once did. The feet of your *yetzer harah* have been immobilized so that you no longer have to go where you used to go. The mind of your *yetzer harah* has been pierced by a crown of thorns so that you no longer have to think the way you used to think. The heart of your *yetzer*

---

[15] The term "sinful nature" is an erroneous translation the NIV uses for the Greek word σαρξος (*sarksos*) 'flesh'.
[16] Genesis 8:21
[17] Though it may seem that "sin nature" and *yetzer harah* are the same thing, there is a profound difference that is beyond the scope of this book to explain.
[18] Ephesians 4:22
[19] Romans 6:6

harah has been impaled so that you no longer have to desire what you once lived for. What was done to Yeshua was done to your *yetzer harah*, that is if you will but believe and embrace it in your heart.

Furthermore, if my sin – the thing that was killing me – has been killed, then I am free to live.

> ... *for he who has died is freed from sin. Now if we have died with Messiah, we believe that we shall also live with Him, knowing that Messiah, having been raised from the dead, is never to die again; death no longer is master over Him. For the death that He died, He died to sin once for all; but the life that He lives, He lives to God. Even so consider yourselves to be dead to sin, but alive to God in Messiah Yeshua...*[20]

Now that I am free, for what shall I live? God forbid that I should return to my old ways since they are dead to me and I am dead to them. To what higher and more noble cause can I dedicate my life than to the One who dedicated Himself to me?

> *...and do not go on presenting the members of your body to sin as instruments of unrighteousness. But present yourselves to God as those alive from the dead, and your members as instruments of righteousness to God.*[21]

A Serpent in the Wilderness

In anticipation of His crucifixion, Yeshua referred to an incident that occurred when the Israelites complained against God and Moses. As a result of their rebellion, God sent poisonous serpents among them and people began to perish. But, when they repented and prayed for deliverance, God instructed Moses to fashion a serpent out of bronze and raise it up on a pole. God said, *".. everyone who is bitten, when he looks at it, he will live."*[22]

Yeshua compared this event to His own impending death when He said, *"As Moses lifted up the serpent in the wilderness, even so must the Son of Man must be lifted up, so that whoever believes will in Him have eternal life."*[23]

---

[20] Romans 6:7-11
[21] Romans 6:13
[22] Numbers 21:8
[23] John 3:14-15

Why did God choose a serpent to be the means of deliverance when serpents were the cause of death in the first place? We must realize that it was not just a serpent that God used as the instrument of deliverance, but a bronze serpent secured to a pole. The picture of Yeshua becoming sin for us is clear. The venomous serpent which inflicts death upon mankind is sin, but sin has been dealt a deathblow through the cross of Messiah.

Let us look at the Hebrew spelling of these words for a dramatic illustration of this truth. God told Moses to make a *"bronze serpent"*. In Hebrew this is *nachash nachashet* (נחש נחשת). The Hebrew word for 'serpent' is נחש (*nachash*). The Hebrew word for 'bronze' is נחשת (*nachashet*). Notice that these two words are identical except for the addition of the letter ת at the end of נחשת. When the 'serpent' (נחש) is fastened to the 'cross' (ת) it forms 'bronze' (נחשת), the material by which deliverance came.

נחש = 'serpent'

נחש+ת = 'brass'

Why did God choose bronze for the material from which Moses should make a serpent? The Bible frequently uses bronze in the context of God's judgment of sin.[24] Examples include the bronze altar used in the Tabernacle for the sin offerings – a picture of God's judgment and removal of sin. God also prophesied in Genesis that a deliverer would come who would crush the serpent's head with His heel.[25] This is fulfilled in Revelation where Messiah is described with feet *"like bronze glowing in a furnace"*.[26] It is through the cross of Messiah (as portrayed by the brazen serpent) that the prophecy in Genesis is fulfilled and the judgment of Revelation is assured.

What a perfect picture God has painted for us! Just as bronze was fashioned into the form of a serpent to provide deliverance from the serpent's poison, so Yeshua became sin for us so that the poison of sin might be neutralized. As the Israelites had to look and live, may we also look to Him that we may have eternal life.

---

[24] Though I generally use the word 'brass' to translate (*nachoshet*) נחשת, I could have used 'bronze' or even 'copper' since the exact translation is uncertain. (Brass and bronze are copper alloys.)
[25] Genesis 3:15
[26] Revelation 1:15

Destroying the Work of the Serpent

In the garden of Eden, the serpent showed himself for the first time when he lured our parents Adam and Eve into sin. Ever since, the serpent has been a symbol of the enemy and his poisonous lies that result in sin.

The book of Revelation provides a glimpse into the serpent's final defeat. There we are told, *"And the great dragon was thrown down, the serpent of old who is called the devil and Satan, who deceives the whole world; he was thrown down to the earth, and his angels were thrown down with him."*[27] How will the serpent be defeated? A few sentences later we are told, *"And they overcame him because of the blood of the Lamb and because of the word of their testimony, and they did not love their life even when faced with death."*[28] John tells us the purpose for Messiah's coming to earth. He writes, *"... The Son of God appeared for this purpose, to destroy the works of the devil."*[29]

Since ancient times the Sages have marveled over an insight revealed by the numeric values of the letters that spell נחש (*nachash*) 'serpent'. If we total the numeric values of these three letters, we derive the number 358.[30] What other Hebrew word has this same value? *Mashiach!*[31] By this phenomenon God is indicating that Messiah's accomplishment exactly negates the works of the serpent.[32]

Making the Bitter Sweet

The principle of the cross is beautifully demonstrated in another wilderness incident. Shortly after the Israelites left Egypt, they came to a place where the water was bitter and undrinkable. Here is the account:

> So the people grumbled at Moses, saying, "What shall we drink?" Then he cried out to Adonai, and Adonai showed him a tree; and he threw it into the waters, and the waters became sweet...[33]

The word the Torah uses for 'sweet' is מתק (*matok*). Note the letter at the center of this word – ת – which represents the cross. So, the question is: what was this word before the 'cross' (ת) was thrown into its midst? It was the word מק (*mak*), which

---

[27] Revelation 12:9
[28] Revelation 12:11
[29] 1 John 3:8
[30] נ = 50; ח = 8; ש = 300; 50 + 8 + 300 = 358.
[31] מ = 40; ש = 300; י = 10; ח = 8; 40 + 300 + 10 + 8 = 358.
[32] In an interesting coincidence, the four letters that appear on a *dreidel* (the traditional toy that is part of the *Purim* celebration) also add up to a total of 358. נ = 50; ג = 3; ה = 5; ש = 300; 50 + 3 + 5 + 300 = 358.
[33] Exodus 15:24-25

means 'putrid' or 'rotten'.[34] What a beautiful picture this provides of the effect the cross has on the rottenness of our sins.

The Sign of the Cross

Tuv's name is the root of the word תוה (*tivah*) 'to make a mark or sign'. According to the *Talmud*, when the Romans destroyed Jerusalem, God ordered Gabriel to put the letter ת on the foreheads of each citizen. If the ת was written in ink, it stood for תחיה (*tachiyah*) "you shall live". But if the ת was written in blood, it stood for תמות (*tamut*) "you shall die".[35]

Though this story is speculative, the Bible does provide an account of God's judgment upon Jerusalem in which He ordered an angel to place a protecting mark upon the foreheads of the devout. When He sent forth the angels of destruction He warned them, *"Utterly slay old men, young men, maidens, little children, and women, but do not touch any man on whom is the mark."*[36] The phrase *"the mark"* is התו (*hatuv*), or *"the tuv"* (ת). Paul may have had this passage in mind when he wrote: *"Having also believed, you were sealed in Him with the Holy Spirit of promise"*.[37]

When we appropriate the grace available to us through the cross of Messiah, we are sealed by God's spirit. Being thus set apart, the Bible calls us αγιοι (*hagioi*) 'saints'.[38] We are not called saints because we are perfect, but because we believe in the One who is.

The words 'writing' and 'saintliness' are connected to *tuv* (ת) in another interesting way. An enlarged ת is found in the book of Esther in the phrase ותכתב אסתר (*vatik'tov Esther*) "so Esther wrote".[39] Since the enlarged *tuv* (ת) is in the word 'wrote', the connection with writing is obvious. But how is this enlarged *tuv* also connected with saintliness? *Tuv* (ת) is the 22nd letter of the alphabet and Esther is the last of twenty-two saintly women found in the *Tanach*.[40]

---

[34] The word מק (*mak*) is used twice in the *Tanach* – Isaiah 3:24 and 5:24.
[35] Shabbos 55a
[36] Ezekiel 9:6
[37] Ephesians 1:13
[38] Or, 'set apart ones'.
[39] Esther 9:29
[40] For a complete list, see Munk, pg.220.

All Truth Points to the Cross

In an earlier chapter we briefly addressed the Hebrew word for truth – אמת (*emet*). It was pointed out that if we were to write all 22 Hebrew letters in a row including the five final forms, the first, middle and last letters would spell the word אמת (*emet*) 'truth', thus demonstrating that truth flows through all of the lessons illustrated by the Hebrew letters from beginning to end.[41] Just as the last letter of אמת is a *tuv* (ת), truth always finds its fulfillment in the cross.

The Focal Point of Time

The cross of Messiah affects all things. There is nothing in this world that is not influenced by it. Paul wrote:

> *For it was the Father's good pleasure for all the fullness to dwell in Him, and through Him to reconcile all things to Himself, having made peace through the blood of His cross; through Him, I say, whether things on earth or things in heaven.*[42]

The cross of Messiah is the focal point of time. Calvary is the central event of human history and all of God's dealings with mankind radiate from it. We have considered the principle of the menorah in other chapters, but the greatest menorah of all is the one stretching across history from the creation of the world to the creation of The World to Come. An abbreviated representation of that menorah pattern is shown in the diagram below. The illustration shows only a few of the most important biblical events arranged in chronological order from top to bottom. But, notice how each event is connected to its corresponding event below. We shall discuss these events one pair at a time.

---

[41] In fact, the final letters of the first three words of the Bible - בראשית ברא אלהים - spell the word אמת (*truth*).

[42] Colossians 1:19-20

262 | In His Own Words

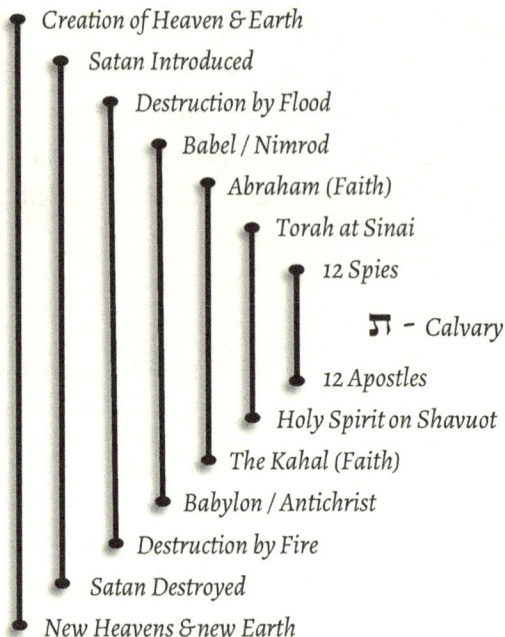

The first event in our list is the creation of the heavens and the earth. God took only six days to do this work and proclaimed that it was good. Nevertheless, this present creation is only a rough sketch and a shadow of the New Heaven and New Earth that are to come. Everything here is temporary and under a curse, but everything there is eternal and there will be no curse.[43]

In the next event we see Satan revealed, whereas immediately prior to the New Heavens and New Earth our enemy will be destroyed. From the Garden of Eden until Calvary we see Satan's kingdom being established, but from Calvary on we see Satan's kingdom being dismantled and God's Kingdom being established in its place.

Not long after Satan made his appearance, the world was destroyed by a flood of water. Prior to Satan's ultimate destruction this present earth will be destroyed by fire. Peter wrote, *"But by His word the present heavens and earth are being reserved for fire, kept for the day of judgment and destruction of ungodly men."*[44] Another connection between

---

[43] Revelation 22:3. In Physics the 'curse' is referred to as *entropy*.
[44] 2 Peter 3:7

these two events is Yeshua's comment that when He returns, conditions on earth will be as they were in the days of Noah.[45]

Shortly after the flood, the first world ruler set up his empire at Babel. The Torah describes Nimrod as a mighty hunter *"in defiance of God"*.[46] Everyone spoke the same language, had the same economy, and obeyed the same dictator. This is also the way it will be when Antichrist makes his appearance near the end of this age to set up his kingdom in Babylon, the same location as ancient Babel.[47]

After God confounded the languages at the tower of Babel, He called Abraham to follow Him into an unknown country. Abraham followed God in faith and became the precursor for every man or woman who follows God in in the same way. Paul wrote that Abraham is a father *"not only to those who are of the Torah, but also to those who are of the faith of Abraham, who is the father of us all."*[48] Paul refers to these spiritual children of Abraham as the *Kahal*, thus the connection shown in the menorah.

Several centuries after God called Abraham, He gave the Torah to Abraham's children on Mount Sinai. On the same date centuries later, God wrote His Torah on the hearts of those gathered in Jerusalem for *Shavuot*. Instead of fire on top of a mountain, He placed fire on the heads of the apostles.[49]

As the Israelites approached the land of Canaan, they sent twelve spies ahead to reconnoiter. Only two of these spies – Joshua and Caleb – returned with a determination to go and conquer the land. However, the other ten spies were filled with fear and dissuaded the people from entering. After His resurrection Yeshua sent forth twelve men *from* the Promised Land – Israel – to carry the Gospel into the world. Out of the original twelve only two were unfaithful – Judas (who killed himself) and Peter (who denied Yeshua, but later repented and died as a faithful martyr).

Do you see the pattern of the menorah as it stretches across human history? And, can you appreciate how these events relate to Yeshua's cross? Both past and future find their focal point at the cross. Yeshua's crucifixion and resurrection are the events to which God would have the world, the angels, and the demons fasten their gaze for it is in the cross of Yeshua that God has spoken forth His message to the universe. This message is life and comfort to those who heed its call, but judgment and death to those who ignore it.

---

[45] Matthew 24:37-39
[46] Genesis 10:9
[47] Revelation 17
[48] Romans 4:16
[49] Acts 2:1-3

The life-giving power of the Yeshua's cross is graphically depicted in one particular word that captures the essence of His sacrifice for us. It is the Hebrew for 'instead'. Let me explain...

...Instead of...

Messiah died on the cross instead of you. He paid the price for your sins instead of you. He took the brunt of the enemy's spite instead of you. Everything about Messiah's cross is a matter of "instead of".

Anyone familiar with the story of Yeshua's crucifixion is aware that He was crucified between two thieves. One repented, but the other did not. One thief mocked Yeshua while the other defended Him. One asked for mercy while the other railed at his circumstances. And between these two men hung Yeshua, who brought peace and comfort to the one, but not to the other.

Look at the Hebrew word for 'instead' – תחת (*tachat*) – it is formed of two *tuvs* with a *chet* (ח) in the middle. Recall that *chet* (ח) represents life and *tuv* (ת) is a 'cross'. We thus see two 'crosses' with the letter of 'life' in the middle.

'Cross' Life 'Cross'

This word – תחת (*tachat*) 'instead' – is used repeatedly in a well-known passage from the Torah:

> "But if there is any further injury, then you shall appoint as a penalty life for life, eye for eye, tooth for tooth, hand for hand, foot for foot, burn for burn, wound for wound, bruise for bruise."[50]

The word translated 'for' in the passage above is תחת (*tachat*) and is shown below in Hebrew:

---

[50] Exodus 21:23-25

ת - *Tuv* | 265

וְאִם־אָסוֹן יִהְיֶה וְנָתַתָּה נֶפֶשׁ **תַּחַת** נָפֶשׁ: עַיִן **תַּחַת** עַיִן שֵׁן **תַּחַת** שֵׁן יָד **תַּחַת** יָד רֶגֶל **תַּחַת** רָגֶל: כְּוִיָּה **תַּחַת** כְּוִיָּה פֶּצַע **תַּחַת** פָּצַע חַבּוּרָה **תַּחַת** חַבּוּרָה:

A more accurate translation would read as follows:

*"But if there is any further injury, then you shall appoint as a penalty life **instead of** life, eye **instead of** eye, tooth **instead of** tooth, hand **instead of** hand, foot **instead of** foot, burn **instead of** burn, wound **instead of** wound, bruise **instead of** bruise."*

Eight is the number of life and new beginnings, and תחת appears eight times in this passage – each one a miniature depiction of Yeshua's life-giving sacrifice standing between two crosses (ת). He died *instead of* you. He was wounded *instead of* you. He was bruised *instead of* you. His hands and feet were nailed to the cross *instead of* yours. He paid the price of your sin *instead of* you.

Though the cross is not an attractive thing, the One who gave His life upon it is attractive beyond description. The Bible states:

Fixing our eyes on Yeshua, the author and perfecter of faith, who for the joy set before Him endured the cross, despising the shame, and has sat down at the right hand of the throne of God.[51]

Contrary to what many claim, salvation is *not* free. It is the most expensive thing in the world. It cost Yeshua His life and it will cost you yours. He endured the cross out of love for us, but will we bear the cross out of love for Him? May God grant that we come to know the Yeshua of the cross as well as the cross of Yeshua so that we may come to the Father through Him. Then we, like Paul, may boast in the cross of our Master – *Yeshua HaMashiach*.

---

[51] Hebrews 12:2

23

א | *Aleph*

Return to Aleph

As we conclude our study of the Hebrew alphabet with its pictures, messages and hidden truths, we return to *aleph* (א) to glean one of its most important lessons. But, we must also be careful not to miss the transcending purpose for all of the insights we have thus far learned from the other letters. And, just as each letter must combine with the others so as to form meaningful words, we too must unite with one another in love so that our message will be spelled out to those who so desperately need to read it. *"By this all men will know that you are My disciples, if you have love for one another."*[1] Unity among God's people is imperative, as reflected in one of Yeshua's last prayers on this earth. He prayed that His disciples would be one just as He and the Father are one.[2]

Chapter 1 ended with the statement that God is 'light' (אור, *or*), 'fire' (אש, *aish*), and 'love' (אהבה, *ahavah*), all of which begin with *aleph* (א). In light of the fact that *aleph*'s numeric value is one, let us consider that which alone can make us one – God's love.

---

[1] John 13:35
[2] John 17:21-23

The Letter of Love and Unity (or, 13 + 13 = 1)

In his wonderful book *The Screwtape Letters*, C.S. Lewis conjectured that in the demonic realm one's identity is developed by either pushing others away (so as to make more room for oneself), or by absorbing others into oneself (like a parasite devouring its host).[3] In contrast, God's principle holds that a person's development depends neither on pushing away nor ingesting, but in loving. Only in this way do we become one with God and one with others in a spirit of unity, while at the same time retaining our individuality.

The Hebrew word for 'one' (אחד, *echad*) begins with *aleph* (א) and so does the word for 'love' (אהבה, *ahavah*). Calculating the numeric values of these two words, we discover that they are identical.

$$\text{ONE} \quad \text{אחד} \quad (\text{א} + \text{ח} + \text{ד} = 1 + 8 + 4) = \mathbf{13}$$
$$\text{LOVE} \quad \text{אהבה} \quad (\text{א} + \text{ה} + \text{ב} + \text{ה} = 1 + 5 + 2 + 5) = \mathbf{13}$$

Why was thirteen (traditionally considered an "unlucky" number) ordained by God to represent both אחד (*echad*) 'one' and אהבה (*ahavah*) 'love'? It has to do with the fact that God's name (יהוה) has a numerical value of 26, which is twice the value of 13.

But if God *is* love, shouldn't the word for 'love' have the same numerical value as God's name? Why is love's value only half that of יהוה? Apparently, it is because love brings unity only when it is practiced by two parties: when A loves B *and* B loves A. God is present whenever brothers dwell together in unity (oneness).[4] Just as 13 + 13 = 26, so *love* (אהבה = 13) and *unity* (אחד = 13) together bear witness to God (יהוה = 26) in our lives. This is what Yeshua meant when He said, "*By this shall all men know that you are My disciples, by your love one for another.*"[5] Mutual love is what identifies us as YHVH's people. When two people truly love one another (2 x 13), YHVH (26) is present.

This is graphically illustrated in the names of the patriarchs and matriarchs of the Jewish people. There are three patriarchs: Abraham, Isaac, and Jacob; and four matriarchs: Sarah, Rebecca, Rachel, and Leah.[6] Below are their names spelled in Hebrew:

---

[3] C.S. Lewis, The Screwtape Letters, Letter XVIII.
[4] Matthew 18:20
[5] John 13:35
[6] The reason there is one more matriarch than patriarch is because Jacob had two wives – Rachel and Leah.

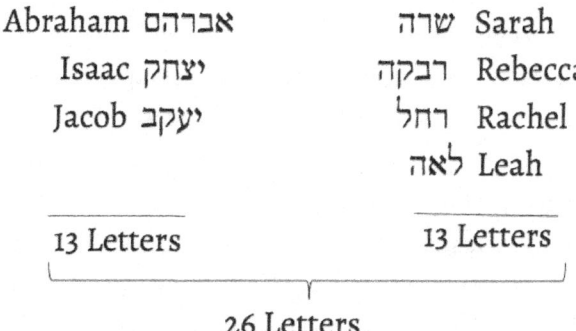

At a glance you will see that the names of the Patriarchs consist of 13 letters, and the names of the Matriarchs also consist of 13 letters. Thus, between them they produce a total of 26, which is the numerical value of יהוה – God's name.

God frequently referred to Himself as the God of Abraham, Isaac and Jacob. But, how could God be the God of these three men only and not of their wives with whom they were one? When we read the Torah's description of God's love for these three great men, we learn of His love for their wives also. Just as when God's name – יה – is formed when man and wife come together,[7] the numerical value of God's full name is formed when the Patriarchs and Matriarchs are joined together.

The Father's Love

God's name – יהוה (YHVH) – consists of two letters that are the same (ה and ה) and two letters that are not (י and ו). If we replace the י and ו with the letters that spell אב (av) 'father', the name יהוה becomes אהבה (ahavah) 'love'.

י ה ו ה   YHVH
↓   ↓
א ה ב ה   ahavah

This similarity reveals that YHVH has a *Father's* love for us. What a beautiful demonstration of the truth that God *is* love – and a Father's love at that.

---

[7] See chapter 1.

As we consider how love produces oneness, let us not confuse unity with uniformity. Love not only leaves ample room for diversity, but even encourages it. Unity is the result of shared convictions, whereas uniformity is merely an external sameness. God is a creator, not a cloner. Therefore, seek the individuality that can be yours only through a proper relationship with God – a relationship based upon yielding to His Word and recognizing His voice.

A fascinating insight into the word 'one' (אחד, *echad*) is found in Yeshua's statement, *"I am the way, the truth and the life."*[8] A Hebrew reader might notice that these three words begin with letters that spell אחד (*echad*) 'one'.

way	= דרך
truth	= אמת
life	= חי
one	= אחד

God's Voice

Though *aleph* (א) is "lord and master" of the alphabet, it is a silent letter. How accurately this reflects the personality of God. He, too, speaks softly – almost silently. Though God once spoke forcefully from the top of Mount Sinai, this so frightened the Israelites that they begged Moses to go up and speak to God alone.[9] Ever since that time, God has spoken only through His Word, His Son, His prophets, His Spirit, and those in whom His spirit dwells. Elijah recognized God's gentle voice thus:

> *And a great and strong wind was rending the mountains and breaking in pieces the rocks before Adonai; but Adonai was not in the wind. And after the wind an earthquake, but Adonai was not in the earthquake. After the earthquake a fire, but Adonai was not in the fire; and after the fire a sound of a small whispering voice. When Elijah heard it, he wrapped his face in his mantle and went out ...*[10]

---

[8] John 14:6
[9] Exodus 20:18-21
[10] 1 Kings 19:11-13

God speaks to us today as He did to Elijah, but His voice is easily drowned out by our clamorous activity. This is why He exhorts us to *"Be still and know that I am God."*[11] God dwells in stillness and we also must be still in order to hear His voice. In fact, this is one of the ways we can recognize God's voice from the voice of our enemy. Satan's voice in our heads is loud and insistent, but the voice of God's spirit is easy to ignore.

The Meekness of God

When Yeshua invited people to follow Him, He said,

> *Come to Me, all who are weary and heavy-laden, and I will give you rest. Take My yoke upon you, and learn from Me, for I am gentle and humble in heart.*[12]

The Father Himself was speaking through Yeshua when He made this declaration. This passage, which so poignantly expresses God's meekness and humility, is captured by the opening word of the book of Leviticus – ויקרא (*vayikra*) "And He called".[13]

An examination of the first word reveals two unusual details. First, the א is in very small print. This is unusual because scribes take great pains to assure that the letters used in Torah scrolls are uniform. Letters must be printed a uniform size with a uniform distance between them. Yet, the *aleph* in the first word of Leviticus is always printed distinctly smaller than the other letters.

וַיִּקְרָא אֶל־מֹשֶׁה וַיְדַבֵּר יהוה אֵלָיו מֵאֹהֶל מוֹעֵד לֵאמֹר:

Secondly, notice that the א is printed above the line: ויקרא. Most Hebrew letters are formed with their broadest strokes at the tops because they are thought of as being suspended from above. In fact, scribes prepare a piece of parchment for a Torah scroll using a bone tool to emboss horizontal indentations and then hand printing the letters *under* them. One of the few exceptions to this rule is the *aleph*, which has a broad, stable base and is considered to rest on its own foundation. This makes the א in Leviticus 1:1 all the more unusual.

---

[11] Psalm 46:10
[12] Matthew 11:28-29
[13] *Vayikra* is also the title of the book of Leviticus in the Hebrew Bible.

Though many explanations have been offered for this ancient tradition, Jewish scholars are not certain why the *aleph* is printed so small, nor why it is printed above the line. But, when one considers that the letters preceding the small א spell ויקר (vayikar) *"And He esteemed / honored"*, then the answers to these two questions become evident. By separating the small *aleph* (א) from the four letters which precede it, we can construct the phrase: א- ויקר, as meaning *"And He esteemed /honored (the small)* א*"*. And what, or who, is the "small א"? Those who know Messiah should find this easy to answer. Paul wrote of Yeshua:

> *Who, although He existed in the form of God, did not regard equality with God a thing to be grasped, but emptied Himself...*[14]

This verse begins a passage which describes the steps Yeshua took to humble Himself; in other words, to make Himself small. In light of the fact that *aleph* symbolizes God's divine image, and Yeshua is the *"image of the invisible God"*[15], it is easy to see how the small *aleph* of Leviticus 1:1 represents Messiah in His humility. And why is the *aleph* printed in an elevated position? Paul continues:

> *... God highly exalted Him, and bestowed on Him the name which is above every name.*[16]

Thus, the *aleph* is "exalted" to a high place. If we, too, lift up and exalt Yeshua, He will fulfill His promise when He said, *"And I, if I be lifted up, will draw all men unto Me."*[17]

א³

We have not yet answered the question: why is the number 26 ordained by God to represent His great name – YHVH? Certainly, He could have chosen any number as *His* number. But, what is so special about 26? Is it only because it is twice 13 - the value of 'love' (אהבה, *ahavah*)?

The answer is found by examining a cube – a solid comprised of 6 identical surfaces, 8 identical corners, and 12 edges of identical length:

---

[14] Philippians 2:6-7
[15] Colossians 1:15
[16] Philippians 2:9
[17] John 12:32

```
  6 surfaces
+ 8 corners
  12 edges
  ─────────
  26 features
```
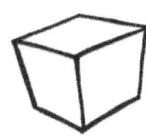

These add up to a total of 26 features – the numeric equivalent of God's name יהוה (YHVH). This connection between God's name and the form of the cube is a profound, though obscure, theme throughout the Bible. In fact, the scriptures refer to three cubes which were ordained by God as dwelling places for His *shekinah* glory. Let's examine each one in turn.

The first cube found in scripture is the Holy of Holies, which was the inner sanctum of the Tabernacle (and, later, the Temple) wherein dwelt God's presence. The sanctity of the Holy of Holies was so great that only the high priest was allowed to enter it, and only once a year on *Yom Kippur*.[18]

The second cube is the New Jerusalem described in the book of Revelation. In his vision John described an angel with a measuring rod and recording the city's dimensions. The city formed a cube approximately 1,500 miles on a side.[19] In this New Jerusalem God will dwell with His people and His *shekinah* glory will radiate from the midst of the city to such a degree that the light of the sun will no longer be necessary.[20]

From the Holy of Holies in the tabernacle to the future New Jerusalem we see God's affinity for the cube as a symbol of His dwelling place – the place where He records His holy name יהוה (YHVH). But, there is one other cube – the smallest of the three – that has been God's dwelling place for the last two thousand years. This cube, of which there are multitudes in existence, is the individual believer in Messiah Yeshua. Paul wrote, *"Do you not know that you are a temple of God and that the spirit of God dwells in you?"*[21] This means that the spirit of the individual believer is actually a Holy of Holies wherein dwells the Holy Spirit.

---

[18] Though the exact dimensions of the Holy of Holies in the tabernacle are not explicitly given in scripture, the fact that it was indeed a cube can be derived from careful examination of the ratios used in its construction. (See The Tabernacle of Israel, by James Strong, Kregel Pub., 1987.) The exact dimensions of the Holy of Holies in the Temple are given in 1Kings 6:19-20, proving that it too was a perfect cube.

[19] Revelation 21:16

[20] Revelation 21:23

[21] 1 Corinthians 3:16

How does the believer resemble a cube? Yeshua said, *"You are the salt of the earth,"*[22] and salt crystals are always cube-shaped – the only cubes found in nature. So, let us effectively bear His name as the salt of the earth.

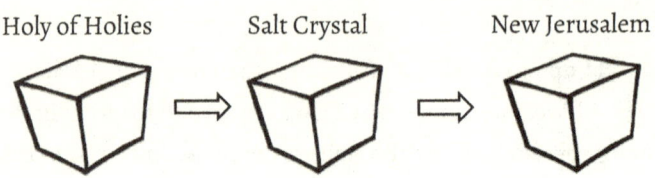

Altar-ations

In addition to these three objects, altars were generally cube-shaped, and I discuss them here because they also bear a distinct connection to the letter *aleph*.

The Torah records instructions for two types of altars.[23] One was an altar made of soil, and the other was an altar made of stone. An altar of soil was just as valid in God's eyes as an altar of stone. In both cases, God said, *"Where I record my name, there will I meet with you."*[24] This means that wherever an altar (whether of soil or stone) was built for the sake of making sacrifices in the name of YHVH, there He recorded His name. Let's read the passage:

> *"'You shall make an altar of earth for Me, and you shall sacrifice on it your burnt offerings and your peace offerings, your sheep and your oxen. In every place where I cause My name to be remembered, I will come to you and bless you. If you make an altar of stone for Me, you shall not build it of cut stones, for if you wield your tool on it, you will profane it. And you shall not go up by steps to My altar, so that your nakedness will not be exposed on it."*[25]

---

[22] Matthew 5:13
[23] These do not include the portable brazen altar that was part of the Tabernacle.
[24] Exodus 20:24
[25] Exodus 20:24-26

We have seen how *aleph* (א) represents God's name, but it is also the first letter of both אדמה (*adamah*, 'dirt' or 'soil')²⁶ and אבן (*evan*, 'stone').²⁷ This pictures how God does indeed record His name (א) in both 'stone' (אבן) and 'soil' (אדמה).²⁸

God is orderly, and just as He requires orderliness in the construction of altars, He requires order whenever believers meet together to worship Him. When believers worship together they create a kind of altar made of living stones whereon they raise up a *"sacrifice of praise"*.²⁹ Therefore, the instructions God provides concerning the construction of altars can benefit us if we apply them to the structure of a faith community.

For instance, let us look at the two warnings God attaches to the construction of the stone altar to see how they apply to the proper order of a fellowship of believers. The two warnings the Torah attaches to the construction of a stone altar are:

1) Do not carve its stones.
2) Do not make the altar so tall that steps are required.

In carving the stones so as to enhance an altar's beauty, people may begin to praise the altar instead of the God of the altar. An altar's permanence could become a temptation to embellish and enlarge it thus making the altar, and not God, the central focus. Similarly, when an altar becomes so tall that it requires steps to reach the top it elevates man instead of God. God warned against elevating one's self *"so that your nakedness will not be exposed"*.

Just as God honors an altar of soil, God honors and recognizes the small, temporary gatherings of believers. But, should a larger and more permanent community be established, like the altar of stone we must begin to exercise caution. We must be careful not to refine it to the degree that we begin to worship it instead of God. Likewise, we must be careful that it is not structured so as to elevate one individual to an exalted position above the rest of the community – a position reserved only for God.

Let us be careful, whether we are part of a small, possibly temporary congregation (like the altar of אדמה, 'soil') or a large permanent congregation (like the altar of

---

²⁶ From this, the name *Adam* is derived
²⁷ Ebony, an extremely hard variety of wood, derives its name from this Hebrew word.
²⁸ The structure of the word *adamah* (אדמה, 'soil') deserves further attention. This word, minus the *aleph* (א) gives us דמה (*damah*) 'resemble'. The message here is obvious: God made *Adam* (אדם) from the אדמה (*adamah*, 'soil') so that he would דמה (*damah*) 'resemble' God (אלהים, *Elohim*) symbolized by the *aleph* (א).
²⁹ Hebrews 13:15

אָבֶן, 'stone'), that we heed the warnings of the Torah so that God will joyfully record His name upon our collective lives.

א and the Ark of the Covenant

Residing in the Holy of Holies was the Ark of the Covenant – the most sacred object in Jewish history. Archeologists dream of discovering its current location. Even Hollywood showed interest when it produced a fictional account of its discovery by Indiana Jones. Whether the ark is rediscovered or not, its description in the Torah holds many beneficial lessons and insights for us.

The ark was a wooden chest overlaid with gold both inside and out. Its cover incorporated sculptures of two gold *cherubim* with wings stretching over the top and touching one another. The wings of the *cherubim* framed an empty space between them from which emanated the glory of God's presence.

The ark contained three objects: the stone tablets upon which God inscribed the ten commandments, a bowl of manna, and Aaron's staff that blossomed.[30] These three objects were reminders of God's righteousness, God's provision, and God's guidance.

Not only did these objects demonstrate God's devotion to man, but also man's sin and rebellion against God. The stone tablets were placed in the ark after the Israelites rejected His authority by committing idolatry with the golden calf, thus depicting their rejection of God's righteous commandments. The manna was placed in the ark after the people complained of not having enough variety in their diet, thus depicting their rejection of God's provision. Aaron's rod was placed in the ark after the people complained about God's choice of Moses and Aaron as Israel's leaders, thus symbolizing their rejection of God's guidance.

The *cherubim* on the ark's lid were positioned so that their gaze was directed downward toward the ark's contents. Putting all of this together, we see two *cherubim* viewing the contents of the ark as symbols of God's love for man, and as symbols of man's rebellion against God.

---

[30] Hebrews 9:4

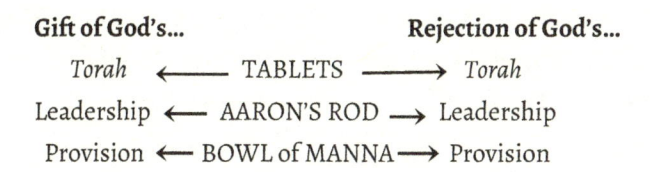

Gift of God's...		**Rejection of God's...**
Torah	⟵ TABLETS ⟶	Torah
Leadership	⟵ AARON'S ROD ⟶	Leadership
Provision	⟵ BOWL of MANNA ⟶	Provision

Though *cherubim* are depicted in popular culture as chubby winged babies, this depiction is entirely wrong. Scripture indicates that *cherubim* are among the angelic elite.[31] They are angels of great power and holiness as well as guardians of God's throne. In fact, Lucifer himself is referred to as a *cherub* in scripture. Speaking to Lucifer, God said, *"You were the anointed cherub who covers, and I placed you there."*[32] As strange as it may seem, Satan was a covering *cherub* who undoubtedly views the objects within the ark as emblems of man's sin and rebellion. No wonder the Bible says that Satan (whose name means 'accuser') accuses the brethren before God day and night.[33]

It is important to mention here that the earthly Tabernacle and its ark were only copies of the originals which exist in heaven.[34] Therefore, Yeshua our High Priest did not enter the Holy of Holies of the earthly Tabernacle, but of the Tabernacle in Heaven. The writer of Hebrews explained it this way:

> *Therefore it was necessary for the copies of the things in the heavens to be cleansed with these, but the heavenly things themselves with better sacrifices than these. For Messiah did not enter a holy place made with hands, a mere copy of the true one, but into heaven itself, now to appear in the presence of God for us.*[35]

Just as the earthly High Priest would annually sprinkle the blood of sacrificial animals before the ark, Yeshua, our high priest, sprinkled His own blood before the heavenly ark. The contents of the ark, once a reminder of man's sins, are now viewed through the sacrifice of Yeshua, our advocate.

---

[31] For a glimpse of the spiritual majesty of *cherubim*, read Ezekiel 10.
[32] Ezekiel 28:14
[33] Revelation 12:10
[34] Hebrews 8:1-5; 10:11-12
[35] Hebrews 9:23-24

What does this discussion about the ark have to do with *aleph* (א)? The Hebrew word for 'ark' (ארון, *a'ron*) begins with *aleph* (א). And, like the ark itself, א represents God's presence. In comparing *aleph* (א) to the ark, one can see similarities between the three components found in each. The long thin *vav* (ו) is similar in appearance to Aaron's rod. One *yud* (י = 10) corresponds to the stone tablets containing the ten commandments. The other *yud* (י = 10) corresponds to the bowl of *manna* – a word that appears in exactly ten verses in the Torah.

An Anchor of the Soul

In this chapter we are once again reminded that the word for 'stone' (אבן, *evan*) begins with א (*aleph*). And we have discussed how Yeshua is the "stone that the builders rejected", and the "chief cornerstone", and the "rock of our faith". But, on a recent trip to Israel I was walking near the Sea of Galilee where I saw several ancient anchors used in fishing boats from the time Yeshua walked where I now walked. I don't remember what I expected an ancient boat anchor to look like, but this is what I saw:

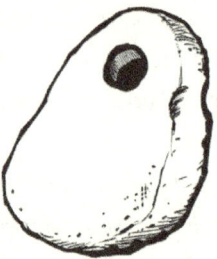

There are two things that struck me about this anchor: it was a stone, and it had been pierced. This simple image – a pierced stone that became an anchor – instantly reminded me of my Messiah, and the words found in Hebrews:

> *This hope we have as an anchor of the soul, a hope both sure and steadfast and one which enters within the veil, where Yeshua has entered as a forerunner for us...*[36]

What an image! Unlike a boat attached by a rope to an anchor at the bottom of the sea, we are souls that have an anchor name Yeshua secured in the eternal spiritual

---

[36] Hebrew 6:19-20

realm – the Holy of Holies in heaven. Regardless of what storms we may encounter in this life, we have a sure anchor in the unshakeable realm above.[37]

Conclusion

Though our journey through the Hebrew alphabet began with א, it never truly ends. As ת led us back to א, even so א leads us on to ב, and ב to ג, and so on. As we have studied these twenty-two holy letters, so let us also walk in the truths they illustrate. My constant prayer is that the reader who does not know Yeshua as his friend and savior may come to know Him thus, and that the reader who does know Yeshua as Lord will come to know Him more intimately.

I hope also that you have seen in these letters and their details a little more of God's greatness as well as His humility so that you will love and obey Him more whole-heartedly. Let me share one final insight from *aleph* (א) to illustrate this. If we take *aleph*'s name in Hebrew – אלף – and spell it backward, we derive the word פלא (*phele*) 'wonder' or 'miracle'. How appropriate that the letter that is the 'lord and master' of the alphabet and most closely represents God should also contain the words 'wonder' and 'miracle'. We can sing with Miriam and the Israelites:

> "Who is like You among the gods, Adonai? Who is like You, majestic in holiness, awesome in praises, working wonders (פלא)?"[38]

But, should you come away only with greater knowledge of Him without a greater heart to follow Him, then you have gained precious little from this book. Obedience to God is of the utmost importance. As the 19th century Scottish novelist, preacher, and poet George MacDonald put it:

> *Men would understand; they do not care to obey. They try to understand where it is impossible they could understand except by obeying. They would search into the work of the Lord instead of doing their part in it – thus making it impossible for the Lord to go on with his work, and for themselves to*

---

[37] An interested aside is that the word for 'I' in Hebrew (אני, *ani*) is, remarkably, also word for 'boat'.
[38] Exodus 15:11

become capable of seeing and understanding what he does.[39] Or, as the Jewish adage goes: a donkey loaded with books is still a donkey.

God does not so much call us to a leap of faith as He does to a leap of action. I pray that this book will help you accomplish both.

---

[39] George MacDonald, Knowing the Heart of God, pg. 213.

Appendices

Appendix: A

The Number 26

Though we have briefly discussed the significance of the number 26, it seemed fitting to devote more space to this topic. Included here you will find not only the information that has already been addressed, but additional information and insights that did not find a home in the body of the book. Thus, this appendix is the collecting point for this information.

Review:

God's proper name is יהוה, which has a numerical value of 26:

$$5 + 6 + 5 + 10 = 26$$

Aleph (א) is called the 'lord and master' of the alphabet because its name – *aleph* – means 'lord' or 'master'. It is also the letter that symbolizes God. It is constructed of three letters: י (*yud*) + ו (*vav*) + י (*yud*):

284 | In His Own Words

The numerical values of these three component letters add up to 26:

$$\text{י } (yud) = 10$$
$$\text{ו } (vav) = 6$$
$$\text{י } (yud) = 10$$
$$\text{Total} = 26$$

God's presence dwelt in the Holy of Holies, which was shaped like a cube. A cube has 26 features:

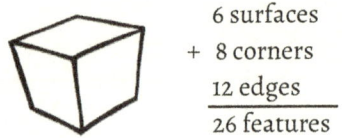

6 surfaces
+ 8 corners
12 edges
26 features

There are three cubes mentioned in scripture which serve as a dwelling place for God's presence:

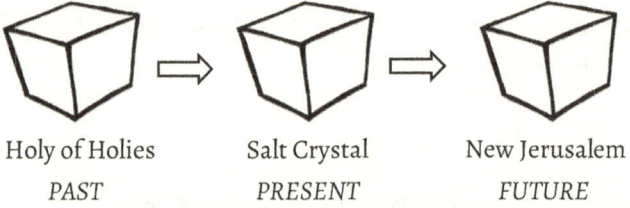

Holy of Holies — Salt Crystal — New Jerusalem
PAST — PRESENT — FUTURE

The number of letters contained in the names of the patriarchs and matriarchs (Abraham, Isaac, Jacob, Sarah, Rebecca, Rachel and Leah) contain a total of 26 letters.

Patriarchs: Matriarchs:
אברהם   שרה
יצחק   רבקה
יעקב   רחל
    לאה

New Information:

French mathematician Pierre de Fermat (1601-1665) discovered that 26 is the most unique whole number on the number line. It is the only number that falls directly between two dimensions. 25 is five squared, and 27 is three cubed. Hence, 26 is a 'bridge between two dimensions'.

$$\ldots 25 \;\; \boxed{26} \;\; 27 \ldots$$
$$(5^2) \quad\quad (3^3)$$

Fermat created a proof that no other number has this property of existing directly between two whole exponents.

There are exactly 26 verses in the *Tanach* that contain all twenty-two letters of the Hebrew alphabet:

Ex. 16:16	Deut. 4:34	Josh. 24:13	2 Kgs. 4:39
2 Kgs. 6:32	2 Kgs. 7:8	Is. 5:25	Is. 66:17
Jer. 22:3	Jer. 32:29	Jer. 32:29	Ezek. 17:10
Ezek. 38:12	Hos. 10:8	Hos. 13:2	Amos 9:13
Zeph. 3:8	Zech. 6:11	Eccl. 4:8	Esther 3:13
Dan. 2:15	Dan. 2:43	Dan. 7:19	Ezra 7:28
Neh. 3:7	2 Chron. 26:11		

The name *Elyon* (עליון) is used 26 times in the *Tanach* in regard to God (*El Elyon*).

A common name for God in the *Tanach* is *El* (אל). We have seen how *aleph* (א) is comprised of three letters whose numerical values add up to 26, the letter *lamed* (ל) is also comprised of letters whose values add up to 26. (כ = 20; ו = 6; 20 + 6 = 26)
The numerical values of the names of Abraham, Isaac, Jacob and Joseph are multiples of 26:

Abraham	אברהם	= 248 = 26 x 9 (+14)[1]
Isaac	יצחק	= 208 = 26 x 8
Jacob	יעקב	= 182 = 26 x 7
Joseph	יוסף	= 156 = 26 x 6

The Greek word πνεθματικος (*pneumatikos*) 'spiritual' appears 26 times in the Apostolic Scriptures.

The word גאל (*goel*) 'redeemer' appears 116 times in the *Tanach*, and גאלה (*goelah*) 'redemption' appears 14 times in the *Tanach*. Together, these total 130 occurrences (130 = 26 x 5).[2]

In Exodus 33:18 Moses requested to see God's 'glory' (כבד, *chavod*). The word כבד (*chavod*) has a numerical value of 26. God's resulting instructions to him (33:20-23) contain exactly 26 words.

God's name of mercy – יהוה – YHVH appears exactly 26 times in the passage of the curses in Deuteronomy 28:15-68. This same passage contains exactly 676 letters (676 = 26 x 26). This passage describe the 'evils' that would befall Israel. רעות (*ra'ot*, 'evils') = 676

If we assign the numerical values of the English alphabet to the word 'God', we discover that G (7) + O (15) + D (4) = 26.

Moses is the 26th generation from Adam.

Isaac's blessing over Jacob (Genesis 27:28-29) contains 26 words.
God's blessings over Jacob (Genesis 28:13-15) contains 52 words. (2 x 26)

---

[1] The number 14 is the value of דוד (*dod*) 'beloved', and '*David*' (Matthew 1:17).
[2] Five is the number of 'mercy' in Scripture.

26 verses in the Apostolic Scriptures contain the words 'faith' and 'love' together.

The *Sukkot* offerings (Numbers 29) include 70 bull, 98 lambs and 14 rams. This makes a total of 182 offerings. (182 = 26 x 7)

Genesis 10 provides the names of the descendants of Noah's three sons: Shem, Ham and Japheth. In regard to *Shem* (from whom the Jewish people descended) the chapter records 26 descendants. This account of Shem's descendants is comprised of 104 words (104 = 26 x 4) and 390 letters (390 = 26 x 15).

In Genesis 1 (the story of creation) the verb 'to be' is used 26 times.

In the story of Noah's Ark, the word 'ark' (תבה, *teivah*) is used 26 times.

Exodus 26 describes the construction of the Tabernacle. It is described as being 20 beams long and 6 beams wide.

Occurrences of 1820 (= 26 x 70)

The name יהוה (*YHVH*) occurs 1820 times in the Torah. (1820 = 26 x 70) The number 70 symbolizes 'completeness', but is also the value of the word סוד (*sod*) 'secret'.[3]

The census in Numbers 1:46 describes the population of the Israelites as 603,550. The census in Numbers 26:51 describes their population as 601,730. The difference is 1,820 (= 26 x 70).

The first word of the Torah is בראשית (*barasheit*) 'in the beginning'. If we spell the name of each letter and add their numerical values, we get a total of 1,820 (= 26 x 70):

---

[3] Psalm 25:14 – "*The secret (סוד) of YHVH is for those who fear him, and He makes known to them His covenant.*"

בית	= 412
ריש	= 510
אלף	= 111
שין	= 360
יוד	= 20
תאו	= 407
	1,820 (= 26 x 70)

The Scriptures describe six rulers of united Israel:

Moses	משה	= 345
Joshua	יהשוע	= 391
Saul	שאול	= 337
David	דוד	= 14
Solomon	שלמה	= 375
Messiah	משיח	= 358
		1,820 (= 26 x 70)

If the number 26 is spelled out in Hebrew, it is עשרים שש (*esrim shesh*). The numerical values of the seven Hebrew letters required to spell out *esrim shesh* total 1,820 (= 26 x 70):

עי	= 130
שין	= 360
ריש	= 510
יוד	= 20
מם	= 80
שין	= 360
שין	= 360
	1,820 (= 26 x 70)

Appendix: B

Fire & Water

Due to their opposing characteristics, fire and water do not dwell in harmony in the natural world. Unless there is some kind of barrier between them, water will quench the fire, or fire will boil off the water. Two of the letters we have discussed – *mem* (מ) and *shin* (ש) – embody these two elements: *mem* (מ) symbolizes water and *shin* (ש) is the letter of fire.

The Hebrew verb that means 'to complete' or 'to harmonize' is שלם (*shaleim*), which begins with ש (the letter of fire) and ends with מ (the letter that means 'water'). Interestingly, this verb – שלם – is the root of the familiar word שלום (*shalom*) 'peace'. Unlike the common notion that peace is merely the absence of conflict, in Hebraic thought, peace is produced by the completion or maturing of a process, or when two dissimilar things come into harmony with each other.

As everyone knows, fire and water have entirely opposite characteristics. One is hot, and one is typically cool. One strives upward, while the other flows downward. One has mass and substance whereas the other does not. Both are necessary for life, but each one can also be deadly. So, what do fire and water symbolize in the Scriptures? For one, they represent two kinds of purification.

Consider the following passage from the Torah:

> Then Eleazar the priest said to the men of war who had gone to battle, "This is the statute of the Torah which Adonai has commanded Moses: only the gold and the silver, the bronze, the iron, the tin and the lead, everything that can stand the fire, you shall pass through the fire, and it shall be clean, but it shall be purified with

> *water for impurity. But whatever cannot stand the **fire** you shall pass through the **water**."*[1]

Note how fire and water are applied in order to purify. If an object can withstand fire, it must be purified by fire. But, if an object cannot endure fire, it must be purified with water. With this in mind, consider John the Immerser's words:

> *"As for me, I immerse you with **water** for repentance, but He who is coming after me is mightier than I, and I am not fit to remove His sandals. He will immerse you with the Holy Spirit and **fire**."*[2]

The same principle applies in this passage as in the one previous. Since human bodies cannot endure fire, John immersed them in water. However, our souls are non-physical, thus they *can* endure the purifying fire of God's spirit. Hence, the Messiah's task was to immerse us in *"the Holy Spirit and fire"*.

From this discussion thus far, I hope that you can see that not only do fire and water picture two kinds of purification, but that they also refer to the physical and the spiritual. Physical things (even the metallic vessels above that were purified by fire) are purified by water,[3] and spiritual things (like our souls) are purified by fire.

Indeed, there are a number of occasions in the Scriptures where these two elements – fire and water – are described as dwelling in harmony. Whenever this occurs, it is a depiction of the physical and the spiritual dwelling together in peace. Behold the human being, for example. Though our bodies are approximately 65% water, we nevertheless have combustion taking place within us. This is why was have body heat. We speak of 'burning calories', but calories are a unit of heat, and our bodies literally burn the stored fuel in a process called slow combustion.

Taking this one step further, when God (who is spirit) interacts with the world (which is, of course, physical) we will often find fire and water together. I continue to discover instances of this amazing and wonderful phenomena when physical and spiritual interact in the Scriptures. So, as we consider the passages that follow, I invite you to stand in awe of our great God and His ways.

---

[1] Numbers 31:21-23 (Emphasis added throughout.)
[2] Matthew 3:11
[3] *"...everything that can stand the fire, you shall pass through the fire, and it shall be clean, but it shall be purified with water for impurity."* (Numbers 31:23)

Examples:

The book of Exodus describes the plagues God sent against Egypt in order to pressure Pharaoh to release the Israelites from slavery. The plagues were also intended to reveal the futility of Egypt's pagan gods, as they revealed the great power and glory of Israel's God.

But, of the ten plagues, number seven is the most unusual. It is introduced with the words, *"For this time I will send all My plagues against you..."*[4] Why does God refer to the seventh plague as *"all My plagues"*? Consider the nature of this plague:

> Now Adonai said to Moses, "Stretch out your hand toward the sky, that hail may fall on all the land of Egypt, on man and on beast and on every plant of the field, throughout the land of Egypt." Moses stretched out his staff toward the sky, and Adonai sent thunder and hail, and fire ran down to the earth. And Adonai rained hail on the land of Egypt. So there was **hail**, and **fire** flashing continually in the midst of the hail, very severe, such as had not been in all the land of Egypt since it became a nation.[5]

Note the strangeness of this plague – hail with fire flashing continually in the midst of the hail. In addition, there are a few other unique things about this plague:

- It is the only plague wherein the Egyptians are given a warning so that they may save their cattle (vv. 19-21)
- It is the only plague that prompts Pharaoh to repent and confess his sin (v. 27)
- It is the only plague in which both of God's names are used together – יהוה אלהים, *YHVH Elohim*. (v. 30)

This last item, I think, is the key to understanding the mixture of fire and water in this plague. As we have learned, God's name *YHVH* is used to emphasize His attribute of divine mercy, and His name *Elohim* is used to emphasize His attribute of strict justice. Here, in the plague of hail and fire, we find both of these attributes mentioned side by side.

---

[4] Exodus 9:14
[5] Exodus 9:22-24

Revelation 1:12-16 provides a description of Yeshua's angel as he appeared to John on the Isle Patmos:

> Then I turned to see the voice that was speaking with me. And having turned I saw seven golden lampstands; and in the middle of the lampstands I saw one like a son of man, clothed in a robe reaching to the feet, and girded across His chest with a golden sash. His head and His hair were white like white wool, like snow; and His eyes were like a flame of **fire**. His feet were like burnished bronze, when it has been made to glow in a furnace, and His voice was like the sound of many **waters**. In His right hand He held seven stars, and out of His mouth came a sharp two-edged sword; and His face was like the sun shining in its strength.

Though Messiah's essence is also God's essence, namely fire,[6] His voice issues forth as the sound of *"many waters"*.

Later in Revelation, a description is provided of God's throne room:

> And I saw something like a **sea** of glass mixed with **fire**, and those who had been victorious over the beast and his image and the number of his name, standing on the sea of glass, holding harps of God.[7]

This seas of glass is not a sea made of glass, but a sea of water that is so calm and undisturbed that it appears as smooth as glass. However, there is fire running through this still water. What an amazing image this provides of the peace that is found in God's presence.

Shortly before Moses' death, he stood before the Israelites and challenged them never to forget their experiences in the wilderness. After this teaching, Moses pronounced a lengthy blessing over the people. This is how it began:

---

[6] Deuteronomy 4:24; Hebrews 12:29
[7] Revelation 15:2

Now this is the blessing with which Moses the man of God blessed the sons of Israel before his death. "Adonai came from Sinai; from Se'ir he dawned on his people, shone forth from Mount Pa'ran; and with him were myriads of holy ones; at his right hand was a fiery law for them..."[8]

The phrase *"fiery law"* (אשדת, *aish'dot*) is actually one word in Hebrew, and used only here.[9] Though translators have puzzled over this word and its meaning, Judaism has traditionally understood this word to be comprised of two shorter words – אש (*aish*) 'fire', and דת (*dot*) 'law'.

However, the word דת (*dot*) is related to the word דות (*dut*) which is a 'cistern' for storing water. Hence, many rabbis have seen in this a hidden reference to God's Torah as having the essence of both fire and water.

Possibly, this is what prompted the following statement in the *Midrash Rabbah*: "The Torah was given in the presence of three things – Fire, Water, and Wilderness."[10]

The Hebrew word for an immersion tank – מקוה (*mikveh*) – is a homophone for 'a burn' – מכוה (*mikvah*).[11]

The Hebrew word for 'Heaven' is שמים (*shamaim*). Note that it consists of the letter *shin* (ש), which is the letter of fire (as discussed in chapter 21), and the word for 'water' (מים, *maim*).

Based upon this insight, one ancient Jewish writing states the following:

The world, too, was created with peace. God created heaven out of **fire** and **water**, though it is obvious that fire and water cannot normally abide

---

[8] Deuteronomy 33:1-2 (CJB)
[9] The word *ash'dot* uses the same spelling as *aish'dot*, but means 'slopes' and appears only in Deuteronomy 3:17 and 4:49.
[10] *Midrash Rabbah* (B'Midbar 1.7)
[11] Leviticus 13:24

together, God made peace between them as we say every day, *"He who makes peace in his heavens [מים+ש]"*.[12]

Psalms also refers to fire and water being used in the creation of the earth:

*He lays the beams of His upper chambers in the **waters**; He makes the clouds His chariot; He walks upon the wings of the wind; He makes the winds His messengers, flaming **fire** His ministers.*[13]

The first test Israel experienced after leaving Egypt was with water:

*Then Moses led Israel from the Red Sea, and they went out into the wilderness of Shur; and they went three days in the wilderness and found no **water**. When they came to Marah, they could not drink the waters of Marah, for they were bitter; therefore it was named Marah.*[14]

However, the first test Israel experienced after leaving Sinai was with fire:

*Now the people became like those who complain of adversity in the hearing of Adonai; and when Adonai heard it, His anger was kindled, and the **fire** of Adonai burned among them and consumed some of the outskirts of the camp. The people therefore cried out to Moses, and Moses prayed to Adonai and the fire died out. So the name of that place was called Taberah, because the fire of Adonai burned among them.*[15]

---

[12] *Zohar Vayikra* 12b (quoting Job 25:2) Note also that the word *'peace'* (*shalom*) is שלום, which begins with ש (*shin* – the letter of fire) and ends with ם (*mem* – the letter of water).
[13] Psalm 104:3-4
[14] Exodus 15:22-23
[15] Numbers 11:1-3

Proverbs teaches that fire and water can also play a part in the way we treat our enemies:

*If your enemy is hungry, give him food to eat; and if he is thirsty, give him **water** to drink; for you will heap **burning coals** on his head, and Adonai will reward you.*[16]

Daniel describes God's throne of judgment as having a river of fire flowing from it:

*"I kept looking until thrones were set up, and the Ancient of Days took His seat; His vesture was like white snow and the hair of His head like pure wool. His throne was ablaze with flames, its wheels were a burning fire. A river of **fire** was flowing and coming out from before Him; thousands upon thousands were attending Him, and myriads upon myriads were standing before Him; the court sat, and the books were opened."*[17]

But, God's throne in the New Jerusalem is described with a river of water flowing from it:

*Then he showed me a river of the **water** of life, clear as crystal, coming from the throne of God and of the Lamb, in the middle of its street. On either side of the river was the Tree of Life, bearing twelve kinds of fruit, yielding its fruit every month; and the leaves of the tree were for the healing of the nations.*[18]

The book of Genesis describes how the world was destroyed by a flood of water.[19] But, Peter describes how in the future the world will be destroyed by fire.[20]

---

[16] Proverbs 25:21
[17] Daniel 7:9-10
[18] Revelation 22:1-2
[19] Genesis 6-8
[20] 2 Peter 3:10-12

Bibliography

Alter, Michael J. *Why the Torah Begins With the Letter Beit* (New Jersey: Jason Aronson Inc., 1998)

Anderson, Neil *The Bondage Breaker* (Oregon: Harvest House Publishers, 1993)

Anderson, Sir Robert *The Coming Prince* (Grand Rapids, MI: Kregel Publications, 1977)

Baal HaTurim Chumash (New York: Mesorah Publications, Ltd., 1999)

Blech, Benjamin *The Secrets of Hebrew Words* (Pennsylvania: Jason Aronson Inc., 1991)

Blech, Benjamin *More Secrets of Hebrew Words* (Pennsylvania: Jason Aronson Inc., 1993)

Bonhoeffer, Dietrich *The Cost of Discipleship* (New York: Macmillan Publishing Co., 1974)

Brown, Francis / Driver, S.R. /Briggs, Charles A. *The Brown-Driver-Briggs Hebrew and English Lexicon: With an appendix containing Biblical Aramaic* (Oxford: Clarendon, 1907. BibleWorks, v.9)

Chitwood, Arlen L. *The Salvation of the Soul* (Oklahoma: The Lamp Broadcast, Inc., 2003)

The Chumash, Stone Edition (Brooklyn: Mesorah Publications, Ltd., 1993)

Church, J.R. & Stearman, Gary *The Mystery of the Menorah* (Oklahoma: Prophecy Publications, 1993)

Davidson, Benjamin *The Analytical Hebrew and Chaldee Lexicon* (Maryland: Hendrickson Publishers, 1990)

The Expanded Artscroll Siddur (Brooklyn: Mesorah Publications, 2010)

Ginsburgh, Rabbi Yitzchak *The Alef-Beit: Jewish Thought Revealed through the Hebrew

Letters (New Jersey: Jason Aronson Inc., 1995)

Glazerson, Matityahu *Letters of Fire* (Jerusalem: Feldheim Publishers, 1991)

Glazerson, Matityahu *Building Blocks of the Soul* (New Jersey: Jason Aronson Inc., 1997)

Goldin, Hyman E. *The Hebrew Teacher* (New York: Hebrew Publishing Company, 1923)

A Guide to Mezuzah (Brooklyn: VAAD MISHMERES STaM, 1984)

Haralick, Robert M. *The Inner Meaning of the Hebrew Letters* (New Jersey: Jason Aronson Inc., 1995)

Harris, R. Laird / Archer, Jr., Gleason L. / Waltke, Bruce K. *Theological Wordbook of the Old Testament* (Chicago: Moody Press, 1980)

Hislop, Alexander *The Two Babylons* (New Jersey: Loizeaux Brothers, 1959)

Kaplan, Aryeh *Tefillin* (New York: National Conference of Synagogue Youth, 1975)

Kaplan, Aryeh *Sefer Yetzirah, The Book of Creation, In Theory and Practice* (Maine:, Samuel Weiser Inc., 1997)

Kolatch, Alfred J. *This is the Torah*,(New York: Jonathan David Publishers Inc., 1988)

Knoch, A. E. *The Problem of Evil and the Judgements of God* (California: Concordant Publishing Concern, 1976)

Kushner, Lawrence *The Book of Letters* (Vermont: Jewish Lights Publishing, 1990)

Lamsa, George M. *Gospel Light* (Philadelphia: A. J. Holman Company, 1967)

Leitner, Dovid *Understanding the Alef-Beis* (Jerusalem: Feldheim Publishers, 2007)

Lewis, C.S. *The Screwtape Letters* (New York: Macmillan Publishing Co., Inc., 1976)

Lightfoot, John *Commentary on the New Testament from the Talmud and Hebraica* (Massachusetts: Hendrickson Publishers, 1989)

Locks, Gutman G. *The Spice of Torah - Gematria* (New York: The Judaica Press, 1985)

Lowin, Joseph *Hebrewspeak* (New Jersey: Jason Aronson Inc., 1995)

Ha-Cohen, Rabbeinu Yisroel Meir *Mishnah Berurah* (Jerusalem: Feldheim Publishers, 1992)

Munk, Rabbi Michael L. *The Wisdom of the Hebrew Alphabet* (Brooklyn: Mesorah Publications, Ltd., 1990)

Nee, Watchman *Spiritual Authority* (New York: Christian Fellowship Publishers Inc., 1972)

Raskin, R' Aaron L. *Letters of Light* (Brooklyn, NY: Sichos in English, 2003)

Richardson, Don *Eternity In Their Hearts* (Bloomington: Bethany House Pub., 2006)

Schneerson, R' Menachem Mendel *HaYom Yom* (Brooklyn, NY: Otzar Hachassidim Lubavitch, 2005)

Shulman, Yaacov Dovid *The Aleph Beit of Rebbi Akiva* (Baltimore, MD: Power Sefer Press, 2018)

Stern, David H. *Jewish New Testament* (Maryland: Jewish New Testament Publications, Inc., 1994)

Stern, David H. *Jewish New Testament Commentary* (Maryland: Jewish New Testament Publications, Inc., 1992)

The Tanach, Stone Edition (Brooklyn: Mesorah Publications, Ltd., 1996)

Trumbull, C. Clay *The Blood Covenant* (Missouri: Impact Books, Inc., 1975)

The Zohar (London, England: The Soncino Press Ltd., 1984)

The Zohar (New York: Yeshivat Kol Yehuda, 2002)

Made in the USA
Coppell, TX
28 November 2023